BOULDER COUNTY
Nature Almanac

BOULDER COUNTY

Nature Almanac

What to See Where and When

Ruth Carol Cushman and Stephen R. Jones
with Jim Knopf

Photographs by Stephen R. Jones

Illustrations by Jim Knopf and Beth Schubert

PRUETT

PRUETT PUBLISHING COMPANY
BOULDER, COLORADO

Cover and book design: Jody Chapel, Cover to Cover Design
Composition by Lyn Chaffee, Amazon Typography

Printed in the United States
10 9 8 7 6 5 4 3 2 1

Library of Congress Cataloging-in-Publication Data

Cushman, Ruth Carol, 1937–
    Boulder County nature almanac : what to see, where and when / Ruth
  Carol Cushman, Stephen R. Jones, Jim Knopf : with illustrations by
  Jim Knopf and photographs by Stephen R. Jones.
      p.   cm.
    Includes bibliographical references (p.   ) and index.
    ISBN 0-87108-819-3 : (pb. : acid free)
    1. Natural history–Colorado–Boulder County. 2. Natural history–
  Colorado–Boulder County–Guidebooks. I. Jones, Stephen R., 1944–
  II. Knopf, Jim. III. Title.
  QH105.C6C87   1993
  508.788′63–dc20   93-6251
                                                              CIP

To Glenn and all others who walk gently on the earth.

— Ruth Carol

To the wildflowers, wildlife, and wild places of Boulder County.

— Steve

To the people of Boulder County who have had the wisdom and perseverance to set aside so much wonderful open space.

— Jim

CONTENTS

Contents

TABLES

ACKNOWLEDGMENTS

The teachers who shared their knowledge of nature with us and the friends and relatives who hiked the trails and shared discoveries are numerous and hold a special place in our hearts. We thank David Armstrong, William Callahan, Mike Figgs, Steve Frye, James Halfpenny, David Hallock, Bill Kaempfer, Nancy Lederer, John Oppenlander, Robert Pyle, Michael Sanders, Marilyn Shaw, Cathy Vaughan-Grabowski, Ann Wichmann, and Bettie Willard, who critiqued portions of the book.

Thanks also go to Rick Adams, Lois Anderton, Frank Beck, Alex and Gillian Brown, Curt Brown, Alexander Cruz, JoAnn Dufty, Paula Hansley, Louise Hering, Rick Ingersoll, and Rich Koopmann, who provided information; to Brian Jones, who provided the drawing of a red-tailed hawk; to Sheryl Morris, who typed large portions of the book; and to Nancy Dawson, who provided sound advice and moral support.

Very special thanks go to Audrey Benedict, Glenn Cushman, and John Emerick, who critiqued the entire book and offered valuable suggestions. We are also grateful to the many volunteers who have worked on natural history projects in Boulder County over the years and for the resources of the University of Colorado Libraries, the Boulder Public Library, the Boulder Carnegie Branch Library for Local History, and the Institute of Arctic and Alpine Research. Finally, we'd like to thank Jim Pruett, publisher; Dianne Russell, editor; and Jody Chapel, book designer.

INTRODUCTION

The purpose of this book is to help readers enjoy nature in Boulder County and experience the thrill of discovery for themselves. The book is not intended as either a field guide or a trail guide. Perhaps you could call it an "awareness guide" or a handbook to the seasons, something to point the way to what is happening: when the bluebirds arrive, when pasque flowers bloom, and when aspen turn to gold.

But don't be surprised if certain flowers do not bloom where and when we specify or if the hummingbirds fail to arrive "on time." Dates in this book are based on records kept by us and by others over a period of years, but nature does not necessarily heed our calendars. For instance, during the year we were writing, an early, warm spring caused wildflowers to bloom three to four weeks earlier than usual. The summer, however, was cooler and cloudier than average; most mushrooms failed to materialize, and trees turned color ahead of schedule.

Another factor that influences seasonal events is altitude. Autumn colors usually peak in the tundra in August, in aspen groves in September, and in urban areas in October. Pasque flowers bloom in March on escarpments near Boulder and in June at higher elevations. Our motto is: Expect the unexpected, but be astonished at everything.

All the trails mentioned hold some special magic at all seasons, so assigning them to a specific month is subjective. We have simply picked our favorite trails to experience at certain times of year, and sometimes we have repeated an area in order to highlight a seasonal event. Because this is not a recreation guide, we have generally omitted information on bicycling, horseback riding, and fishing and have concentrated on foot power. When you go slowly and silently, you see more.

Introduction

We hope readers will use this book month by month to explore the natural wonders of Boulder County, and that "almanackers" will let us know what we have missed (send suggestions to us in care of our publisher). Each chapter starts with a scene-setting essay followed by a weather box, flora and fauna essays, a Where To Go section, and a Month at a Glance summary. Information boxes and snippets offer facts that fascinated us but that didn't seem to fit elsewhere.

The maps listed in Suggested Reading pinpoint places mentioned in the text and are essential if you're not familiar with the territory. We've tried to minimize use of botanical names in the text, but a complete, cross-referenced index of botanical and common plant names appears on page 317. Our primary sources for plant names are *Hortus Third*; *Flora of the Great Plains*, by Ronald McGregor and T. M. Barkley; and *Catalog of the Colorado Flora: A Biodiversity Baseline*, by William A. Weber and Ronald C. Wittman.

ABBREVIATIONS USED IN THE TEXT

CR: County Road, SR: State Road, US: United States Highway, NCAR: National Center for Atmospheric Research

CLIMATE HIGHLIGHTS

CITY OF BOULDER
(See the weather chart on page 23 for sources.)

HEAT

Overall highest temperature	104°F (23 July '54 and 11 July '54)
Average number of days above 90°F	33
Greatest number of days above 90°F	60 (1952)
Fewest days above 90°F	0 (1906)
Highest winter temperature	79°F (8 February 1954)
Highest overnight temperature	82°F (20 July 1930)

Introduction

COLD

Overall lowest temperature	−33°F (17 January 1951)
Average number of days reaching <32°F	134
Lowest summer temperature	30°F (2 June 1951)
Most consecutive hours of 0°F or less	62 (December 1983)
Lowest daytime high temperature	−12°F (4 February 1989)

FROST-FREE PERIOD

Longest	207 days (1940)
Shortest	111 days (1951)
Average	153 days

WIND

Highest gusts	147 mph at NCAR
	165 mph at Marshall Mesa

PRECIPITATION

Highest annual	29″ (1939)
Longest wet spell	15 days
Average annual	18.24″
Lowest annual	8.8″ (1893)
Longest dry spell	55 days
Earliest snow	2 September 1973
Latest snow	13 June 1969
Heaviest 24-hour snowfall	76″ Silver Lake near Ward
(world record!)	14–15 April 1921

SUNSHINE

Average percentage of possible sunshine varies from 75% in September to 64% in May, but it can be nearly 100% for as long as a month, or as low as about 25% for a month.

Average annual number of cloudy days	118
Average annual number of partly cloudy days	129
Average annual number of totally sunny days	118

The intensity of the sunshine is also significant. Ultraviolet light is about 100% greater at 6,000 feet than at sea level.

DAILY TEMPERATURE RANGES

This tells another tale relevant to life that can't come indoors.

63°F change	(61°F to −2°F)	20 January 1943
61°F change	(33°F to −28°F)	8 February 1936
52°F change	(70°F to 18°F)	17 December 1979
50°F change	(73°F to 23°F)	8 April 1917

There have also been numerous days with less than 1°F of temperature change.

Introduction

BOULDER AND LONGMONT COMPARED

	BOULDER		LONGMONT	
Average Daily Highs and Lows (°F) (1947–87)				
Jan.	45°	20°	41°	12°
Feb.	49°	24°	46°	17°
Mar.	53°	27°	52°	23°
Apr.	63°	36°	62°	33°
May	72°	45°	71°	43°
Jun.	82°	54°	82°	51°
Jul.	88°	59°	89°	56°
Aug.	86°	58°	86°	54°
Sep.	78°	49°	78°	44°
Oct.	67°	40°	67°	33°
Nov.	54°	29°	52°	23°
Dec.	47°	23°	44°	15°

Average Number of Days at More Than 90°F

BOULDER	LONGMONT
33	38

Average Number of Nights at Less Than 0°F

BOULDER	LONGMONT
4	13

	BOULDER		LONGMONT	
Record Highs and Lows (°F) (1951–1980)				
Jan.	72°	−22°	71°	−34°
Feb.	79°	−15°	76°	−36°
Mar.	79°	−3°	82°	−18°
Apr.	83°	−3°	86°	−7°
May	93°	22°	94°	24°
Jun.	104°	30°	105°	32°
Jul.	104°	42°	106°	40°
Aug.	101°	43°	101°	38°
Sep.	97°	22°	99°	20°
Oct.	90°	10°	90°	0°
Nov.	79°	−7°	80°	−16°
Dec.	76°	−16°	73°	−27°

Frost

BOULDER		LONGMONT
9 May–6 Oct.	(average first and last frost dates)	9 May–30 Sep.
153	(average number of frost-free days)	144

Precipitation

	BOULDER	LONGMONT
MAX.	29 inches (1939)	20.3 inches (1967)
AVE.	18.24 inches	12.6 inches
MIN.	8.8 inches (1893)	7.0 inches (1954)

EXPLORING
BOULDER COUNTY

There are some who can live without wild things, and some who cannot. For us of the minority, the opportunity to see geese is more important than television, and the chance to find a pasqueflower is a right as inalienable as free speech.

—Aldo Leopold

Boulder County is a place where edges meet: where East meets West, and where the plains meet the mountains. The resultant diversity makes this 750-square-mile plot of land a place of infinite wonder. In spite of the incursions of "civilization," Boulder County is still an ideal place to study nature, to absorb its nuances, and to feel the joy that comes from communion with the natural world.

The climate is volatile and invigorating, with weather representing all four seasons sometimes occurring in a single day. Mountain lions occasionally roam through subdivisions on the western edge of the city of Boulder while golden eagles nest within sight of the county courthouse. Wildflowers may bloom any month of the year.

Astonishing natural occurrences are commonplace. No one was too surprised when 23 inches of snow fell on the fourth and fifth of May, 1978, or when a vermilion flycatcher, a rare tropical species, was seen perched on a snow-covered tree limb near White Rocks in December 1987. Nor is anyone shocked if spring beauties bloom in January or Easter daisies unfurl in February.

Lying near the geographical center of North America and straddling the interface between the Great Plains and the Rocky Mountains, Boulder County

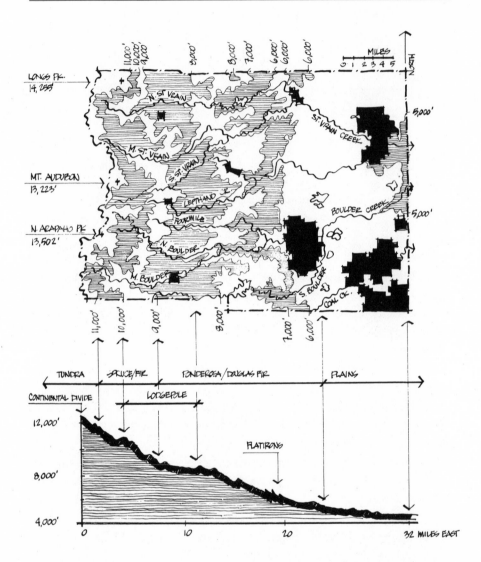

Boulder County Topography in Plan and Section

collects weather, flora, and fauna from all four directions. Arctic air masses can drop winter temperatures to as low as −30°F, and warm westerlies can melt half a foot of snow in minutes. In summer, warm subtropical air rising up over the mountains clashes with the cold air aloft to spawn spectacular thunderstorms that produce damaging hail and tornadoes as they rumble eastward across the plains.

If you sit in a cottonwood grove along Boulder Creek watching white-tailed deer and listening to blue jays calling from the treetops, you can absorb some of the ambiance of the eastern deciduous forest. Thirty miles west, you can explore an environment that could pass as Alaska. In terms of climate and vegetation change, the 25-mile drive and walk from the city of Boulder to Arapaho Pass is analogous to a 2,500-mile journey from Boulder to Fairbanks.

The convergence of life-forms in Boulder County creates endless possibilities for bird-watching, mammal-watching, or botanizing. In North St. Vrain Canyon, mule deer, white-tailed deer, elk, and bighorn sheep forage within a few miles of one another. Over the seasons and years at Sawhill Ponds, you can see more than two hundred species of birds, including a dozen species of warblers. In the Boulder Mountain Park, six species of conifers thrive on the same ridge-top between South Boulder Peak and Bear Peak, and ten species of wild orchids bloom in nearby canyons.

Boulder County's remarkable elevation range (from 4,920 feet along St. Vrain Creek to 14,255 feet at Longs Peak) and its complex topography combine to create an array of unusual microhabitats. One of the joys of exploring this area is discovering these hidden, secret places: a shady canyon in the foothills where ferns grow waist-high and ovenbirds sing in streamside hazelnut shrubs; a cottonwood grove on the plains where bald eagles roost in winter; or a waterfall in the mountains where fairy-slippers bloom and black swifts dart through the mist.

ECOSYSTEMS OF BOULDER COUNTY

Boulder County's diversity of topography and climate is reflected in its flora. More than fifteen hundred species of vascular plants have been identified along Colorado's Front Range—over six hundred in the Boulder Mountain Park alone. Some plants, such as creeping mahonia, thrive in a wide variety of habitats and elevations. Others, such as Bell's twinpod, which grows only on foothills shale outcrops, are confined to a single ecological setting. Understanding ecosystems helps in appreciating the distribution and habitat requirements of plants, birds, mammals, and other wildlife.

An ecosystem is a distinct community of plants and animals functioning as an interconnected unit. Ecosystems are living entities, made up of millions of organisms, ranging from bacteria to ferns to birds to trees. These organisms have co-evolved to create a dynamic equilibrium. The loss of a single species can cause irreversible changes to the entire system.

In ponderosa pine forests, Abert's squirrels contribute to tree regeneration by scattering seeds but also limit the amount of regeneration by ingesting most of the seeds they find. Ponderosa pines "control" populations of Abert's squirrels and other seed predators by occasionally producing below-normal cone crops. When seeds are not available, the squirrels subsist on the soft inner bark of ponderosa twigs and on truffles growing symbiotically with the ponderosa roots. By harvesting the truffles, the squirrels may help to spread the fungus's spores throughout the forest. The lives of the trees, the squirrels, and the truffles are intertwined in a complex web of interdependent and competitive relationships.

Geographical distribution of ecosystems is determined by a variety of factors, including soil texture and chemistry; moisture; temperature; elevation; slope; effects of wind, fire, and erosion; and interactions between plants and animals. Ecosystems constantly shift and evolve. Only fifteen thousand years ago the region of Boulder County that we now consider prairie was probably a mosaic of coniferous forests, tallgrass savannahs, marshes, and thickets populated by camels, mammoths, and saber-toothed cats. Much of the present-day tundra was covered with ice, and tree line was significantly lower.

Over the past 150 years, human-caused disturbances such as fire, overgrazing, introduction of exotic plants, logging, and urbanization have significantly altered Front Range ecosystems. Most of the grasslands and old-growth forests are gone. Nevertheless, all the ecosystems briefly described below can still be found in a more or less natural state in parts of Boulder County. For more detailed descriptions of local ecosystems, see *From Grassland to Glacier*, by Cornelia Mutel and John Emerick, and *The Southern Rockies*, by Audrey Benedict.

The **plains grasslands** that once covered most of eastern Boulder County and beyond still flourish along South Boulder Creek and at Rock Creek Farm and Rabbit Mountain. Wetter areas support tallgrasses such as big bluestem, switchgrass, and Indian grass; drier sites support blue grama, buffalo grass, and western wheatgrass. Prairie dogs, badgers, coyotes, thirteen-lined ground squirrels, Swainson's hawks, ferruginous hawks, grasshopper sparrows, and many other native species still thrive in our remaining grasslands.

Plains riparian woodlands, dominated by plains cottonwoods and willows, occur along Boulder Creek, St. Vrain Creek, and their tributaries. This ecosystem supports an array of cavity-nesting and foliage-nesting birds, as well as streamside mammals such as white-tailed deer, raccoons, and red foxes. **Prairie ponds** and **marshes** sustain a variety of uncommon plants and provide critical nesting habitat for many birds found nowhere else in the county, including northern harriers, least bitterns, and yellow-headed blackbirds.

In the foothills (approximately 5,500 to 8,000 feet elevation), the grasses of the plains merge with the coniferous forests of the mountains to form a mosaic of ecosystems that support a high diversity of birds and mammals. **Foothill shrublands,** with a dense growth of deciduous mountain mahogany,

hawthorn, three-leaf sumac, chokecherry, and wild plum, are important foraging and nesting areas for black bears, gray foxes, and many species of birds.
Ponderosa pine/Douglas fir forests are the dominant forest type in Boulder
County between 6,000 and 9,000 feet. The drought-resistant ponderosa pines
dominate on sunny south-facing slopes, and the shade-tolerant Douglas firs
prevail on cooler north-facing slopes. Over fifty species of mammals and over
seventy species of breeding birds have been documented in these forests,
where seeds, fruits, berries, and insects are particularly varied and abundant.
Typical mammals and birds of ponderosa pine forests are Abert's squirrels,
flammulated owls, solitary vireos, and pygmy nuthatches. In the shadier
Douglas fir forests, look for chickarees (pine squirrels), Cooper's hawks, hermit
thrushes, and blue grouse.

In the high mountains, the ponderosa pine/Douglas fir forests give way
to several other forest forms, including aspen woodlands, lodgepole pine
forests, and spruce/fir forests. **Aspen woodlands** occupy disturbed sites (by
both natural and human activity) between about 7,000 and 11,000 feet.
Because aspen groves are full of light, they support a rich understory of grasses,
wildflowers, and small trees. Small mammals abound, as do cavity-nesting
birds such as red-naped sapsuckers, house wrens, tree swallows, and mountain
bluebirds.

Lodgepole pine forests also occur on disturbed sites. Lodgepole pines tend
to grow close together, forming shady, even-aged groves with little undergrowth. To regenerate, lodgepoles depend partly on fire to open their tough,
resinous cones, to disperse the seeds, and to create sunny openings where
seedlings can grow. Because the pine seeds are hard to extract and fruits are
scarce, wildlife is less abundant here than in other forests. However, the lack
of undergrowth makes lodgepole pine forests good places for tracking small
mammals such as snowshoe hares, short-tailed weasels, and porcupines.

Engelmann spruce/subalpine fir forests occur between about 9,500 and
11,000 feet, in the region of deep winter snows and frequent summer

thunderstorms. This is the typical "fairy-tale forest," with tall, robust trees; mossy, lichen-covered logs; and a rich undergrowth of blueberries, wintergreens, and arnica. In terms of wildlife, the spruce/fir forest is a poor second to the ponderosa pine/Douglas fir forest, supporting fewer than half the species of birds and mammals. Harsh winters and the short summer growing season restrict the number of species that can survive there. Among the common birds are hermit thrushes, gray jays, ruby-crowned kinglets, yellow-rumped warblers, and pine grosbeaks. Typical mammals include pine martens, snowshoe hares, black bears, chickarees, and long-tailed weasels.

Mountain riparian woodlands are dominated by narrowleaf cottonwoods, willows, and smaller deciduous trees. Yellow warblers, black-capped chickadees, and warbling vireos nest in the cottonwoods and willows. Black bears and other mammals forage in the shrub understory. Beavers build lodges and dams and feed on the nutritious bark of willows and aspen. **Mountain meadows** and **wetlands** are scattered across the mountains in wet or disturbed areas where conifers cannot survive. Mountain meadows containing willow thickets are one of the richest breeding-bird habitats in all Colorado. Common species include soras, Wilson's warblers, MacGillivray's warblers, and Lincoln's sparrows.

The upper limit of tree growth in Boulder County occurs around 11,500 feet. Here the spruce/fir forest thins and becomes stunted, forming a **krummholz** (German for "twisted wood") of gnarled, windswept trees growing only a few feet high. Slightly higher on the mountainsides, the krummholz gives way to **alpine tundra**. The tundra is a treeless ecosystem dominated by grasses, perennial herbs, low shrubs, mosses, and lichens. Included are plants of cold northern climates, such as the Arctic gentian, as well as miniature versions of plants found at lower elevations, such as mertensias. Most birds and large mammals of the tundra are summer visitors that move down the mountainsides with the approach of winter. Year-round residents include heather voles, northern pocket gophers, pikas, marmots, and a few male ptarmigan.

Nearly everyone who lives in Boulder County has a favorite ecosystem. For many, it is the tundra or the verdant spruce/fir forest. For others there is nothing prettier than the tallgrass prairie on a dewy August morning, or the ponderosa pine/Douglas fir forest when snowflakes whisper down through evergreen needles. Encountered in a natural state, free of human disturbance, each ecosystem is a source of delight.

WATCHING WILDLIFE

Someone once said that if you stood anywhere in North America for a long-enough time, you would eventually see every North American bird. In most parts of the continent, this would probably take about as long as what the pro-verbial six monkeys would need to type the complete works of Shakespeare, but in Boulder County you might be able to do it within a few lifetimes. More than 350 bird species have been sighted since the Boulder Audubon Society began keeping formal records in 1975. About 220 species are reported each year; of these, about 170 species breed regularly within the county.

The county's avifauna consists of year-round residents (about eighty species), summer residents (about ninety species), winter residents (about twenty-five species), and migrants (about forty-five species). (See Appendix 3, page 298, for a detailed checklist.) Year-round residents include a few birds, such as great horned owls, that may stay in the same general area all year, as well as those, such as Townsend's solitaires and horned larks, that undertake vertical migrations from the high country to lower elevations. Many of our summer residents arrive with the onset of warm weather in the spring and head south by the end of September.

The composition of Boulder County's breeding-bird population has changed gradually over the past hundred years. Sharp-tailed grouse, American wood-cocks, and long-billed curlews disappeared as their breeding habitat was altered or destroyed. Eastern blue jays, least flycatchers, and brown-headed cowbirds colonized our area from the east, while common ravens moved in from the north and west. The most dramatic change has been the arrival and flourishing of exotic species from Europe, including rock doves, starlings, and house sparrows (see May Fauna for details). Two species, burrowing owls and long-eared owls, currently are on the verge of disappearing from Boulder County, and peregrine falcons have only recently become reestablished after a thirty-five-year hiatus.

Bird-watching provides insights into ecological relationships because birds are powerful indicators of environmental conditions and environmental change. It's also a good way to get outdoors and meet people. Several Boulder County organizations offer free bird-watching trips throughout the year (see Appendix 5, page 311, for addresses).

Boulder County also boasts an extremely diverse mammal population. Eighty-two naturally occurring species have been documented, and nine additional species are believed to live here. Mammals have colonized our area from all directions: rock squirrels and bushy-tailed wood rats from the Southwest, fox squirrels and white-tailed deer from the East, and chickarees and pine martens from the North.

Some mammals, including mule deer, badgers, and deer mice, are distributed throughout most of the county. Others, such as Abert's squirrels in ponderosa pine forests, are largely restricted to a single ecosystem. Still others, such as black bears and elk, migrate from one ecosystem to another.

Before European-American settlement, the rich grasslands and shrublands at the base of the Rocky Mountains attracted herds of elk, bison, pronghorn, and bighorn sheep. Packs of gray wolves followed these herds. Grizzly bears foraged along the banks of prairie streams while river otters and mink fished in the clear waters. Almost all of these mammals were extirpated by human activity. Even mule deer and elk, now considered common, disappeared temporarily from much of the Front Range.

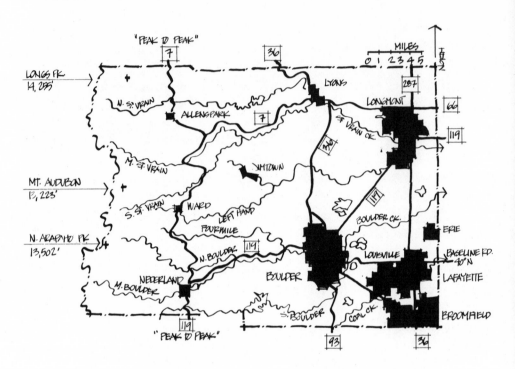

Boulder County Major Roads and Towns

Although many mammals are coming back, loss of habitat has eliminated the possibility of ever re-creating the richness of the presettlement fauna in Boulder County. Remaining grasslands may not be extensive enough to permit reintroduction of bison or pronghorn. Low instream flows in local creeks may preclude recolonization by river otters. Fragmentation of coniferous forests by roads and subdivisions threatens the viability of black bear and elk populations.

Today, remote areas of the county, such as the alpine tundra and spruce/fir forest, probably offer the best opportunities to observe mammals in a natural setting. Pika and marmot colonies are particularly productive because they attract long-tailed weasels, red foxes, and other predators. Foothills canyons are good places to look for large carnivores, including black bears, coyotes, bobcats, and mountain lions. In fall 1992, there were more than thirty black bear sightings in the Boulder Mountain Park alone.

On the plains, wetlands and grasslands attract a surprising variety of wildlife. At Sawhill Ponds you can almost always scare up a red fox or white-tailed deer; and at Boulder Valley Ranch you can watch coyotes stalking meadow voles, deer mice, thirteen-lined ground squirrels, cottontails, white-tailed jackrabbits, and black-tailed prairie dogs.

Observing mammals requires patience but connects us with the rhythms of nature. When elk bugle in the fall, we sense their excitement. In spring when young foxes frolic, we grin with delight. When marmots yawn, we sometimes catch ourselves yawning back. These moments more than compensate for the hours of waiting and watching.

TREADING LIGHTLY

There's no shortage of hiking trails or outdoor places to go in Boulder County. Unfortunately, there's also a superabundance of people. To put things into perspective, there are 250,000 humans and only a couple of dozen black bears; 110,000 human dwellings and only about 10 golden eagle nest sites; 60 retail florists and only a half-dozen known specimens of white adder's-mouth, one of our rarest orchids.

Whenever we go out into nature we run the risk of loving it to death. Although anyone who would read this book probably already walks lightly on the land, here are a few suggestions to help preserve the places we cherish.

• Comply with signs regarding pets. Dogs can be especially disruptive to wildlife and other hikers. Even the scent of a dog can stress wild animals. Remember that regulations vary. In some areas, no dogs are allowed; in others, they must be leashed; and in still others, they must be under voice control.

• Comply with signs regarding vehicles and mountain bikes, which are prohibited on many trails because of erosion problems. Refrain from using bikes on muddy slopes where deep ruts develop quickly, and yield to other trail users.

• Avoid shortcutting trails, as shortcuts destroy vegetation and cause erosion. Be especially careful when conditions are muddy and in areas where unusual or rare plants grow. On narrow trails, walk single file rather than several abreast, and try to avoid congregating large groups in sensitive areas.

• Don't pick wildflowers or dig up plants; it's illegal in all parks, and permission is needed on private land. Be judicious in picking fruit and leave some for wildlife.

- Campfires are becoming controversial. Build fires only when and where permitted, and never leave one unattended.

- Bury human waste and bury or burn toilet paper.

- Leave gates as you find them, unless signs instruct otherwise.

- In heavily used areas, such as the Boulder Creek Path, keep to the right to avoid collisions. Bikers need to be especially careful in passing pedestrians and should give warning of their presence.

- Give right of way to horses, keeping to the downhill side. The same rule applies to all large mammals, who will become stressed if you remain above them.

- Horses should be kept on trails and should not be allowed to graze except where expressly permitted.

- Avoid disturbing nesting birds, and comply with closures designed to protect plants or animals.

- If you are photographing or observing wild animals and they become nervous, you are too close. Back away.

- If you feel like doing a good deed, carry out litter left by others.

No matter how careful we are, our actions have an impact on the natural world, and as our human population grows, negative impacts become more and more severe. If you are interested in learning more about our environment and in working to preserve it, join one or more of the organizations listed in Appendix 5, page 311.

"Walk in peace and beauty always"—Navajo greeting

Canada Geese, Sawhill Ponds

JANUARY

New Year's Day. It's the beginning of a new year, and we celebrate with an old tradition – ski touring where there's snow, hiking where there's not. The champagne we drink is the sparkling cold air filled with prismatic ice crystals that some skiers call "fairy dust." The resolution we make is to enjoy and care for our natural world during the next twelve months, each of which is filled with its own special miracles and magic.

Alpenglow is one of the miracles of this month of slowly lengthening days when the sun, paradoxically, rises at the latest hour of the year (see sunrise/sunset chart on page 284). Because of this timing, most of us are up before dawn and can watch the low light touch the peaks and paint the Flatirons. Alpenglow occurs when rays of sunlight reflect off summits, causing them to glow with an ethereal pink radiance. The effect is even more dazzling when fresh snow has fallen. In locations where mountains are to the east, watch for alpenglow as the sun sets. The moment when mountains blush is brief, but it's worth venturing out into the cold to see.

When the temperature is below 0°F and the bare ground seems to have disappeared until May, a warm wind may sweep down from the mountains. It's affectionately (or disparagingly) known as "chinook" or "Snow Eater." This downslope wind can raise the temperature thirty degrees in thirty minutes, thawing the snow like a hair dryer. When a chinook ceases, temperatures may crash just as drastically. Its cousin, the cold wind from the north, is called "bora," and bores right through to the bone.

Even warm winds can chill, making you feel much colder than the thermometer reads. The "windchill index" is a way of measuring the combined effect of wind and temperature on exposed human flesh. For example, if the thermometer reading is 0°F and the wind velocity is 40 mph, energy loss from bare skin is equivalent to −49°F with no wind. (See the wind chill table on page 21.)

The variability of the weather − proverbial in Colorado − is dramatic in January, when the most violent winds of the year occur. An example is the gale of January 1988. Gusting at over 90 mph, it knocked down part of an overpass bridge under construction in Boulder. Another windstorm in 1971 gusted to 147 mph at the National Center for Atmospheric Research (NCAR) and reached 165 mph at Marshall Mesa. Some of the earliest photographs of homes in Boulder and in Caribou show stout poles, like flying buttresses, supporting the cabins against these fierce winds.

During this coldest month, many creatures are fired with passion. Beavers and coyotes mate, and great horned owls begin to court. We frequently hear an owl duet at Sawhill Ponds, where we go to watch the first full moon of the year rise as the sun sets.

This is a month when much of the color seems to be in the sky: pink alpenglow, rose-gold moonrises, fiery sunrises and sunsets, and one of our favorite atmospheric astonishments − iridescent clouds sometimes called sundogs, mock suns, or parhelia. This phenomenon occurs when ice crystals in cirrus clouds near the sun refract the sunlight into opalescent colors. The brightness is enhanced when the crystals are more numerous and uniform in size.

Even snow on the ground is not entirely white. When a sunny day follows a bitter cold night and the surface crystals are large, it looks as though someone had scattered glitter across the snow. If you rotate your head, the colors change like a kaleidoscope. At other times the snow is blue, especially where it has been fractured. The reason for the predominance of blue is that most other wavelengths of light are absorbed by the snow.

Small details also provide bits of brilliance. Watch for the golden crowns of kinglets, the scarlet caps of pine grosbeaks and finches, orange lichen on rocks, and gray-green "old-man's-beard" (*Usnea* lichen) festooning the Douglas firs. Rising sap tints

WILD CHILL TABLE

Indicates the Wind Chill Index (equivalent in cooling power on exposed flesh)

AIR TEMPERATURE (°F)

WIND SPEED (MILES/HOUR)	35	30	25	20	15	10	5	0	-5	-10	-15	-20	-25	-30	-35	-40
	COLD			VERY COLD				BITTER COLD				EXTREME COLD				
4	35	30	25	20	15	10	5	0	-5	-10	-15	-20	-25	-30	-35	-40
5	32	27	22	16	11	6	0	-5	-10	-15	-21	-26	-31	-36	-42	-47
10	22	16	10	3	-3	-9	-15	-22	-27	-34	-40	-46	-52	-58	-64	-71
15	16	9	2	-5	-11	-18	-25	-31	-38	-45	-51	-58	-65	-72	-78	-85
20	12	4	-3	-10	-17	-24	-31	-39	-46	-53	-60	-67	-74	-81	-88	-95
25	8	1	-7	-15	-22	-29	-36	-44	-51	-59	-66	-74	-81	-88	-96	-103
30	6	-2	-10	-18	-25	-33	-41	-49	-56	-64	-71	-79	-86	-93	-101	-109
35	4	-4	-12	-20	-27	-35	-43	-52	-58	-67	-74	-82	-89	-97	-105	-113
40	3	-5	-13	-21	-29	-37	-45	-53	-60	-69	-76	-84	-92	-100	-107	-115
45	2	-6	-14	-22	-30	-38	-46	-54	-62	-70	-78	-85	-93	-102	-109	-117

Wind speeds greater than 40 MPH have little additional cooling effect.

Example: A 30 MPH wind, combined with a temperature of 30°F, can have the same effect as a temperature of -2°F when it is calm.

Source: U.S. Department of Commerce, National Oceanic and Atmospheric Administration Climate Analysis Center.

willow twigs yellow and red, and the first silvery pussy willow buds and the tight red buds of mountain maples start to swell.

These minutiae remind us of how colorful and varied nature is in Boulder County, where one season is snugly wrapped within another but may unfurl at unexpected times and places.

FLORA

SNUGGLED UNDER SNOW

"A blanket of snow" is more than a metaphor. Snow provides insulation for both plants and animals wintering underneath it in an environment called "subnivean." In *Wandering Through Winter*, Edwin Way Teale tells of an experiment in which a thermometer was placed in the snow. At the surface, the temperature registered −27°F, but 7 inches below the surface, the temperature was 24° *above* zero—a difference of fifty-one degrees.

In *Snow*, Ruth Kirk writes of a study showing that with a 6-inch snow cover, frost penetrated less than an inch into the soil, whereas adjacent snow-free fields were frozen more than a foot deep. Tiny air pockets insulate the earth in the same way that dressing in layers provides extra insulation for people.

Snow cover also helps prevent the extreme fluctuations in temperature that damage plants, and—surprisingly—it also supplies fertilizer. Kirk says that nitrate spread on fields by an average winter snowfall has been valued at twenty dollars an acre. On the debit side, snow can restrict light penetration and, possibly, the exchange of gases.

Winter ecologist James Halfpenny says that some plants, such as kinnikinnick, remain green all winter under the snowpack and continue to carry on photosynthesis. Although subnivean light levels are much reduced, the little light that does penetrate is of a wavelength that is near optimum for photosynthesis. Some snow-covered sedges put out new leaves, some seeds germinate under several feet of snow, and many perennials bloom through their white blanket. Next spring look for the yellow flowers of snow

JANUARY WEATHER

JANUARY 1

Sunrise: 7:21 AM MST
Sunset: 4:46 PM MST

	Boulder	**Allens Park**	**Niwot Ridge**
	5,445'	8,500'	11,565'
Ave. Max.	41°F	35°F Ave. January high	16°F Ave. January high
Ave. Min.	18°F	15°F Ave. January low	+5°F Ave. January low

JANUARY 31

Sunrise: 7:09 AM MST
Sunset: 5:18 PM MST

Ave. Max.	45°F	35°F Ave. January high	16°F Ave. January high
Ave. Min.	20°F	15°F Ave. January low	+5°F Ave. January low

JANUARY CHANGES (January 1–January 31)

Day Length: 9 hours, 25 minutes to 10 hours, 9 minutes=change of +44 minutes

Change: Max.	+4°F	−2°F	0°F
Change: Min.	+2°F	−2°F	0°F

JANUARY EXTREMES

Max. Temp.	77°F	62°F	See note
Min. Temp.	−33°F	−38°F	See note
Max. Wind	147 mph	99 mph	Not available
Ave. Precip.	.55 in.	1.1 in.	6.3 in.
Max. Precip.	2.5 in.	2.4 in.	11.4 in.
Min. Precip.	00 in.	.1 in.	2.7 in.
Ave. Snow	9 in.	20 in.	Not available
Max. Snow	35 in.	38 in.	Not available
Min. Snow	00 in.	.3 in.	Not available

Note. 77°F is highest for any summer and −31°F is lowest for any winter on Niwot Ridge.

NOTES AND SOURCES

1. "Colorado's Climate, Meteorology & Air Quality," PEDCO-Environmental, Inc. Cincinnati, Ohio, for Bureau of Land Management. 1951–1981.
2. The Niwot Ridge/Green Lakes Valley long-term Ecological Research Program, INSTAAR (1951–81).
3. *The Boulder Weather Log.* Bill Callahan, Boulder, Colo.: Upslope Press.
4. MST is used due to split months and because dates of change from standard time vary with political whim.
5. Niwot Ridge wind data are from 1983–1990.
6. Niwot Ridge precipitation data are complicated by frequent wind-driven snow conditions.
7. *Climate of the States.* 1951–1980. Detroit, Mich.: Gale Research Co.

I'D RATHER SWIM AT 20°C THAN AT 20°F

Gabriel Fahrenheit developed the Fahrenheit scale during the eighteenth century, basing it on a freezing point for water of 32° and a boiling point of 212° at sea level. At about the same time, Anders Celsius did the same thing, basing his scale on 0° for the freezing point and 100° for the boiling point of water at sea level.

In Boulder County, water boils at 201.9°F at a 5,500-feet elevation, and at 197.5°F at 8,000 feet. This makes a lot of difference in cooking; just imagine, a three-minute egg at sea level becomes a five- or six-minute egg on the plains of Boulder County! The rate of change is about one degree Fahrenheit for every 550 feet of elevation change. The freezing point of water changes very little with changes in elevation.

Because the Fahrenheit scale is still the most familiar one in the U.S., we are using it in this book. Like many other North Americans, we have some difficulty converting to the Celsius (or centigrade) scale and tend to think in broad terms, as illustrated in the following table:

```
-10°C = bitter cold =  14°F
  0°C =  freezing   =  32°F
 10°C =    cool     =  50°F
 20°C =    mild     =  68°F
 30°C =    hot      =  86°F
 40°C = very hot  = 104°C
```

An interesting bit of trivia: −40° is the same on both scales.

buttercups and glacier lilies poking through the edges of snowfields in alpine and subalpine areas.

EVERGREENS

When other trees are bare and herbaceous plants are dormant, evergreens – symbol of hope – catch our fancy. We sing carols to their "faithful branches" and decorate our homes with them. In Colorado we proclaim the Colorado blue spruce our state tree. Sometimes we wonder why the conifers remain green and fragrant throughout the year.

There is a Cherokee legend that says when the trees were first made they were told to stay awake and keep watch for seven nights. The only ones who succeeded were cedar, pine, spruce, fir, holly, and laurel. As a reward, they were allowed to remain forever green.

In reality, northern evergreens have evolved several adaptations to withstand severe winter conditions. Their sap has a low freezing point, and the chlorophyll in their green needles allows them to carry on some photosynthesis throughout the winter. The presence of chlorophyll in the bark tissues of aspen allows this species also to continue limited photosynthesis in winter, enabling it to compete successfully with conifers during the long leafless season. Although deciduous trees tend to break when snow accumulates on branches that are still leafed out, most evergreen branches slope downward, allowing the snow to slide off. This pattern is especially noticeable in spruce trees.

Conifer needles have a waxy coating and a streamlined shape with a minimum of surface area. This design helps to prevent desiccation, the main factor in winterkill. As Ann Zwinger writes in *Land Above the Trees*, these needles are "elegantly engineered for survival in a cold, dry climate."

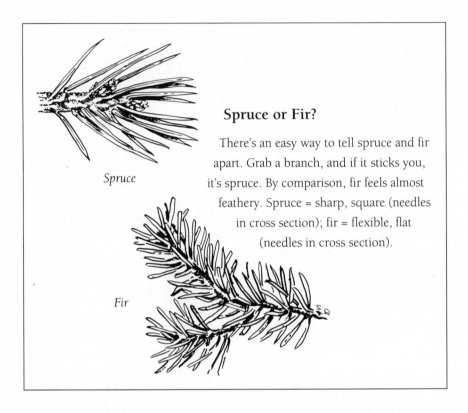

Spruce or Fir?

There's an easy way to tell spruce and fir apart. Grab a branch, and if it sticks you, it's spruce. By comparison, fir feels almost feathery. Spruce = sharp, square (needles in cross section); fir = flexible, flat (needles in cross section).

Spruce

Fir

FAUNA

CAT TRACKS

Although January is the driest month of the year, it's also the month when snow usually stays on the ground the longest. Because most plants are dormant and most birds are absent then, January is a good month for tracking animals.

The high country has the deepest snow, but the foothills probably have the greatest diversity of mammalian life. At

26

CONIFERS OF BOULDER COUNTY

Species	Location	Identification
Ponderosa Pine *Pinus ponderosa*	Relatively dry, often south-facing sites; 5,500–9,000 feet	Long (4–7") needles in clusters of two or three; textured, reddish bark on older trees
Lodgepole Pine *Pinus contorta*	Disturbed sites; 7,000–11,000 feet	Short, twisted needles in clumps of two; tall, straight trunk
Limber Pine *Pinus flexilis*	Rocky, windswept ridges and exposed slopes; 7,500–11,000 feet	Short needles in bundles of five; trunks often gnarled and twisted
Rocky Mountain Bristlecone Pine *Pinus aristata*	Dry, windswept slopes west of Caribou; 10,000–11,000 feet	Short, twisted needles, five to a clump, flecked with white pitch; gnarled, twisted trunks; bristle-tipped cone scales
Engelmann Spruce *Picea engelmannii*	Areas of permanent winter snow; 9,000–11,500 feet	Dark green four-sided needles; tall trees; reddish, scaly bark; cones hang down
Colorado Blue Spruce *Picea pungens 'Glauca'*	Moist habitats, often along foothills streams; 5,500–10,000 feet	Bluish four-sided, sharp needles; Christmas-tree-like shape; cones hang down
Douglas Fir* *Pseudotsuga menziesii*	Shaded, often north-facing, sites; 6,000–10,000 feet	Short, flat needles; female cones hang down and have 3-pronged bracts protruding from between cone scales
Subalpine Fir *Abies lasiocarpa*	Areas of permanent winter snow, usually in association with Engelmann spruce; 9,500–11,500 feet	Flat, short, blunt needles; upright purple-black cones on upper branches; whitish bark
Rocky Mountain Juniper *Juniperus scopulorum*	Relatively dry, often rocky sites; 5,500–9,000 feet	Stout, shrublike tree growing 10–20' high; green to bluish purple berrylike cones; scalelike foliage
Mountain Common Juniper *Juniperus communis saxatilis*	Understory of dry forests; 5,500–10,000 feet	A low shrub with sharp, needlelike foliage; berrylike cones

*Douglas fir is not a true fir at all, but is a member of a separate genus found only in western North America and the mountains of eastern Asia.

Mammal Tracking

Because many mammals are nocturnal and secretive, we must learn about them by "reading" their tracks. It can become a great game of gathering clues and guessing imaginatively.

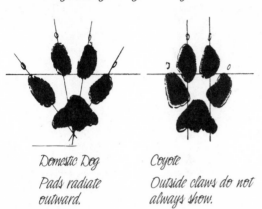

Domestic Dog
Pads radiate outward.

Coyote
Outside claws do not always show.

Cat Family
No claw marks, prints appear round, or wider than long...Two lobes on plantar pad, front side.

places like Rabbit Mountain, North St. Vrain Canyon, and Walker Ranch, you can find tracks of more than a dozen species. The tracks create a vivid picture of the relative populations of herbivores and predators. Mouse, vole, rabbit, raccoon, and squirrel tracks are abundant; deer tracks are common; weasel, fox, and coyote tracks are scattered about; mountain lion and bobcat tracks are uncommon.

During the first half of this century, there were no documented mountain lion sightings in Boulder County. Today,

lion sightings are reported to local wildlife agencies almost weekly, and lion-human interactions are becoming more commonplace. Nevertheless, lions are difficult to find. Adults occupy home ranges of 100 square miles or more, and they are usually secretive and wary of humans. A set of fresh tracks in the snow, or a "scratching post" where bark has been scraped from a tree trunk or log, may indicate only that a cougar is somewhere within ten or fifteen miles.

The recent increase in mountain lion sightings in Boulder County probably results from elimination of bounties, an increase in local mule deer populations (the cougar's preferred prey), and a greater human presence in the mountains. Humans are spending more time hiking in the rugged foothills country frequented by lions. More houses are being built in these regions, and pets and pet food may attract lions to developed areas.

James Halfpenny and Kristen McGrath, of the University of Colorado's Institute for Arctic and Alpine Research, and Michael Sanders, of Boulder County's Parks and Open Space department, compiled a list of known lion sightings in Boulder County from 1950 to the present and solicited mountain lion reports from Boulder County residents. Numbers of mountain lion sightings have increased significantly, as have numbers of aggressive interactions between mountain lions and humans. Of the more than three hundred lion sightings reported in the Boulder area between 1986 and 1991, thirty-seven (11.5%) included "lion-dominant behaviors" indicative of aggressiveness.

Lions are occasionally seen in urban areas. Reports included a pair of cougar cubs found under a house in Boulder near Fourth and Arapahoe, a cougar seen stalking deer in the Martin Acres subdivision in South Boulder, and frequent cougar observations along the Mesa Trail in the Boulder Mountain Park.

As cougar populations increase and some cougars lose their fear of humans, cougar attacks may become more common. In 1990 a high school student jogging in the forest near Idaho Springs was killed by a female mountain lion. During the same year, a woman jogging in the foothills west of Boulder received minor scratches when two young cougars stalked her and followed her up into a tree. Two lions were shot and killed by mountain residents who said they feared for the safety of their pets and children.

Some experts recommend an aggressive program to restore the cougars' natural fear of people. Some animal rights advocates believe lions have been persecuted too much already and should be left alone. The state of California, where several lion attacks occurred during the late 1980s and early 1990s, has nevertheless placed a moratorium on all hunting of mountain lions.

While local mountain lion populations have increased recently, two other members of the cat family may not have fared so well. Bobcats, which inhabit the foothills and mountains of Boulder County, are reported less frequently than are mountain lions. They have been trapped throughout this century, and the Colorado Division of Wildlife lists their status as "uncertain, requiring further study." Bobcats are seen occasionally in the Boulder Mountain Park, North St. Vrain Canyon, the foothills near Lyons, and in Lykins Gulch north of Boulder.

The Canada lynx is listed as an endangered species in Colorado. Because lynx resemble bobcats and are about the same size, lynx "sightings" are often questionable. Although there have been no clearly documented lynx observations in Boulder County in this century, Canada lynx have been seen in other parts of the state. James Halfpenny and Richard Thompson recently confirmed observations of Canada lynx tracks near the Vail ski area. Lynx are boreal mammals, inhabiting the subalpine forests of Canada, the northern United States, and the northern and central Rockies. In Boulder County they would most likely be found in spruce-fir forests above 10,000 feet.

Although the odds of finding any wild cat are slim, tracking offers a good excuse to go hiking, skiing, or snowshoeing in remote areas of the county. And the discovery of a set of cat tracks in a snowy, isolated canyon can stimulate an adrenalin rush sufficient to warm the extremities on the coldest January day.

HOW DANGEROUS ARE MOUNTAIN LIONS?

In 1990, when an Idaho Springs high school student was killed by a mountain lion and a Boulder jogger was forced up a tree by two mountain lions, some people began to wonder about the advisability of hiking or jogging alone in the Front Range foothills. But what are the real dangers, and how can they be avoided?

James Halfpenny, Michael Sanders, and Kristen McGrath estimated the chances of being attacked by a mountain lion in Boulder County on a given day as 1 in 35,000,000 – approximately seven times less than the chances of winning the Colorado Lottery. To come up with this figure, they multiplied the population of Boulder County by the number of days in a year and divided the total into the average number of attacks per year (two attacks between 1985 and 1991).

Paul Beier, of the University of California at Berkeley's forestry department, summarized all available accounts of mountain lion attacks on humans in North America between 1890 and 1990. He concluded that there were fifty-five documented attacks during that period, resulting in ten human fatalities. Nine of the ten fatalities reported by Beier were children under the age of fourteen. More than half of the attacks were directed at unaccompanied children, and eleven of the seventeen adult victims were also alone at the time of the attack. Over half of the documented attacks have occurred since 1975.

The table below shows the approximate number of U.S. deaths per year from various natural hazards.

Clearly, the chances of being attacked by a mountain lion are minimal, even in areas where mountain lion populations are high. If a cougar stalks or confronts you, experts recommend the following actions:

- Respond aggressively, by shouting, swinging a stick, waving your arms over your head, or throwing rocks.
- Make yourself appear as large as possible.
- Do not run away. Fleeing may stimulate the cougar's aggressive instincts.

In almost every case, victims who responded aggressively have been

Hazard	Injuries/year	Deaths/year
Mountain Lions	0–3	0–2
Black Widow Spiders	–	0–5
Rattlesnakes	5,000	10–15
Domestic Dogs	200,000	10–20
Honey Bees	–	30–50
Lightning Strikes	–	50–100

Sources: Paul Beier, "Cougar attacks on humans in the United States and Canada," *Wildlife Soc. Bull* 19 (1991):403–412; National Center for Health Statistics, *Vital Statistics of the United States 1979*, vol. 2 "Mortality" (Washington: GPO, 1984), part A–5; J. J. Sacks, R. W. Sattin, and S. E. Bonzo, "Dog bite fatalities from 1979 through 1988," *Journal of the American Medical Association* 262 (1989):1489–92; R. Weiss, "Researchers foresee antivenin improvements," *Science News* 138 (1990):360–62.

successful in repelling cougar attacks. Lying down and playing dead (the advice generally given for bear attacks) does not seem to work with cougars. To be doubly safe, it might be a good idea to avoid hiking or jogging alone in remote areas of the foothills around dawn and dusk. Children should never be left alone in areas where cougars are believed to be present. Cougars with prey should never be disturbed or approached.

WHERE TO GO IN JANUARY

ELDORA SKI AREA

Eldora, the only downhill ski area in the county, also contains 45 kilometers of groomed Nordic trails that make loops, figure eights, and various other trail permutations, so cross-country skiers seldom need to retrace their steps. Although trail fees are charged, this area is a good choice if you're skiing alone because help is never far away. (One trail, "Deadman's Gulch," is so called because two of Fremont's men were buried here in 1845–46, not because this steep, narrow run suddenly makes a 90-degree turn.)

For those who want to observe snowshoe hares or listen for owls at night, the Tennessee Mountain Cabin, 3 miles from the trailhead, is available for rent from the Nordic Center. Guinn Mountain Cabin (also called the Arestua Hut) lies outside the ski area and is maintained by the Colorado Mountain Club (CMC). It's always kept open, but donations are requested for overnight use. If you wish to avoid the trail fees, ski up the beginner's slope about a mile and take a 3-mile marked forest service trail to the Guinn cabin. Wildlife has become especially tame at Eldora because of frequent encounters with humans. On one trip we encountered eight chickarees and lunched a few feet from a motionless showshoe hare. Gray jays and mountain chickadees ate from our hands.

Peterson Lake, which can be seen to the left just before reaching the ski area on CR 140, is one of the few places in the world where Rocky Mountain capshell snails live. First identified in 1920 by Junius Henderson, curator of the Henderson Museum at the University of

WORDS FOR WINTER

Why use ten words when one will do? In English, we must say "bowl-shaped depression in snow around the base of trees." However, the Inuit Indians in Alaska have just one word for that concept: Qamaniq. Many snow scientists use the vocabulary of peoples from the far north because of its conciseness and expressiveness. In her book *The Secret Language of Snow*, Terry Tempest Williams writes about terminology for different types of snow. For instance, the Inuit call falling snow "Annui"; snow on the ground, "Api"; snow that swirls like smoke above the ridges, "Siquoq"; and snow that collects on trees, "Qali."

Scientists have also developed their own vocabularies. The International Snow Classification System describes ten different categories of crystals, including *stellar*, *spatial dendrite*, and *needles*. Stellar crystals with six delicately embellished points are probably the most beautiful and most familiar of the crystals. An even more detailed classification scheme, devised by C. Magono and C. W. Lee, describes one hundred crystal types with such fine distinctions as *hollow bullet*, *solid bullet*, and *columns with dendrites*.

Many regions also have pet names for wind. In Boulder we call warm downslope winds "chinook," a term first used in the Pacific Northwest to refer to a warm moist wind off the Pacific Ocean that blew from the direction of the Chinook Indian camp. Other names for warm downslope winds are "Santa Ana" in Southern California, "foehn" in the Alps, and "warm braw" in New Guinea.

Colorado, this tiny mollusk may be on the edge of extinction and is found in only a few other lakes in Canada and Montana.

From the southwest end of Nederland take CR 130 to the Lake Eldora Ski Road, which dead-ends at the parking lot, or take the RTD bus.

CONEY FLATS ROAD

An old jeep road makes a broad, not-too-steep ski/snowshoe trail to Coney Flats, just below tree line and about 3 miles from Beaver Reservoir. The trail, protected from wind by lodgepole pine forests and a few aspen groves, opens out at Coney Flats, where strong winds usually prevail. The view of Sawtooth Mountain is worth braving the bluster. If weather permits, you can ski up the valley toward Buchanan Pass or Red Deer Lake, looking for ptarmigan at and above tree line. We have also seen flocks of more than three hundred rosy finches at the reservoir, and, once, a bald eagle.

From the lower end of Beaver Reservoir you can take the Sourdough Trail, with one branch leading to Camp Dick on Middle St. Vrain Creek and the other branch leading to Brainard Lake. To reach Beaver Reservoir, turn west from

Ptarmigan

Because of their superb seasonal camouflage coloring, ptarmigan usually see us long before we see them.

SR 72 at the Tahosa Boy Scout sign about 2 miles northwest of Ward. Coney Flats Road takes off from the northwest end of the reservoir just beyond the spillway.

BRAINARD LAKE AREA

Probably the most popular outdoor site in Boulder County, Brainard Lake is the chief gateway into the Indian Peaks Wilderness, with numerous trails originating in the vicinity. It's equally delightful summer or winter, but in winter boreal owls may call and pine martens and short-tailed weasels may dash across the trail.

In January the road is usually closed below Red Rocks Lake, and skiing and snowshoeing trails lead in every direction. (The forest service prohibits dogs on Little Raven, Waldrop, and the CMC South trails during the skiing season.) We strongly recommend a map if you are unfamiliar with this area; once a group followed our tracks without checking a map and ended up miles from their intended destination. Here are a few easily accessible trails:

• *Henry Waldrop Trail* parallels the road to the north and leads to the Colorado Mountain Club cabin in 2.8 miles. The cabin is open on weekends for skiers to purchase hot cider. Overnight accommodations can be rented from CMC (phone number in Appendix 5, page 311). At about 2 miles the trail forks, with the left branch going to the cabin. The right fork becomes the South St. Vrain Trail and later branches again, with the right branch returning to the parking lot via the Sourdough Trail while the left branch goes on to Beaver Reservoir.

• *CMC South Trail* parallels the other side of the road and is the easier route to Brainard Lake and the cabin. It's also possible to ski the road if there's sufficient snow and you don't object to snowmobiles. From Brainard Lake, strong skiers can continue to Lake Isabelle or Blue Lake or to the top of Mt. Audubon.

• *Sourdough Trail* goes north and south from the road. The north branch connects with other trails that lead to either Brainard Lake or Beaver Reservoir; the south branch goes to the Rainbow Lakes Road (CR 116).

• *Little Raven Trail*, starting at the Sourdough Trail and crossing Left Hand Park Reservoir Road, leads to Brainard Lake in about 2.5 miles.

• *Left Hand Reservoir Trail* connects the road to the reservoir.

BEWARE OF AVALANCHES

Snow avalanches kill several people each year in Colorado. They are characterized as being either "loose snow" avalanches that start from a specific point, grow as they descend, and remain relatively fluffy; or "slab" avalanches that start when a large slab of compacted snow begins to slide from a fracture line.

Although avalanches are complex and difficult to predict, here are a few danger signals: slopes exceeding 30 degrees (avalanches are most common on slopes of 30 to 45 degrees); convex slopes where there are no trees or brush to anchor the snow; sustained high wind; snow falling at the rate of 1 inch per hour or more; small pellet- or needle-shaped crystals rather than stellar crystals; rapid changes in weather. Backcountry skiers or snowshoers should consider taking a class on winter safety.

The road to Brainard Lake (CR 102) heads west from Ward. Turn off SR 72 at the sign. A network of higher-elevation trails starting in the vicinity of Brainard Lake is described in the July chapter.

VALMONT RESERVOIR

Unfrozen lakes are hard to find in January, so Valmont Reservoir with its open water (warmed by hot-water emissions from the power plant) is popular with both birds and birders. Rarities such as wood ducks and common loons come to this 536-acre lake, and a large prairie dog town attracts raptors. A spotting scope is useful and can be set up at Legion Park on the highest point, once called "Goodview Hill" because it served as a lookout for early Native Americans and white settlers. Cannon Loop Trail, 1 mile, circles the perimeter of Legion Park.

To reach Legion Park from Arapahoe Road, turn north onto a short gravel road east of the power plant and half a mile west of 75th. Another viewing point is just west of Legion Park at the turnaround behind several commercial buildings.

JANUARY OUT-OF-COUNTY EXCURSION

Rocky Mountain Arsenal was once called "the most polluted place on the planet" and is now the nation's largest urban National Wildlife Refuge. For forty years the U.S. Army produced chemical weapons on this 27-square-mile site that is only fifteen minutes from downtown Denver, often dumping toxic wastes into the open, lakelike basins. Later, Shell Oil Company produced Aldrin and Dieldrin here. Now bald eagles spend the winter at this wildlife area, preying on large populations of prairie dogs. Badgers, coyotes, deer, hawks, owls, and many other animals live here, although a high percentage are contaminated with toxic chemicals. To see how refuse is changing into refuge, take an escorted bus tour through the refuge. Phone the Arsenal for reservations: (303) 289-0132.

JANUARY AT A GLANCE

MAMMALS

- Beavers breed in January or February.
- Coyotes breed from January to March; young are born in about sixty days and emerge from the den in another three weeks.
- Black bear cubs are born while their mothers are dormant.

BIRDS

- Rosy finches flock by the hundreds at higher elevations.
- Great horned owls court.
- Large flocks of Bohemian waxwings feed on juniper and mountain ash berries in urban areas. Because they follow the fruit crop, their arrival cannot be predicted and therefore they are called "erratic."
- Rare ducks show up on Valmont Reservoir, often the only open water; other rarities may include redpolls and snow buntings.

OTHER CRITTERS

- Some grasshoppers, revved up with "antifreeze" (elevated levels of glycerol), remain active, providing food for coyotes, foxes, and owls.

PLANTS

- Some buds, such as pussy willow and Rocky Mountain maple, start to swell.
- Easter daisies may begin to bloom in lower Bear Canyon.

SPECIAL EVENTS

- The Indian Peaks bird count, conducted by the Boulder County Nature Association, takes place early in the month.

IN THE SKY

- Quadrantid meteor shower peaks around January 3. Look low in the northwest after sunset.
- Orion, The Great Hunter, is high in the southern sky around 9:00 P.M. Orion contains the Great Nebula, observable with binoculars, and the first-magnitude stars Rigel and Betelgeuse. Rigel is 460 light years distant but is fourteen thousand times brighter than our sun. The red giant Betelgeuse has a diameter of 215 million miles, greater than the diameter of Earth's orbit around the sun.

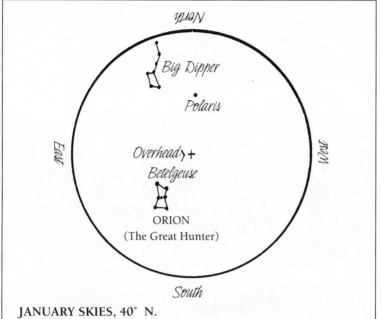

North

Big Dipper

Polaris

Overhead ⟩ +
Betelgeuse

ORION
(The Great Hunter)

East

West

South

JANUARY SKIES, 40° N.
Hold chart overhead

9 PM MST - Early Jan.
8 PM MST - Late Jan.

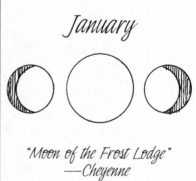

January

"*Moon of the Frost Lodge*"
—*Cheyenne*

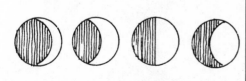

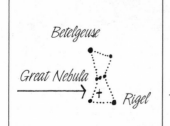

Betelgeuse

Great Nebula →

Rigel

ORION (The Great Hunter)

39

Raccoon in Russian Olive

FEBRUARY

Skiers and snowshoers revel in some of the best snow of the year in February. The snow base has had time to accumulate, and blizzards keep adding extra layers (unless there's a warm spell) until snow depth can reach 5 or 6 feet in the high country. The maximum depth measured in the city of Boulder watershed, in the forest at 10,300 feet, was 96.9 inches in April 1957; at Martinelli snowbank (on 11,000-foot Niwot Ridge) it was 60 feet.

Since this is the third coldest month of the year, the snow typically remains firm. It squeaks underfoot–a sound that means cold snow, fast snow. This sound may be due to the dryness of cold snow, according to James Halfpenny. With nothing to lubricate the space between crystals, friction may create the squeak, which occurs when the snow temperature (not the air temperature) is about 0°F. With rising temperatures, the crystals become silent once more.

True winter bliss is schussing through Colorado "champagne powder," a light, dry snow, as compared to "Sierra cement" or "Cascade concrete." However, snow behaves more like plastic than powder or concrete. It flows. It creates sinuous, curving sculptures. Tree stumps are topped with marble busts. Bird nests filled with snow look like bowls of ice cream. Heavy scallops of snow hang suspended from branches and from the eaves of houses. Cornices curl over mountain ridges. Above tree line and in open areas, wind hardens the plastic snow into sheets of "boilerplate" and into sharp frozen waves specified by the Russian term "sastrugi."

February

Snow is still the master artist of February's landscape. But in a typical Colorado paradox, hikers compete to find the first flowers on south-facing slopes. Because they receive more sun, these slopes are often warmer than are level areas at lower elevations. A tip for flower stalkers: Large rocks often create warmer microenvironments for early bloomers.

Spring beauties, small white flowers with pink veining, have been found as early as February 13 at Rabbit Mountain, and filarees, tiny magenta flowers also called storksbill, have been found on Valentine's Day. Creeping mahonia, sometimes called Oregon grape or holly grape, with yellow flowers and red-and-green leaves, is another colorful early bloomer. In urban areas, the first crocuses poke through the snow early in this month of intermingling flowers and snowflakes.

It's hard to miss the yellow and purple crocus, but many people never notice the blooming of tall deciduous trees such as maples, aspen, and elms. It's a spectacle worth craning your neck to see. The flowers are relatively inconspicuous until backlit by a low sun that makes them as resplendent as apple blossoms in May.

A few early migrants arrive from the south. We see our first bluebirds, often perched on last year's mullein stalks. We hear a few tentative love songs, such as the plaintive two-note call of chickadees or the house finch arias that seem to end with a question mark, as though doubting this prespring spring. Boreal owls begin calling at Brainard Lake, and lowland owls begin to nest.

It's an exciting month to go "owling" along the Mesa Trail during the full moon. At dawn the moon sets and the sun rises to the singing of pygmy or saw-whet owls or to the yipping of coyotes. Coyotes, sometimes called "song dogs," often respond to human vocalizations. We have elicited an electrifying chorus with a taped owl call, and an exuberant skier once let out a yodel that turned into a duet with "Don Coyote."

On the plains, listen for the breakup of ice on frozen lakes, a sound like the shattering of champagne glasses. A close-up look at the disintegrating ice reveals honeycombed fragments gradually pulling apart and bumping into one another to produce the crystalline music that signals the end of winter.

FEBRUARY WEATHER

FEBRUARY 1

Sunrise:	7:08 AM MST		
Sunset:	5:19 PM MST		

	Boulder	**Allens Park**	**Niwot Ridge**
	5,445'	8,500'	11,565'
Ave. Max.	44°F	36°F Ave. February high	18°F Ave. February high
Ave. Min.	20°F	15°F Ave. February low	+6°F Ave. February low

FEBRUARY 28

Sunrise:	6:35 AM MST		
Sunset:	5:51 PM MST		

Ave. Max.	47°F	36°F Ave. February high	18°F Ave. February high
Ave. Min.	23°F	15°F Ave. February low	+6°F Ave. February low

FEBRUARY CHANGES (February 1–February 29)

Day Length: 10 hours, 11 minutes to 11 hours, 16 minutes=change of +1 hour 5 minutes

Change: Max.	+3°F	+1°F	+2°F
Change: Min.	+3°F	0°F	+1°F

FEBRUARY EXTREMES

Max. Temp.	77°F	63°F	See note
Min. Temp.	−28°F	−32°F	See note
Max. Wind	115 mph	105 mph	Not available
Ave. Precip.	.77 in.	1.2 in.	5.3 in.
Max. Precip.	1.93 in.	1.9 in.	9.4 in.
Min. Precip.	Trace	.2 in.	1.6 in.
Ave. Snow	10 in.	22 in.	Not available
Max. Snow	28 in.	34 in.	Not available
Min. Snow	Trace	7 in.	Not available

Note. 77°F is highest for any summer and −31°F is lowest for any winter on Niwot Ridge.

FLORA

EARLY BLOOMERS

Cartoonist Jeff MacNelly once characterized February as "that four month period between January and March." February does bring some of the year's dreariest weather, and the days can plod interminably toward spring. Small bursts of color on the plains and in the foothills are especially welcome.

Early blooming wildflowers tend to appear in those areas where we would most expect to find them: south-facing hillsides, exposed mesas, and dark-colored, sparsely vegetated shale beds that absorb above-average amounts of solar radiation. Many early bloomers are perennials that store nutrients in their roots or tubers over the winter, enabling them to sprout and grow quickly when the ground thaws and the sun's warmth intensifies. Many grow only a few inches high and thrive on bare ground or gravelly soils. Some appear to benefit by growing rapidly in moist spring soil that may have more nitrogen than will be available later.

Early growth and blooming give plants a head start in competition for nutrients but exposes them to the risk of not completing their reproductive cycles. Frost damage is one potential obstacle. Another is the relative scarcity of pollinators such as bees, moths, and hummingbirds. Some early bloomers, including the yellow violet, are self-pollinating. Others depend on wind to carry pollen from plant to plant.

Wildflower blooming times typically vary by several weeks from one year to another, but there can be a difference of two months between when a plant blooms in an "early" year versus a "late" year. The plants listed below usually bloom between early February and late April.

Early Easter daisies (*Townsendia hookeri* and *T. exscapa*) grow on dry slopes on mesas and in the foothills. These small composites with narrow white ray flowers often appear long before Easter.

Pasque flowers (*Anemone patens*) occur from the plains to the high mountains, with first-bloomers found on the mesas or in the foothills.

Sand lilies (*Leucocrinum montanum*) are abundant on open hillsides and in

NCAR
(National Center for Atmospheric Research)

With a good all-weather road and ample parking, this is one of the most accessible sites from which to look out over eastern Boulder County or to begin hikes along the Mesa Trail.

disturbed prairies. Their delicate, white star-shaped flowers taste like honeysuckle (picking them, however, may produce bad karma and is not recommended).

Spring beauties (*Claytonia rosea*) grow in a variety of settings on the plains and in the foothills. Their small pink-and-white flowers are abundant along streams, in moist grasslands, and in ponderosa pine forests.

Filarees (*Erodium cicutarium*) are tiny magenta geraniums that grow in disturbed areas. These winter annuals de-velop leafy rosettes in October, enabling them to complete their growth and bloom quickly in early spring.

Yellow violets (*Viola nuttallii*) appear on the plains, mesas, and foothills and were eaten by the Plains Indians.

Bell's twinpod (*Physaria bellii*) is a rare mustard that grows only on shale outcrops along the northern Front Range foothills. Look for the bright yellow flowers growing outward from a pale green rosette on shale slopes north of Boulder. These plants should not be disturbed under any circumstances.

FAUNA

NESTING OWLS

During the coldest time of the year, when trees are bare and the ground still frozen, great horned owls begin an activity usually associated with spring— the selection and preparation of nest sites. By early February great horned owls on the plains are sitting on eggs, and by mid-March the first young have hatched. Other owls begin nesting in March and April. The nesting season for owls extends into September or early October, when the last barn owl chicks fledge.

Because owls do not build nests, they must lay their eggs in existing nests, stumps, tree cavities, burrows, or on ledges. Great horned owls often recycle nests previously constructed by hawks, crows, or magpies. To find great horned owls on the plains, look for bulky stick nests, slightly flattened on top, high in cottonwoods or willows. The incubating female's tail feathers, or her round cat-like face with the distinctive "horns," are usually visible.

On the plains, great horned owls de-fend nesting territories of about 1 square mile. In the foothills and mountains, where prey is probably scarcer, nesting territories may be slightly larger. A pair of horned owls will nest in the same area year after year. Over a twelve-year period during the 1980s and early 1990s, great horned owls in a small woodlot at Sawhill Ponds used seven different nests, and no nest was used more than two years in a row. This territory fledged an average of 1.5 chicks per year. A pair of horned owls nesting in ponderosa pine forest on Marshall Mesa used the same nest three years in a row, fledging a total of six young.

Great horned owl young usually leave the nest in May or early June. Unable to fly, they scramble around on tree branches. Fledglings engaged in first flights often end up on the ground, where they become easy prey for foxes, coyotes, and domestic dogs. People sometimes pick them up thinking the young owls have been abandoned by their parents. Actually the parents are usually close by and may squawk and scream if you get too close to their young.

Great horned owls thrive in a variety of habitats. In Boulder County they inhabit every ecosystem except the alpine tundra. Suburban horned owls nest on building ledges and feast on squirrels, rats, skunks, and domestic cats.

Local great horned owl populations have probably increased as disturbed ecosystems have replaced natural ecosystems, whereas populations of such relative specialists as long-eared owls and burrowing owls have declined. A checklist of Boulder County birds compiled by Junius Henderson in 1909 listed long-eared owls and burrowing owls as "common" and great horned owls as "rather common." Now long-eared owls and burrowing owls each nest in only a few locations in the county.

In February and March, northern saw-whet owls and northern pygmy owls begin to establish nesting territories in the foothills and mountains. The monotonous, hollow whistles of male pygmy and saw-whet owls can be heard from mid-February through late May, but not every night. These tiny, cavity-nesting owls are vulnerable to predation by goshawks, Cooper's hawks, and great horned owls, so they call infrequently. Once females have begun incubating, calling may cease entirely.

Saw-whet owls are entirely nocturnal and almost impossible to see in the daytime, when they roost in heavy foliage. You can attract male saw-whets at night by whistling or by playing a tape recording of their territorial song. However, too much whistling or tape-playing can disrupt nesting activity. It's best to try once or twice in a particular location and then leave the owls alone for the rest of the breeding season. It's also advisable to wear glasses or goggles. While playing territorial calls, we've been buzzed by small owls that apparently mistook us for gargantuan rivals. Watch out for northern goshawks, as well. They may interpret your tape recording as an invitation to dinner.

Northern saw-whet owls are found throughout the coniferous forests of Boulder County from 6,000 to 10,000 feet. Saw-whets nest almost every year on Green Mountain West Ridge and on Enchanted Mesa in the Boulder Mountain Park. We've also found saw-whets annually along the Brainard Lake Road, between Ward and Red Rock Lake, and in lower Sunshine Canyon.

Northern pygmy owls are sometimes visible in the daytime when they perch in the tops of conifers or flutter through foothill canyons looking for songbirds, mice, lizards, and insects. Though of small stature (about 8 inches high), northern pygmy owls are ferocious predators. They can kill birds larger than themselves and have even been observed attacking magpies and grouse.

Songbirds have no love for pygmy owls. In fact one way to locate pygmy owls (or other owls) is to listen for the "mobbing" sounds of chickadees, nuthatches, juncos, jays, and robins. It's a wonder the owls ever get any sleep. In spring and early summer, listen for a high twitter that pygmy owls make around the nest. Nests are located 10 to 40 feet up in dead or dying ponderosa pines, aspen, and Douglas firs.

Northern pygmy owls appear occasionally at urban bird feeders. One winter, West Boulder resident Susan Ward noticed a feral pink parakeet at her feeder. Later she peered out her back window and saw a pygmy owl perched on a tree limb with the parakeet in its talons.

One of the first northern pygmy owl nests ever documented in Boulder County was found in 1985 by Andreas Zetterberg, a seventeen-year-old volunteer working on a small-owl study sponsored by the Boulder County Nature Association. Zetterberg was hiking on Enchanted Mesa when a pygmy owl flew by with what appeared to be a white lab rat in its talons. The owl carried its catch to a small nest cavity located high in a ponderosa pine. Coincidentally, Zetterberg also found a saw-whet nest a few yards away when he knocked on a dead tree and a roosting saw-whet poked its head out of a hole only 8 feet off the ground. Finding small-owl nests is not supposed to be so easy.

Of all the small cavity-nesting owls in Boulder County, boreal owls are probably the most difficult to observe. These 10-inch-tall relatives of the saw-whet owl (both are members of the genus *Aegolius*) nest in spruce-fir forests at high elevations. Their bell-like territorial call is almost identical to the "winnowing" sound that common snipe make with their tail feathers. More than one local boreal owl sighting has turned out to be a low-flying snipe. The snipe "winnow" while diving through the air and owls sing from stationary perches, so it shouldn't be difficult to tell the two species apart.

Until recently, maps of the boreal owl's distribution in North America showed its breeding range extending only as far south as the U.S.-Canadian border. During the early 1980s, biologists at Colorado

NESTING OWLS OF BOULDER COUNTY

Species	When and Where	Vocalizations
Common Barn Owl	June–September; plains	Hisses and rattles
Eastern Screech Owl	March–June; riparian corridors, plains and foothills	High trill or horselike whinny
Great Horned Owl	February–May; plains, foothills, and mountains	Low, resonant hoots: "wh-whoo, whoo-who"
Flammulated Owl	May–July; foothills ponderosa pine and aspen forests	Soft, resonant hoot, single or in threes: "hoot, hoot, wh-wh-hoot"
Northern Pygmy Owl	March–June; coniferous forests in foothills and mountains	High, hollow whistles, sometimes paired: "toot-toot, toot, toot, toot-toot"
Burrowing Owl	May–July; prairie dog colonies on plains	A soft "coo-coooo," or a jaylike rattle
Long-eared Owl	March–July; dense thickets, plains and foothills	A resonant hoot, loud squawks, moans and squeals
Northern Saw-whet Owl	April–June; mostly coniferous forests, plains, foothills, and mountains	High, hollow whistles, two or three notes, higher-pitched than pygmy and seldom paired: "toot-toot-toot-toot"
Boreal Owl	March–June; spruce/ fir forests above 9,500 feet	A short series of rapid, hollow "hoo" notes, reminiscent of winnowing snipe

State University, assuming logically that boreal owls would be found in boreal (cold northern) forests, began looking for them in the Cameron Pass area north of Rocky Mountain National Park. In the winter of 1983–84, David Palmer, Ronald Ryder, and other field workers found thirty-six singing boreal owls in the Cameron Pass area. The first nest ever documented in Colorado was observed during the spring of 1984. Now the "official" range of this owl has been extended south into northern New Mexico.

The first observation of singing boreal owls in Boulder County was reported by Dave Hallock in 1985. Since then, boreal owls have been heard in the Red Rock Lake area, west of Ward, and on Bryan Mountain, near Hessie. The owls have probably been around for thousands of years, but it was only recently that bird-watchers took to skiing at night into remote areas of the county listening for owl calls. It makes you wonder what else might be out there waiting to be discovered.

GOLDEN EAGLES

While hiking in the foothills many years ago, Boulder naturalist Mike Figgs saw several large black birds circling overhead. Figgs snapped a photo of the birds, thinking they were turkey vultures. Later he realized they were golden eagles. "At the time I didn't know golden eagles nested in Boulder County," says Figgs. "I wanted to find out more about them."

In 1980 Figgs met Nan Lederer, who had monitored golden eagle nests in Alaska's Denali National Park. They began looking for golden eagle nests in Boulder County, following up on tips from local bird-watchers. At the University of Colorado's Norlin Library, Figgs and Lederer discovered a set of field notes written by nineteenth-century Boulder-area naturalist Denis Gale. Gale reported observing golden eagle eyries in about a dozen locations along the Front Range, including a cliff in Lefthand Canyon now known as the Palisades. A 1943 Ph.D. dissertation by University of Colorado graduate student M. T. Jollie described the Palisades site and mapped five golden eagle nesting territories in the foothills of Boulder County. Each territory contained several nest sites located on high cliffs or in ponderosa pines.

During the early 1980s, Figgs and Lederer visited the territories mapped by Jollie and found all but one still active.

Near Linden Avenue, north of Boulder, eagles had apparently been displaced by a housing development. Figgs, Lederer, and other volunteers from the Boulder County Nature Association (BCNA) also mapped at least three additional nesting territories in the county.

Figgs concluded that the local golden eagle population is "at or near capacity," and that there are probably about as many eagles nesting locally now as there were one hundred years ago. However, increasing urbanization and recreational use of the mountains threaten the viability of several golden eagle eyries. The most serious problems are housing developments encroaching on territories and rock climbers inadvertently disturbing nests. "There's hardly an eagle nest in the county that isn't under some kind of threat from developers or rock climbers," says Figgs. Housing developments on the plains are rapidly eating up hunting areas as well.

BCNA volunteers who monitor golden eagle nests each year have observed climbers on or within a few feet of nests on Eldorado Mountain, in the Boulder Mountain Park, and on the Lefthand Palisades. Lederer has seen incubating eagles nervously peering over the edge of the cliff at approaching climbers and

leaving the eyrie when the climbers got too close.

The Boulder County Nature Association and the Boulder County Audubon Society have worked with local government agencies and climbing groups to limit disturbance of nesting eagles. Seasonal climbing-route closures have been instituted, and volunteers monitor active nests. Nest monitors perch at least one-quarter mile away and view the eagles through spotting scopes. Hikers and photographers are also encouraged to keep their distance, since close approaches may frighten the eagles and lessen the chances of nesting success.

Golden eagles nesting in the foothills fly out onto the plains to hunt prairie dogs and rabbits. A single pair may hunt over a territory of 25 square miles or more. Golden eagles also eat carrion, squirrels, snakes, and birds. Boulder physicist Tom VanZandt observed a peregrine falcon carcass and a wild turkey carcass in a Lefthand Canyon nest.

In Boulder County, golden eagles begin breeding in late February. Over a period of years a pair of eagles will construct several nests on a single cliff. Some nests are used only once, others cyclically from year to year. Fresh greenery (pine and spruce boughs) may indicate that the nest is currently in use. One of the nests visible on the Palisades has been used off and on since at least 1886. It is approximately 10 feet across and 6 feet high.

Eagle chicks usually hatch in April, fledging in late June or early July. Young eagles are fed by their parents for several months after fledging. At two to three years of age the young eagles disperse, and when they have reached maturity at about five years of age, they establish their own nesting territories.

Throughout this century, golden eagles have managed to overcome a variety of threats to their existence. In the early 1900s, Front Range egg collectors frequently raided eagle nests. Before golden eagles gained federal protection in 1946, they were routinely shot by trophy hunters and some ranchers. Even today, hundreds of golden eagles nationwide are shot, electrocuted on power lines, or run over by cars each year.

Given this history of abuse, the apparent stability of the county's golden eagle population is impressive. "I am continually amazed by the tenacity of the will to survive demonstrated by wildlife," says Figgs.

WHERE TO GO IN FEBRUARY

FOURTH OF JULY ROAD AND HESSIE

At higher elevations the snow is almost always excellent on these trails, but watch for bare spots on sunny, windy sections at lower elevations. From the town of Eldora, continue on CR 130 to where it is blocked by snowdrifts. At this point you encounter the most difficult aspect of these trails: parking. Every year more No Parking signs go up, more cars are towed, and the rules change. Our best advice is to look for off-road parking that is not posted. Then ski the road to the signpost at the "Y" junction.

From here the main road is a gentle 4-mile climb to Buckingham Campground (also known as Fourth of July Campground), below South Arapaho Peak. Hardy skiers can continue on toward the peak but should watch for avalanche danger. The left fork goes past

Red-Tailed Hawk

This is Boulder's most common raptor,
occurring year-round in all habitats.

the ghost town of Hessie and past frozen waterfalls to Woodland Flats. There it forks again with three alternatives: Lost Lake, King Lake, or Jasper Lake.

EAST PORTAL

Although most of this area lies in Gilpin County, we're including it because it's just barely over the county line and its high elevation usually means good snow and good views. It also offers a variety of terrain for all levels of cross-country skiers. Boreal owls may be abroad at the higher elevations. We once saw one in the middle of the day below Heart Lake.

From SR 119, turn west at Rollinsville onto the Rollins Pass Road (CR 149). In 7.5 miles the road forks, with the left fork leading to the East Portal of Moffat Tunnel and the beginning of the trail system. Cross the tracks, climb the gate, and head for the trailhead at the far side of the meadow. The first mile of the trail goes through private property. (A way of saying thanks is to bring back any litter you spot along the way.)

The trail follows the creek (with an exciting dip where it crosses a side creek) to an open meadow with a few dilapidated cabins. This first mile is easy skiing, and the meadow is ideal for lunching or for practicing turns and downhilling. From the meadow two main trails diverge. The left trail climbs steeply to Heart Lake (4 miles); the right trail (not quite as steep) goes to the first of the Forest Lakes in 3 miles. Finding Forest Lakes can be a test for orienteering skills, so bring a topo map; even oldtimers get lost. Unmarked side trails lead to the Arapaho Lakes (off the Forest Lakes fork) and to Crater Lakes (off the Heart Lake fork).

SOUTH ST. VRAIN TRAIL

From SR 72, about 2 miles north of Ward, turn west at the sign for the Tahosa Boy Scout Camp and park just beyond the creek. After an icy, steep stretch near the beginning of the trail, it's mostly smooth skiing through aspen and conifer forests. This trail is especially good for animal tracks. We once found fresh bobcat tracks and scat that was still steaming. Skiers with endurance can go all the way to Brainard Lake (6 miles) and beyond, but less ambitious skiers might want to turn around at the Baptist Camp.

BOULDER RESERVOIR AND COOT LAKE

These lakes and wetlands are always good for off-season hiking, and the solitude is a pleasant contrast to the busy activities of summer crowds. You may see a few ice fishermen and you're almost certain to see hawks, eagles, and prairie dogs. Great horned owls sometimes nest in the vicinity, and in 1992 a barn owl was seen on the Christmas Count. On a warm day listen for the early spring songs of red-winged blackbirds and for the breakup of ice along the shore.

Several trails skirt the lakes or lead to the shorelines. It's possible to walk from the Coot Lake parking area on CR 39 to 51st Street (about 1 mile) and enjoy a variety of habitats along the way, ranging from wetlands to prairie.

Both lakes lie west of the Diagonal Highway (SR 119) between 51st Street and CR 39. There are several marked parking areas.

PANAMA RESERVOIR

As many as sixteen bald eagles have been sighted at this lake in early spring, just before they head north for nesting, so it's worth checking out even though there is no hiking. The reservoir is on private land, but there are several pull-offs where you can watch for eagles and for waterfowl. This is also a good place to see pelicans in summer. The reservoir is northeast of the junction of US 287 and CR 52; dirt roads circle the lake.

RANGEVIEW TRAIL AND TENDERFOOT LOOP

Most foothills trails provide "windows" through which to view the Indian Peaks, but Rangeview Trail from Flagstaff Road to Artist's Point (0.5-mile) is one continuous view—a view that is especially dramatic in winter. The Tenderfoot Loop (2.5 miles) branches to the left and heads downhill. Watch for blue grouse and red crossbills in the conifer forests. Both trails start at Realization Point, where a barricade usually closes Flagstaff Road a half-mile below the summit in winter. Park at the barricade. If there's good snow, you can ski the road to the top of Flagstaff Mountain and enjoy the view of Boulder and the plains.

A Paiute Story

The Great Spirit colored all the birds and animals but forgot one bird. This bird flew up into the sky to protest his drab coat. Bits of the sky stuck to his feathers and he became our mountain bluebird.

FEBRUARY OUT-OF-COUNTY EXCURSIONS

Because of the consistently good snow, February is (usually) the best month for hut-hopping on skis or snowshoes. The 10th Mountain Trail System, dedicated to the skiing soldiers of World War II, stretches from Aspen to Vail to Leadville and includes more than 300 miles of interconnecting trails. The cabins, a vigorous day's skiing apart, are available for rent from November to early April. Contact the 10th Mountain Trail Association, 1280 Ute Avenue, Aspen, Colorado 81611, or phone (303) 925-5775 for reservations or a list of guide services.

If you've ever said, ". . . when Hell freezes over" and wondered just what such a paradox would look like, go ski touring or showshoeing in Yellowstone. It's a fire and ice paradise. It's also a unique opportunity to see bison, elk, and other wildlife up close. Phone Yellowstone (1-800-421-3401) for reservations.

FEBRUARY AT A GLANCE

MAMMALS

- Gray foxes mate February through March; young are born in about nine weeks.
- Raccoons mate in February and March.

BIRDS

- Bluebirds arrive.
- Great horned owls and golden eagles nest.
- House finches and red-winged blackbirds begin singing.

OTHER CRITTERS

- On warm days the first mourning cloak butterflies may emerge from crevices behind bark where they spend the coldest part of winter.

PLANTS

- First crocuses bloom in urban gardens.
- First wildflowers (filarees, Easter daisies, creeping mahonia, and spring beauties) may be found (if the weather cooperates).

IN THE SKY

- Candlemas, the approximate halfway point between the winter solstice and the vernal equinox, is celebrated on February 2. This festival, a precursor to Ground Hog Day and Valentine's Day, honors the stirrings of new growth and passion that accompany the waxing light of late winter.
- Taurus, The Bull, is almost directly overhead at 9:00 P.M. Taurus contains the spectacular star cluster known as the Pleiades, or Seven Sisters, and the red giant Aldebaran.

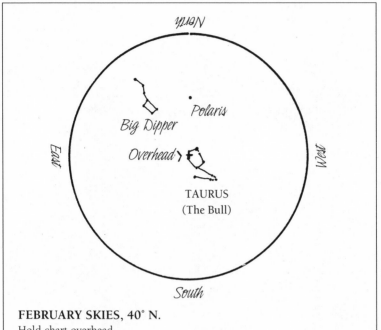

North

Polaris

Big Dipper

East

Overhead

West

TAURUS
(The Bull)

South

FEBRUARY SKIES, 40° N.
Hold chart overhead

9 PM MST - Early Feb.
8 PM MST - Late Feb.

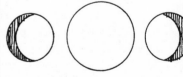

February

"Crust of Snow Moon"
—Ojibwa

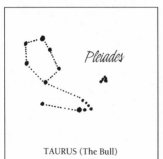

Pleiades

TAURUS (The Bull)

Pasque flowers

Coyotes at National Center for Atmospheric Research

MARCH

March is the month of melting and of mud. The poet e. e. cummings caught its flavor when he wrote: "In Just-spring when the world is mud-luscious . . . when the world is puddle-wonderful." At Walden Pond, Henry Thoreau also enjoyed the patterns and colors of the earth springing to life and wrote: "Few phenomena gave me more delight than to observe the forms which thawing sand and clay assume in flowing down the sides of a deep cut."

These puddles, ponds, and other shallow wetlands give rise to one of the great spring concerts late in March. The striped chorus frogs start to sing. Scarcely longer than an inch, these frogs expand balloonlike throat sacs to emit a noise any percussion section would envy. The larger the frog, the lower the voice; and the warmer the weather, the faster the tempo.

Although the heaviest snows of the year tend to come now, rising temperatures (sometimes in the seventies) quickly melt them. Hiking trails may be filled with pure white snow one day and run rivers of golden mud the next. March is a transitional month. We may ski one day, ignoring the fact that the snow may be sticky or icy, and search for wild-flowers the next.

During these days of emerging wildflowers, hikers rediscover the thrill of childhood Easter-egg hunts. Whoever finds the first pasque flower calls friends to share the excitement – and to exult in being the first to discover this pale lavender bloom that even looks a bit like an Easter egg before the petals unfold. We also stalk the first sand lilies and Nuttall's violets.

(And don't let wildflower enthusiasts claim that "botanizing" is a noncompetitive hobby!)

By mid-March there are enough blooms to attract butterflies, bees, and other insects. Mourning cloak butterflies (dark velvety brown wings edged with ivory) overwinter here in crevices and under bark and are now active. Ladybugs are eating pests in the garden, and ticks may be out. The ticks, which can carry Colorado tick fever and Rocky Mountain spotted fever, will become more prevalent as the weather warms. When you return from the out-of-doors, check for these round, brown blood suckers before they have a chance to dig in.

By the end of the month, eager gardeners have planted early vegetables – snow peas, lettuce, onions, and radishes – and are uncovering purple violets, dwarf iris, daffodils, scilla, and snowdrops. We tour our yards and are surprised by forgotten flowers peeking out from piles of moldy brown leaves. Sometimes a decaying leaf is actually pierced by a new shoot, and a blue scilla bud appears to arise from a tattered maple leaf. At the same time, new green leaves unfurl from honeysuckle bushes.

A lot of the action this month takes place underground. Not only are seeds coming to life, but many animals are giving birth or nursing their young in carefully chosen dens. Although "dirty" mud and "pure" snow seem to be opposites, they are equally good media for preserving tracks, so this is a month to play detective and to try to read the prints – sometimes called "the oldest writing in the world." If they lead to a hole in the ground or in an embankment, kneel down and sniff. A faintly pungent odor is typical of a fox den, and a full-bodied bouquet means skunk.

A favorite sign of a western spring is the song of the meadowlark. In winter, meadowlarks are silent and skulk along roadsides gathering grit, their feathers drab and dingy, but by March they have regained their brilliant yellow vests. They perch on telephone wires and fence posts to proclaim that the yellow sun and yellow birds are once again in ascendance.

MARCH WEATHER

MARCH 1

Sunrise: 6:34 AM MST
Sunset: 5:52 PM MST

	Boulder 5,445'	**Allens Park** 8,500'	**Niwot Ridge** 11,565'
Ave. Max.	48°F	39°F Ave. March high	22°F Ave. March high
Ave. Min.	24°F	16°F Ave. March low	9°F Ave. March low

MARCH 31

Sunrise: 5:46 AM MST
Sunset: 6:23 PM MST

Ave. Max.	57°F	39°F Ave. March high	22°F Ave. March high
Ave. Min.	30°F	16°F Ave. March low	9°F Ave. March low

MARCH CHANGES (March 1–March 31)

Day Length: 11 hours, 18 minutes to 12 hours, 37 minutes = change of +1 hour 19 minutes

Change: Max.	+9°F	+3°F	+4°F
Change: Min.	+6°F	+1°F	+3°F

MARCH EXTREMES

Max. Temp.	83°F	60°F	See note
Min. Temp.	−13°F	−23°F	See note
Max. Wind	105 mph	105 mph	Not available
Ave. Precip.	1.56 in.	1.9 in.	7.43 in.
Max. Precip.	5.06 in.	3.2 in.	11.48 in.
Min. Precip.	.05 in.	.2 in.	4.40 in.
Ave. Snow	15.8 in.	30.7 in.	Not available
Max. Snow	56.7 in.	66 in.	Not available
Min. Snow	Trace	4 in.	Not available

Note. 77°F is highest for any summer and −31°F is lowest for any winter on Niwot Ridge.

SPRING NOTES:

	Boulder
Frost: Earliest last spring killing frost:	10 April 1956
Latest last spring killing frost:	13 September 1947
Earliest fall killing frost:	9 September 1929, 1941
Latest fall killing frost:	10 November 1907
Longest frost-free season:	207 days (12 Apr. 1940–5 Nov. 1940)
Shortest frost-free season:	111 days (2 Jun. 1951–21 Sep. 1951)

MARCH WEATHER (continued)

SPRING NOTES:

Boulder

Frost: Ave. last spring killing frost: 8 May
Ave. first fall killing frost: 12 October
Ave. frost-free season: 158 days

Snow: Ave.last snowfall: 30 April
Latest last snowfall: 13 June 1947
Earliest last snowfall: 28 February 1918
Latest first snowfall: 26 November 1978
Earliest first snowfall: 3 September 1961

Temperature Change (City of Boulder): −1°F March 1989 to +62°F 6 March 1989=63°F and matched the all-time 24-hour record.

FLORA

SURVIVING SPRING

"Don't plant your corn before oak leaves are the size of squirrels' ears." "Hold the cantaloupes until the catalpas bloom." "Always plant your peas on March 17 (St. Patrick's Day)." How is a gardener to know what to do in a climate as unpredictable as ours? A better question might be, How do the local plants know when to leaf out, sprout from seed, or bloom? Usually nature has an uncanny way of assuring that these things happen at the right time – without digital watches, Gregorian calendars, or the latest in computer-generated weather forecasts.

Spring plant development is chiefly determined by warming temperatures. However, in our erratic climate, early blooming plants risk perishing in late cold snaps. To assure successful fertilization and reproduction, most plants must bloom at the right time to attract the right insect and hummingbird pollinators. This juggling act seems impossible, but it works for native and for well-adapted introduced plants.

Some plants adapt better than others. Apples, which need relatively more heat than other fruit trees, bloom late enough to avoid freezing almost every year. Peas are able to bloom early each year because they have a high tolerance for cold temperatures. On the other hand, apricots (introduced from Asia, where they are sheltered from late Arctic cold spells by the surrounding mountains) need relatively little heat to bloom but have poor tolerance for late freezes. Consequently, in Colorado they bloom early, the blossoms are usually killed by frost, and the trees fail to fruit.

Other plants cope by growing a second, and even a third, set of leaves if they lose the first set. Grapes sometimes respond to frost damage by growing a second set of leaves but probably do not produce fruit when this happens. Some plants manage to set enough seed during good years to compensate for not fruiting during bad years. Gambel's oak (*Quercus gambelii*) in Aspen, Colorado, skipped an entire year recently when a late June freeze destroyed the first set of leaves and replacements failed to develop.

Knowing how plants cope with extremes in the weather makes life interesting rather than frustrating when the weather behaves "normally" and hits us with extremely abnormal conditions. Clever local gardeners can put this knowledge to use by waiting until the catalpa trees have well-developed flower buds before planting crops like melons and cucumbers or buffalo grass lawns. The heat needed to bring catalpas to bloom is almost the same as is needed to warm the ground enough for cukes and melons to germinate.

Because spring development of plants is so dependent on temperature, and because temperature changes fairly regularly with latitude and altitude, it is possible to anticipate spring plant development at different locations with the following formula:

100 feet higher: 1 day later in spring and (less certainly) 1 day earlier in fall.

100 feet lower: 1 day earlier in spring and (less certainly) 1 day later in fall.

1 degree of latitude=70 statute miles=300 feet higher or lower=3 days, especially in spring.

Precipitation is another important aspect of a Boulder spring. The high concentration of available moisture during spring enables our soils to support a greater amount of vegetation than might be expected in a semiarid environment. In fact, March, April, and May could be called "the season of great storms," beginning in March with major snowstorms and tapering off in June with monumental thunder- and hailstorms.

For Boulder, however, generalities about the weather should be considered with caution, bearing in mind that "always" and "never" should "seldom" be taken seriously. Abnormal, in fact, might be considered normal, and normal abnormal, with averages only a numerical result of mathematical calculations. "Be prepared and take it as it comes," might be the best attitude.

THE EASTER FLOWER

The pasque flower (*Anemone patens*) has been a favorite sign of spring since at least 1597 when it was first described by John Gerard in *The Herbal*. In his chapter titled "bastard anemones, or Pasque flowers," he wrote: "The first of these pasque floures hath many small leaves finely cut or jagged, like those of carrots: among which rise up naked stalkes, rough and hairie; whereupon doe grow beautiful floures bell fashion, of a bright delaied purple colour: in the bottome whereof groweth a tuft of yellow thrums . . ."

This member of the buttercup family (Ranunculaceae) is sometimes called wind flower, anemone, wild crocus, and prairie smoke, but most often it's called pasque flower, from the French for "Easter flower." Some authorities think it's the biblical lily of the field.

One of the pasque flower's endearing characteristics is its fuzziness. The soft, silky gray hairs that cover the buds and stems are thought to protect the flower from the intense rays of the sun by reflecting light and providing shade. They also protect it from dehydration by reducing wind velocity. The flower buds rise from a buried root crown before the lobed leaves unfurl. These leaves contain a volatile oil used by western Native Americans in poultices as a counterirritant for rheumatism.

Walker Ranch (Open Space) represents early settlement in ponderosa pine/Douglas fir ecosystem.

Lavender flowers are the norm, but on rare occasions pure white blooms occur. When the flowers have "pasqued" their prime, the styles lengthen into a feathery cluster of fruits looking like an unruly head of hair. You can almost hear one of them saying to another, "I just washed it and can't do a thing with it!"

Although they look fragile, they thrive in gravelly soil from 4,000 to 10,000 feet and have even been found above tree line. Because pasque flowers lead spring up the mountains, they can be found in warm microclimates along the Mesa Trail in March and above Rainbow Lakes in June. They are one of the first flowers of spring—and one of the last.

FAUNA

YOUNG ONES IN THE DEN

At Sawhill Ponds Wildlife Refuge, the resident red fox pair has been digging out the multiple entrances of the den in preparation for the birth of this year's young. If the foxes follow form, their den will be located on a conspicuous earthen mound overlooking a small cattail marsh. This site has been used off and on by several generations of red foxes at Sawhill for at least twenty years. A well-worn trail frequented by hikers and joggers passes within a few feet of the den entrance. Most passersby seem unaware of the foxes' presence. Those who come looking for them rarely see more than a flash of red streaking through the cattails or vanishing over the hill.

Red foxes are legendary for their ability to coexist with people. The same species survived deforestation and persecution in England for centuries and now thrives in semiurban settings throughout much of North America and Eurasia. In some instances red foxes have benefited from human settlement; by removing large predators such as cougars, wolves, and coyotes, we have created niches they can occupy without much competition.

What makes red foxes so adaptable? They eat almost anything, from mice, rabbits, snakes, and disabled waterfowl to apples, chokecherries, and grasshoppers. They can construct their dens wherever there is soft earth to dig in. They are small (adults weigh around 10 pounds) and can hide easily in shrubs or long grasses. Perhaps most important, they can control their own populations by adjusting litter sizes. Red foxes raise from one to twelve young per year, depending on the availability of food and open territory. When food is particularly scarce, embryos are absorbed into the pregnant female's body.

Red foxes range throughout Boulder County from the plains to the tundra, but they seem most abundant on the fringes of urban areas. Look for them at places like Sawhill Ponds, South Boulder Creek east of Boulder, and the Longmont Municipal Airport. When snow is on the ground, red foxes are easily tracked to their dens. Their tracks resemble those of a small dog, but their behavior is decidedly more purposeful. Dens are used for sleeping as well as for rearing young. Dens containing young usually have multiple entrances for quick escape in emergencies.

On the plains, red fox pups are usually born in March, and they make their first appearance above ground in early April. For a few days the young foxes seem oblivious to danger, but they quickly acquire the wariness characteristic of their species. By the time they are about six weeks old they will scurry into the den at the sight of an approaching person.

Foxes are acutely aware of movement but less adept at discriminating stationary objects. If you sit motionless within view of a fox den, you can watch the family activities without creating a disturbance. The young pups snarl and snuffle as they engage in mock combat on the earthen mound in front of the den. The parents appear from time to time with scraps of food, receiving wild bounding greetings and licks to the face. Sometimes the whole family will take long naps together, the pups lying on the earthen mound while their parents sleep nearby.

Adults display surprising bravery. We've watched them leading large dogs on merry chases away from the den or rushing out to bark at humans who get too close to their pups. At night they bark at anyone who comes by. They seem to think the woods belong to them once the sun goes down.

Residents of Lyons and West Boulder occasionally see gray foxes at their doorsteps scrounging for dog food or for garbage. Gray foxes, which mostly inhabit shrubby areas in the foothills, are much less common locally than are red foxes. Numbers of sightings fluctuate considerably from year to year. During the mid-1980s, gray foxes were seen regularly on

Flagstaff Mountain in the Boulder Mountain Park. In fact, one hiker videotaped a gray fox and reported it to the authorities as a mountain lion! But a canine distemper outbreak apparently felled most of the population. Contact with humans, and with their pets, may be having a detrimental effect on this species.

Gray foxes often den in hollow logs or burrows located in heavy brush. Young (usually two to five) are born in March, April, or May. The young disperse in the fall and are able to breed the following winter.

One of the highlights of each spring season is the first appearance of coyote pups at the National Center for Atmospheric Research in Boulder. In January and February, the adults sometimes court in the meadow below the NCAR buildings. The amorous coyotes race around in the snow, rising up on their hind legs to touch forepaws, or stand quietly together, sniffing and nuzzling.

About two months after breeding, the female gives birth to a litter of two to twelve pups. At NCAR, dens are located in ravines or brushy hillsides near water. Coyotes frequently use dens excavated by other species, including skunks and badgers.

Compared to red foxes, denning coyotes seem more sensitive to human disturbance. At NCAR we once set up a spotting scope 400 yards from the den and watched the comings and goings of the adults for three days. On the fourth day the coyotes had vanished. We never found the new den.

A number of other carnivores give birth to their young during the spring months. Badger, mink, and short-tailed weasel young appear above ground in April, May, and June. Bobcat kittens are usually born in May and June. Black bear cubs first appear outside the den in spring, but the sows give birth to in midwinter. Remarkably, black bear sows nourish their cubs for many weeks while subsisting on body fat stored the previous summer and fall.

Mammals with newborn young may expose themselves to dangers not faced during other times of their lives. To provide enough food for their offspring, coyotes may increase daylight hunting or become more bold around humans. Just as hummingbirds will chase hawks or eagles away from their nesting territories, bobcats will attack coyotes, dogs, and even bears that come too close to their dens. A female badger with young will take on all comers, including curious humans.

Coyotes

This adaptable predator can be found in all parts of Boulder County. The name appears to be derived from the Aztec word "Coyotl."

DENNING TIMES AND LOCATIONS
FOR BOULDER COUNTY CARNIVORES

Species	When	Where
Coyote	May–June	Burrow near water; plains, foothills, mountains
Red Fox	March–June	Burrow excavated in earthen mound or bank; plains, foothills, mountains
Gray Fox	March–June	Burrow or hollow log in heavy brush; foothills
Black Bear	November–March	Caves, rock crevices, burrows; foothills, mountains
Raccoon	April–May	Hollow tree or burrow; plains, foothills, mountains
Marten	March–May	Log, rock pile, or stump; mountains
Long-tailed Weasel	March–May	Burrow lined with grass and hair; plains, foothills, mountains
Short-tailed Weasel	April–May	Burrow under rock or tree; mountains
Mink	April–May	Hollow log, burrow, beaver or muskrat house; plains, foothills, mountains
Badger	March–May	Burrow; plains, mountains
Spotted Skunk	April–June	Hollow log or burrow; foothills
Striped Skunk	May–July	Under rocks or buildings, in hollow logs; plains, foothills, mountains
Mountain Lion	All year, most often in midsummer	Rock shelters, caves, eroded banks; foothills
Canada Lynx*	April–June	Hollow log, rock shelter, fallen tree; mountains
Bobcat	All year, peaks May–June	Hollow log, rock shelter, fallen tree; foothills, mountains

*Rare species, poorly documented in Boulder County.

Sources: David Armstrong, *Rocky Mountain Mammals*; National Audubon Society, *Audubon Field Guide to North American Mammals.*

What stimulates such acts of bravado? Call it parental investment, nurturing instinct, or a blind desire to pass the genes along. It's a powerful stimulus familiar to humans, and one often felt this time of year.

FUR TRAPPING

Fur trapping is still practiced in Boulder County. Commercial trappers catch bobcats, coyotes, foxes, mink, and beaver in snares or leg-hold traps and sell the pelts. In addition, farmers, ranchers, and health department officials trap "nuisance animals" including mountain lions, coyotes, skunks, and muskrats.

Proponents of trapping say it is a longstanding tradition in Colorado, a livelihood for many professional trappers, and a humane means of controlling predator populations. They say predator control is necessary to protect domestic animals. Opponents argue that trapping with leg-hold traps is cruel, unnecessary (predators don't need to be controlled), and a danger to pets, people, and nontarget species. They add that these traps have been banned in more than one hundred countries worldwide.

Several local organizations are involved in the trapping controversy. The Colorado Trappers Association, the Colorado Wildlife Federation, and the Colorado Division of Wildlife support the use of leg-hold traps. The Boulder County Humane Society, the Boulder County Audubon Society, and Speak Out for Animals have lobbied against the use of these traps.

Most commercial trapping is done during winter months, when animal pelts are in prime condition. Hikers and skiers occasionally free animals found caught in leg-hold traps – an act considered a crime under Colorado State statutes.

WHERE TO GO IN MARCH

RAINBOW LAKES ROAD

Because it's wide and relatively flat, the Rainbow Lakes Road is a good choice for ski touring or snowshoeing when conditions are marginal, a common problem in March. It's also a good choice for beginners. This south-facing road receives lots of sun, so beware of sunburn and

COLORADO DIVISION OF WILDLIFE
TRAPPERS SURVEY, 1986–91

Species	Number Trapped in Colorado 1986	Number Trapped in Colorado 1988	Number Trapped in Colorado 1991
Beaver	5,913	4,033	3,151
Marten	1,160	3,006	1,191
Mink	235	246	134
Muskrat	22,930	11,715	6,292
Ring-tailed Cat	584	237	147
Long-tailed Weasel	126	287	56
Short-tailed Weasel	34	29	10
Badger	847	424	331
Gray Fox	940	879	373
Kit and Swift Fox	1,062	265	375
Red Fox	1,366	1,496	1,114
Opossum	52	48	20
Spotted Skunk	484	167	67
Striped Skunk	4,520	2,052	1,021
Bobcat	1,238	936	538
Raccoon	4,798	2,446	1,907
Coyote	11,492	5,798	4,721
Totals	57,781	33,994	21,448

Boulder County Numbers (1991): Beaver 18, Marten 3, Muskrat 10, Long-tailed Weasel 2, Badger 2, Red Fox 3, Spotted Skunk 5, Bobcat 2, Raccoon 23, and Coyote 31.

Source: Voluntary trapper survey conducted by Colorado Division of Wildlife. Not all trappers responded, so actual numbers of mammals trapped may be higher.

sticky snow. It's also where we found the earliest tick of the year while picnicking on pine needles during a March ski tour.

From the Peak to Peak Highway halfway between Nederland and Ward, turn west onto CR 116 at the CU Research Station sign. Drive about a mile on the gravel road to the fork, where there is roadside parking. The right fork leads to the research station, and the unplowed left fork (4.2 miles) to the Rainbow Lakes Campground. See the August chapter for a description of trails originating at the campground. From the fork you can backtrack 0.4-mile to the branch of the Sourdough Trail that goes to the Brainard Lake winter parking area.

SIX-MILE FOLD

Clam and oyster fossils and some of the earliest wildflowers are found in the Niobrara and Pierre shale outcroppings (marine deposits of the Cretaceous Period) just north of the former Beech Aircraft facility. Hundreds of Easter daisies bloom on the ridge, sometimes by mid-February. Later in spring, look for Drummond milk-vetch, Lambert's locoweed, Nuttall's violets, and a variety of mustards.

Several rare plants, such as Bell's twinpod (*Physaria bellii*, a rosette of blue-green leaves with bright yellow flowers), bloom here in spring. This species is endemic to scattered shale outcrops along the Front Range and is being considered for federal listing as an endangered plant. In August the ten-petal blazing-star (*Mentzelia decapetala*) blooms at night (it can also be seen in early morning) and is the unquestioned star of the show. These, as well as other species, thrive in road cuts and on shale due to the lack of competition. Because of their rarity, it is especially important not to disturb these species.

In 1990 the Olde Stage Road Fire spread almost down to the highway, making this a fascinting place to observe regeneration as well as geologic phenomena, such as a dramatic folding in the earth's crust. A nearby prairie dog town lures coyotes and raptors, and once we saw a bobcat prowling in the chokecherries and hawthorns along the road.

Park at the Beech Open Space lot at Neva Road and the North Foothills Highway. Most of this land is Open Space, owned by either the county or the city. Check an Open Space map before visiting. An inspection of other roadcuts may reveal additional treasures.

NORTH FOOTHILLS TRAIL

Somewhat similar to the nearby Six-Mile Fold, this area consists of rolling grasslands and a burned-over hogback. The gravelly ridges are good for early wildflowers and for raptor viewing. Later in the spring some of the slopes are covered with blue and magenta penstemons. One segment of the trail circles Wonderland Lake, which is a wildlife refuge.

Trail access points are located at the Foothills Nature Center (4201 North Broadway); the Foothills Trailhead, 0.4-mile north of the intersection of SR 36 and Broadway; Lee Hill Road, about 0.5-mile west of Broadway; and the west end of Utica Street. Because of the multiple trailheads, several loops or car exchanges are possible. A hike from the Foothills Nature Center to the Foothills Trailhead is about 3 miles; a loop from Lee Hill Road around the hogback and down to the Foothills Trailhead is 3.2 miles. These trails also connect to a

trail system at Boulder Valley Ranch, another good area for early wildflowers.

MARSHALL MESA, COMMUNITY DITCH, AND GREENBELT PLATEAU

Great horned owls frequently nest in the ponderosa pines on Marshall Mesa, where sandstone formations provide habitat for early wildflowers. Meadowlarks sing from old yucca stalks, and some of the first chorus frogs sound off from the temporary wetlands below Community Ditch, which flows into privately owned Marshall Lake.

Odd chunks of orange sandstone, hollow in the center with matching spherical concretions, are sometimes found scattered about the ridge like fossilized bird nests and eggs. The concretions, high in iron content, accumulated many eons ago around bits of organic matter. Both these sandstone concretions and coal formed under similar poorly oxygenated conditions.

The town of Marshall was once a coal-mining and iron-ore center that had a larger population than Boulder. Ruins of some of the mining buildings can still be seen, and underground coal fires have been burning for more than a century. An attempt was made many years ago to douse the fires by running an irrigation ditch into one of the mines for an entire summer, but it failed. On cold days, plumes of steam still may rise from the abandoned tunnels. Some former mine areas are dangerous and closed to the public.

Several trails interconnect in this area, so various loops and permutations can be made if you follow the Boulder Open Space map. These trails also connect with Doudy Draw, described in the May chapter. Park at either the Marshall Mesa trailhead south of Marshall Road, 0.9-mile east of SR 93, or at the Greenbelt Plateau trailhead, 0.1-mile east of 93 on the north side of 128.

DRY CREEK TRAIL AND BASELINE RESERVOIR

A trail crosses Dry Creek (which usually isn't dry) and a grassy field to a crest above Baseline Reservoir. The view across the lake to the mountains is spectacular, and many waterbirds frequent the lake. Some of the rarities sighted here include swans, loons, and a Eurasian wigeon. The reservoir itself

is privately owned, but there are many pull-outs along Cherryvale and Baseline roads where you can stop to observe birds.

For hiking, park at the trailhead south of Baseline Road and east of the reservoir, about a mile east of Cherryvale Road.

NIWOT TRAIL

This level trail follows the Boulder/ White Rocks irrigation ditch for about a mile through agricultural land to a Niwot subdivision. Cottonwoods, willows, and Russian olives line the trail and may harbor a great horned owl and/or early-spring migrants. Park at the trailhead on 79th Street north of SR 52.

SOMBRERO MARSH

This small pond and cattail marsh, estimated to be twenty thousand years old, is one of the last prairie potholes in Boulder County and is a popular place to look for rare birds. Birders from all over the U.S. congregated here in the spring of 1992, when a garganey (a European duck rarely seen in this

Robins

Contrary to popular belief, robins are not a sign of spring in Colorado. Although most of our robins do migrate south, some of them usually stay 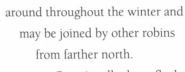 around throughout the winter and may be joined by other robins from farther north.

Occasionally, large flocks of robins can be seen here in midwinter.

country) dabbled about with cinnamon teal for several weeks.

Access for viewing is at the Lark Circle cul de sac in The Reserve subdivision east of Cherryvale and south of Arapahoe, or at the end of 63rd Street just south of Arapahoe.

LYKINS GULCH

This brushy ravine is privately owned but is protected by a conservation easement held by the Boulder County Land Trust. For over twenty years Allegra

Collister banded birds here in the 1950s and 1960s; that work is now being carried on by volunteers from the Foothills Audubon Club, the Colorado Bird Observatory, and other conservation organizations.

Long-eared owls and bald eagles usually roost here through March. Come back in May to see both lazuli and indigo buntings, blue grosbeaks, yellow-breasted chats, and Virginia warblers nesting. At various times of the year more than one hundred species, including the rare scissor-tailed flycatcher and Calliope hummingbird, have been observed.

Although permission from Boulder County Nature Association is necessary to walk into the gulch, many birds can be seen and heard from the road.

A series of several ravines shown on county maps are known as "Lykins Gulch," named for David Lykins, Boulder's first beekeeper, who settled here in the early 1860s when the Denver area became too crowded for him. Stone points and ancient campfire rings show that this area has been used by humans for many centuries.

The Lykins Gulch that is designated as a wildlife sanctuary is north of Old St. Vrain Road, half a mile east of the North Foothills Highway.

MARCH OUT-OF-COUNTY EXCURSIONS

Sandhill crane migration peaks toward the end of the month, precipitating a bird-watcher migration to an 80-mile stretch of the Platte River near Kearny, Nebraska. Half a million sandhills and a few whoopers pause for several weeks along the riparian sandbars and in the nearby grain fields before heading north for nesting. (The main whooping crane flock comes through a few weeks later than do the sandhills.) Best viewing is at dawn and dusk from the blinds at the National Audubon Society's Lillian Annette Rowe Bird Sanctuary. These blinds are so popular that advance reservations must be made by phoning (308) 236-7574. The sound and sight of thousands of cranes flocking together is worth the eight-hour drive.

In recent years, withdrawal of water from the North and South Platte river systems for agricultural and municipal use has decreased seasonal flooding needed to preserve sandbars from encroaching vegetation. Cranes depend on these sandbars for roosting. In a complex web of relationships, damming the rivers endangers the ancient migration patterns of the cranes.

The sandhill crane spectacle (in lesser numbers) can also be witnessed in Colorado at the Monte Vista National Wildlife Refuge. About two thousand cranes stop at these wetlands in the San Luis Valley each spring. During the 1980s, biologists tried to create a new flock of whooping cranes by using the sandhills as foster parents. The whoopers failed to reproduce, and the cross-fostering was discontinued. But it's still possible to see a few of the snow-white whoopers mixed in with the sandhill flocks at Monte Vista.

MARCH AT A GLANCE

MAMMALS

- Snowshoe hares and long-tailed weasels begin their prevernal molt. From now through April they will gradually turn from white to brown.
- Black-tailed prairie dogs are born. They leave their parents in about ten weeks and attain full size in about six months.
- Fox and badger babies are born.
- Raccoons may try to establish nurseries in house chimneys.
- Black bears emerge from dormancy and begin to forage voraciously for food.

BIRDS

- Meadowlarks and canyon wrens start to sing.
- Wintering bald eagles leave for nesting areas farther north.
- Red-tailed hawks nest.

OTHER CRITTERS

- Chorus frogs start to sing.
- Rainbow trout spawn.
- Ticks reappear.
- Bee and butterfly numbers multiply.

PLANTS

- First pasque flowers, creeping mahonia, and Nuttall's violets usually bloom in the wild, and daffodils bloom in towns.
- Early vegetables are planted.
- Winter wheat, planted in the fall, greens up on farms in the eastern part of the county.
- First green leaves appear on shrubs and trees.

IN THE SKY

- The vernal equinox occurs around March 21. Days and nights are of approximately equal length, and spring officially begins on most modern calendars.
- Leo (The Lion) lies high in the eastern sky just north of the ecliptic at 9:00 P.M. The head and neck of the lion, also known as The Sickle, form a distinctive backward question mark. The first-magnitude star Regulus lies at the bottom of the question mark.

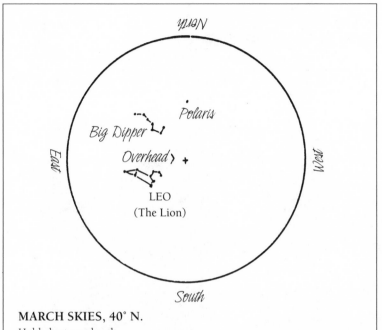

MARCH SKIES, 40° N.

Hold chart overhead

9 PM MST - Early Mar.
8 PM MST - Late Mar.

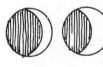

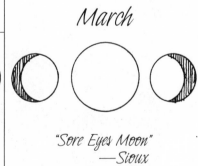

March

"Sore Eyes Moon"
—Sioux

LEO (The Lion)

81

Cottonwoods near White Rocks

APRIL

Shiny new leaves create a haze of soft green in the treetops. New grass is fast replacing the tan shreds of last year's growth. The land is now steeped in gradations of green ranging from the chartreuse of willows to the silver-green of sage to the emerald feathers of hummingbirds—a welcome transformation after the spare colors of winter.

In March we paused to marvel at each new sign of spring. Now we are inundated by its arrival. Instead of one pasque flower, we find hundreds. We catch a spicy whiff of antelope bitterbrush even before we spot its small creamy yellow flowers. Mouse-ear chickweed, mertensia, snowball saxifrage, and various species of milk-vetch, locoweed, and mustard begin to bloom.

Box elder blossoms dangle from male branches like tassels of pink embroidery thread terminating in maroon knots, and miniature pairs of red wings begin to develop on female box elders. Their tiny leaves are also red, a common phenomenon of newly emerged leaves in the spring before chlorophyll becomes dominant.

In towns, flowering fruit trees—crabapple, redbud, and plum—start their show. We pick the first mint for juleps and iced tea. Home gardens yield the year's first harvest—rhubarb—and we savor the season's first fresh fruit pie.

As flowers begin to bloom and sap to flow, the broad-tailed hummingbirds return. They announce their arrival late in the month with an insect-like trill made by the males' wings. Other eagerly awaited arrivals include

The courtship of western grebes involves scooting across the water with necks outstretched.

chipping sparrows, green-tailed towhees, ruby-crowned kinglets, house and rock wrens, tree swallows, and yellow-rumped warblers.

Many water and wading birds–eared and western grebes, pelicans, and avocets–also return in April. Check the lakes and ponds in the eastern part of the county for newcomers, and be prepared for surprises. On one memorable April morning, as yellow-headed blackbirds called from the cattails, thirty-five white-faced ibis wheeled overhead and landed in a wet meadow near Sawhill Ponds. Most birds now sport their fanciest feathers and are arrayed in breeding plumage.

Breeding has already taken place for red foxes. If you located their den in March, now is the time to watch for the pups to emerge and romp about. Marmots sun themselves on boulders encrusted with orange lichen as chipmunks scamper about. But April is not just rhubarb pie, returning birds, and gamboling foxes. Misty gray days, heavy rains, and blizzards also occur. In fact, Boulder County made *The Guinness Book of Records* for the snowstorm that occurred on April 14 to 15, 1921, at Silver Lake. A world record of 76 inches of snow fell in twenty-four hours.

APRIL WEATHER

APRIL 1
Sunrise: 5:45 AM MST
Sunset: 6:24 PM MST

	Boulder	**Allens Park**	**Niwot Ridge**
	5,445'	8,500'	11,565'
Ave. Max.	56°F	48°F Ave. April high	28°F Ave. April high
Ave. Min.	31°F	24°F Ave. April low	14°F Ave. April low

APRIL 30
Sunrise: 5:02 AM MST
Sunset: 6:53 PM MST

Ave. Max.	63°F	48°F Ave. April high	28°F Ave. April high
Ave. Min.	38°F	24°F Ave. April low	14°F Ave. April low

APRIL CHANGES (April 1–April 30)
Day Length: 12 hours, 39 minutes to 13 hours, 51 minutes=change of +1 hour 12 minutes

Change: Max.	+7°F	+9°F	+6°F
Change: Min.	+7°F	+8°F	+5°F

APRIL EXTREMES

Max. Temp.	88°F	72°F	See note
Min. Temp.	−3°F	−10°F	See note
Max. Wind	127 mph	85 mph	Not available
Ave. Precip.	2.55 in.	2.10 in.	5.96 in.
Max. Precip.	9.18 in.	7.30 in.	11.9 in.
Min. Precip.	.15 in.	.20 in.	.60 in.
Ave. Snow	11.4 in.	28.1 in.	Not available
Max. Snow	44 in.	78 in.	Not available
Min. Snow	00 in.	4 in.	Not available

Note. 77°F is highest for any summer and −31°F is lowest for any winter on Niwot Ridge.

FLORA

THERE'S THREE FEET OF SNOW ON THE TULIPS; IT MUST BE SPRING

This month of seesawing weather is a good time to note which plants are well adapted and which are ill adapted. Daffodils and hybrid tulips, originally from milder climates, are regularly crushed by snow, but crocus and wild tulips from Central Asia do well because they evolved in a climate similar to ours. Native pasque flowers and mertensias are relatively unaffected by spring snows and freezes.

April is also a month to check on local microclimates–those shady or sunny places where plants seem to be ahead of or behind the norm. For instance, grass greens up quickly at the edges of pavement, the same place it browns out first in hot weather. Sunny walls on south sides of buildings also give plants a head start. However, night temperatures usually drop just as low here as elsewhere, so plants that progress rapidly may be damaged at a later,

vulnerable stage in their development. Exceptions are canyon country plants, such as evergreen species of mountain mahogany, that evolved in sunny, rocky areas and thrive next to urban walls. "Generalists," such as creeping mahonia (*Mahonia repens*) flourish in almost every situation.

Large boulders on south-facing slopes create microclimates for early wild-flowers. In the foothills above Lyons, antelope bitterbrush (*Purshia tridentata*) fans out against pink sandstone boulders as though espaliered. In April the branches touching the rock are often in full bloom while the branches a few inches away are still in bud.

On clear nights, cold air (denser than warm air) flows toward low areas on the plains, often following creek corridors from the foothills. Conversely, the "Boulder Banana Belt" (higher areas along the base of the foothills) is relatively warm. At times the temperature in the higher areas is ten to twenty degrees warmer than in the cold pockets. An example is the Anne U. White Trail, which follows a creek corridor. It's possible in April to find prolific blooms at the top where the canyon opens out, and very few flowers in the cold pockets near the bottom.

The Mesa Trail offers showcase examples of contrasting microclimates and their plant communities. Look for creeping mahonia to bloom in early March in the warmest environments and to finish in May in the coolest.

COTTONWOODS

In a land where trees are scarce, the cottonwood is cherished. In summer its large leaves provide shade, in autumn it rivals the aspen for color, and in spring it brings an explosion of green to the plains.

Cowboys and westering pioneers welcomed the sight of cottonwoods across the prairie, a sign that water was near. They scraped the twigs for a sweet pulp called "cottonwood ice cream"—a treat also enjoyed by the Plains Indians and by horses, who grazed on the young saplings. Native Americans ate the young buds in the spring and made yellow dye from them. Both the buds and the bark contain salicin and populin (both are related to acetylsalicylic acid, the primary ingredient in aspirin), which were used to control pain. Children made toy tepees from the heart-shaped leaves, and Pueblo Indians still carve the root to make sacred Kachinas.

Cottonwoods bear two types of sticky winter buds: a slender, pointed leaf bud and a plump terminal flower bud. When the flower buds bloom in early April, it's fun to compare the male and female flowers, which are borne on different trees. The male flower looks like a red chenille tassel, whereas the female flower resembles a string of pale green beads. Later, the cotton fluffs out, transforming the female catkin into an elongated powder puff. Shortly after the blooms mature, flying cotton fills the air like a spring snowstorm—an efficient method of seed dispersal.

Although there are numerous species of cottonwoods, the one we think of first in Boulder County is the plains cottonwood (*Populus deltoides*), a massive tree with deeply furrowed gray bark and "deltoid" shaped leaves. Species occurring in the mountains and foothills are: narrowleaf cottonwood (*P. angustifolia*); lanceleaf cottonwood (*P. deltoides X P. angustifolia*), a natural hybrid between the plains and the narrowleaf cottonwood; and balsam poplar (*P. balsamifera*), a possible relict of the glacial period.

Cottonwood

The narrowleaf cottonwood is sometimes confused with the peachleaf willow. However, the darker green cottonwood has a straight central trunk as opposed to the more outwardly spreading, somewhat crooked willow trunk. The willow also lacks a terminal twig bud. The leaf buds are another key to distinguishing the two species: cottonwood buds have overlapping scales, whereas willows have a single bud scale.

There are more cottonwoods in many areas on the plains now than there were prior to white settlement. (Formerly, bison, prairie fires, and stream-bank erosion controlled the expansion of the trees.) The increased numbers of cottonwoods may have enabled species from eastern deciduous forests to spread westward along riparian corridors. White-tailed deer and eastern blue jays, scarce twenty years ago, are now frequently seen in Boulder County, and sightings of Virginia opossums have

been reported.

At the same time cottonwoods were extending their range, the shrub understory, faced with increasing shade, decreased. A subsequent decline in some bird species, such as shrub-nesting willow flycatchers and American redstarts, has been noticed.

Recently, many streams have been channelized or drained, and plains cottonwoods, which need flooding to germinate properly, are not regenerating well. In addition, overgrazing by cattle is destroying saplings. The ecological story of cottonwoods is complex and unfinished. It will be interesting to see what the future holds for this tree and for the animal community dependent on it.

Sawhill Ponds or the White Rocks area are good places to see cottonwoods, as well as white-tailed deer and blue jays. If you see a possum, let us know.

FAUNA

MIGRATION

It begins in February when flocks of mountain bluebirds line up along telephone wires and fence posts. A few weeks later, ducks and shorebirds begin to converge on the county's lakes and ponds. By early April, kettles of turkey vultures and red-tailed hawks can be seen riding the warm thermals that rise up where the mountains meet the plains. Finally, in May, the songbirds arrive en masse. Warblers, vireos, thrushes, finches, and sparrows, some coming from as far away as Argentina and Chile, bring song and color to the greening landscape.

"Migration season" is a bit of a misnomer, because most birds are on the move throughout much of the year. Crossbills wander from month to month, seeking out areas with abundant conifer seeds. Some duck species take several months to complete their "fall migration," arriving in "wintering areas" just long enough to turn around and head slowly back north. Bobolinks make a direct flight from Colorado to South America and then spend the winter months roaming in flocks throughout several million square miles of Brazil and Argentina, feeding on cultivated rice and other seeds. Only a small minority of species, such as the northern mockingbird and Townsend's solitaire, maintain distinct winter territories in addition to summer breeding territories.

Migration is complex. Some Canada geese winter in Boulder County and summer far to the north. Others breed here in the summer and then head south for the winter. Still others may remain here throughout the year. Some songbirds, including golden-crowned kinglets and horned larks, make a "vertical migration" from the high country in summer down to the plains and foothills in winter.

A few species travel different routes to and from breeding areas. Rufous hummingbirds, which winter in Mexico, nest from the Pacific Northwest to Alaska. They optimize nectaring opportunities by migrating north along the Pacific lowlands, where spring wildflowers are abundant, then returning south over the central Rockies, where the flower bloom peaks in summer. We see them in Boulder County during July and August, when they defend foraging territories established around feeders or flower gardens.

Spring migration might be characterized as a series of waves, most flowing south to north and some from east to west, washing across eastern Colorado and breaking up as songbirds disperse to nesting territories throughout North America. During late April and early May, these waves tend to converge in Boulder County, where it is possible to see more than one hundred avian species in a single day.

The Boulder County Audubon Society "Birdathon," where participants raise money for conservation based on how many bird species they see, is usually held the first Saturday in May. Over the years birdathon participants and other bird-watchers have ferreted out the best places to look for migratory birds. These include Sawhill and Walden ponds (shorebirds, herons, and warblers); St. Vrain Creek in Lyons (rare warblers and flycatchers); Prince Lakes near Lafayette (ducks and shorebirds); Union Reservoir east of Longmont (pelicans, gulls, terns, and ducks); Boulder Reservoir (ducks, songbirds, and sparrows); and Gregory Canyon in the Boulder Mountain Park (warblers, grosbeaks, and vireos).

A highlight of spring migration is the flight of thousands of eagles, hawks, and falcons over the Front Range foothills during the last week of March and the first two weeks of April. From the summits of Bear Peak, Green Mountain, or Rabbit Mountain you can see as many as thirty raptors per hour soaring northward. Golden eagles, red-tailed hawks, northern harriers, Cooper's hawks, turkey vultures, prairie falcons, and many other species take advantage of the strong thermals that rise up over the foothills on warm spring days.

Hawk-watching is best around midmorning. Later in the day the birds are soaring so high they are no longer visible. Numbers of eagles and buteos (large soaring hawks) usually peak around the first of April. Falcons and accipiters (small gliding hawks) pass through our area a little later in the month.

Freeman Hall, a meteorologist who studied hawk migration patterns in Boulder County, found that soaring raptors indicate areas where thunderstorms are developing. The strong, warm updrafts that enable raptors to soar effortlessly also create the conditions necessary for thunderstorm formation. Hall noted that when you see one circling hawk you usually see several others, all riding the same warm-air column.

Some of the raptors that fly into Boulder County in April stay for the summer, while others continue northward. Swainson's hawks traveling in flocks of two hundred individuals or more complete a 5,000-mile journey from Argentina. Swainson's hawks often return to the same nest site year after year. One pair nested in the same tree near the corner of 47th Street and Jay Road for three consecutive years.

Biologists believe migrating birds use a variety of navigational clues, including topographic features, wind, stars, odors, sun direction, and the earth's magnetic field. Behavioral ecologist Stephen Emlen studied songbird reliance on stellar cues by observing caged indigo buntings in a planetarium. Around the time of spring migration, the buntings hopped and fluttered restlessly in the general direction of the North Star. When the position of the North Star was changed, the birds reoriented in that direction. Emlen concluded that young buntings recognize the area of the sky with least stellar rotation (the area around the North Star) and use that part of the night sky as a navigational fix.

In another experiment, homing pigeons fitted with opaque contact lenses and released several miles from their roost found their way back. Pigeons probably use their sense of smell and an acute sensitivity to the earth's magnetic field to perform these remarkable feats of "blind navigation."

Migration enables birds to maximize foraging opportunities, to escape harsh weather conditions, and to take advantage of latitudinal and seasonal variations in day length. Snow buntings nesting in the region of continual daylight north of the Arctic Circle can forage twenty-four hours a day. They arrive in the Arctic just as insects become active and fly south just before the onset of winter. Swainson's hawks enjoy the best of two

Burrowing Owls

This appealing little owl is mysteriously disappearing from Boulder County grasslands even where prairie dog colonies have been protected by open space programs.

worlds—perpetual summers on the plains of North America and in the pampas of Argentina. But they pay a price: Because these hawks travel in large flocks, they become relatively easy prey for golden eagles and rifle-toting humans.

Watching and listening to migrating birds fosters a deeper appreciation of the rhythmic progression of the seasons. The arrival of ducks and shorebirds from the south coincides with the melting of frozen lakes as the days lengthen and the sun's warmth intensifies. Flocks of warblers and vireos appear just as buds are opening and most insects are becoming active. In June, when lesser goldfinches finally begin to make their way up into the foothills, seeds are ripening and hot days are upon us. In July, the first arrival of Franklin's gulls and shorebirds from the north reminds us that summer is slowly turning toward fall.

FIRST ARRIVAL DATES FOR
SELECTED SUMMER RESIDENT BIRDS

Species	When*	Where
Black-crowned Night Heron	January 25–April 16	Lakes and ponds; plains
Blue-winged Teal	February 14–April 1	Lakes and ponds; plains
Turkey Vulture	March 16–April 14	Plains, foothills
Swainson's Hawk	March 18–April 24	Grasslands and cotton-woods; plains
Spotted Sandpiper	March 29–April 30	Lakes, ponds, and streams; plains, foothills, mountains
Mourning Dove	March 31–April 12	Shrubby areas, cottonwood groves, coniferous forests; plains, foothills
Burrowing Owl	March 27–May 1	Prairie dog colonies; plains
White-throated Swift	March 27–May 9	Cliffs and canyons; foothills
Broad-tailed Hummingbird	April 16–April 25	Shrubby areas and coniferous forests; foothills, mountains
Williamson's Sapsucker	March 24–April 30	Aspen and coniferous forests; mountains
Cordilleran Flycatcher	April 30–May 25	Coniferous forests; foothills, mountains
Tree Swallow	March 19–April 24	Lakes, aspen, and coniferous forests; plains, foothills, mountains
House Wren	March 30–May 5	Conifer and riparian under-story; plains, foothills, mountains

(Continued on page 94)

FIRST ARRIVAL DATES FOR SELECTED
SUMMER RESIDENT BIRDS (Continued)

Species	When*	Where
Mountain Bluebird	January 10–March 10	Open forests and fields; plains, foothills, mountains
Hermit Thrush	April 26–May 9	Dense coniferous forests; foothills, mountains
Warbling Vireo	May 5–May 27	Cottonwoods and willows; foothills, mountains
Yellow Warbler	April 17–May 9	Cottonwoods and willows; plains, foothills
Black-headed Grosbeak	April 20–May 13	Cottonwoods, willows, and coniferous forests; foothills
Green-tailed Towhee	April 22–May 10	Shrubby areas and open forests; foothills, mountains
Chipping Sparrow	April 5–April 25	Riparian woodlands, coniferous forests, and shrubby areas; plains, foothills, mountains
Northern Oriole	May 2–May 12	Cottonwoods and willows; plains, lower foothills
Lesser Goldfinch	April 23–May 31	Cottonwoods, shrubby areas, and meadows; plains, foothills

*Range of earliest arrival dates reported to Boulder County Wildlife Inventory (Boulder County Audubon Society 1983–91).

BURROWING OWLS
ON THE EDGE

Where have all the burrowing owls gone? These 10-inch-high diurnal raptors, which lay their eggs in abandoned rodent burrows, were once common in Boulder County. Early twentieth century observers reported seeing as many as thirty burrowing owls in a single prairie dog colony.

Burrowing owl populations in the county decreased throughout the first half of this century and then rebounded slightly during the 1960s and 1970s as prairie dog colonies reappeared. By 1980 there were about a dozen active nest sites within the county. Then the owls began to vanish. By the early 1990s, only a couple of sites remained active.

Some nesting areas have been destroyed. One nest near Boulder Reservoir was disturbed when the surrounding prairie dog colony was used as a parking lot for the annual Kinetic Conveyance Race. A second site, on private property north of the reservoir, was converted into a winter-wheat field. But most of the historic nest sites remain viable; the owls just aren't coming back to them.

Some biologists attribute part of the decline of high plains burrowing owl populations to pesticide use in Mexico. Many of the owls winter in Mexico, where they consume poisoned grasshoppers and other insects. Predation by great horned owls may also take a toll. Great horned owl numbers in eastern Colorado have increased over the years as humans have disturbed natural ecosystems; by planting trees and telephone poles in and around prairie dog colonies, we've created ideal hunting perches for horned owls. For whatever reason, burrowing owls appear to be on the verge of extinction in Boulder County.

You can help local volunteers to better understand and possibly save this species by reporting any sightings to the Boulder County Audubon Society or the Boulder County Nature Association (see Appendix 5, page 311). Look for burrowing owls from April to October in prairie dog colonies at Boulder Reservoir, Rabbit Mountain, Lagerman Reservoir, Davidson Mesa, Rock Creek Farm, and along Coal Creek near Lafayette.

WHERE TO GO IN APRIL

CHAUTAUQUA PARK

Kites, frisbees, hikes, picnics, concerts, bird-watching, botanizing—Chautauqua means many things to many people. A good starting point for naturalists is the Ranger Cottage next to the parking area. Here a knowledgeable staff answers questions and provides brochures. A wildflower garden with labeled plants native to the mountain areas of Boulder surrounds the cottage. A butterfly garden, also composed of native plants, is specially designed to attract butterflies and caterpillars.

Started by vacationing Texans in 1898, Chautauqua now attracts hundreds of people daily. However, because the park is the hub of an extensive trail system, visitors fan out in all directions. The star of this system is the Mesa Trail, described below.

The turnoff to Chautauqua is just west of 9th on Baseline in Boulder.

MESA TRAIL AND LATERALS

This trail, probably the most popular in the county, is the granddaddy of Boulder's trail system. It goes up- and downhill, across mesas, and into canyons for 6 miles, from the historic Doudy-Debacker-Dunn House on the south end to the Bluebell Shelter on the north. Hikers on the trail pass below such well-known flatiron rock formations as Seal Rock, Devil's Thumb, the Maiden, and the Matron. Because the trail goes through habitats ranging from ponderosa pine forests to grasslands to wetlands, the variety of wildflowers and wildlife is tremendous even though there is little elevation change. Look for micro-climates and check side canyons for evidence of cold-air drainage. On a hot day, it's pleasant to feel the increased coolness at the mouth of these small canyons.

Deer are abundant, and black bears, coyotes, foxes, and mountain lions are often sighted. Look for marmots on the old stone walls near the Dunn House and for Abert's squirrels in the ponderosa pines. Most of Boulder County's owl species have been recorded along this trail. Golden eagles and prairie falcons nest in the cliffs and, in 1991, peregrine falcons returned to nest near the Flatirons after an absence of over thirty years.

The two main access points are Chautauqua and the South Mesa Trailhead on Eldorado Springs Drive 2 miles west of SR 93. There are many other access points, such as the National Center for Atmospheric Research or the McClintock Trail. Check a trail map for other possibilities. Also check a map for the many lateral trails, which are usually less crowded than the Mesa Trail. Here are a few of our favorites:

- *Royal Arch.* The only known large natural arch in Boulder County.
- *Mallory Cave.* A small sandstone cave.
- *Bear Creek.* A trail that passes through mossy, moist glades, aspen groves, and red rock slabs.
- *Fern Canyon.* A fern-filled gulch where prairie falcons and Cooper's hawks nest.
- *Shadow Canyon.* Another ferny place where flammulated owls nest and where the Boulder Mountain Park's largest known Douglas fir (about 40 inches in diameter) grows.
- *Towhee and Homestead.* Filled with chokecherry, alders, and willows, these connecting trails are especially good for "brush birds" such as towhees. In late spring look for lazuli and indigo buntings and yellow-breasted chats.

It's possible to do many loops or figure eights on the Mesa Trail network. By connecting the Mesa Trail with other City of Boulder trails and streets, you can hike all the way from North Boulder to south of Eldorado Springs.

MT. SANITAS

A steep 1.2-mile climb passes red sandstone formations to culminate at one of the best overlooks of the city of Boulder. Because of the 1,200-foot elevation gain, you see wildflowers at vastly different stages of development, a fitting illustration of the principle that spring climbs the mountains at about 100 feet per day. Look for nesting raptors and listen for canyon wrens.

The mountain takes its name from the sanitarium, built in 1895, that preceded the present hospital. Some of the first trails in the area were used by tuberculosis patients who came to Boulder for its beneficial air.

The trailhead is west of Community Hospital's Mapleton Center at Mapleton and 4th Street. It's possible to return by a different route via some rock quarries and a fire road.

RED ROCKS AND ANEMONE HILL

The gothic-looking red rock formation at the mouth of Boulder Canyon has attracted rock scramblers ever since the first gold seekers camped below here on October 17, 1858. To escape the urban view, head west up Anemone Hill. An old irrigation ditch that skirts the base of Anemone Hill offers good examples of micro-climates with some extremely early blooming flowers. On April 23, 1992, we found the first-of-season wild phlox, blue flax, boulder raspberry, white stemless evening primrose, spiderwort, and wild geranium along this ditch. All of these species were blooming a month earlier than expected.

Park on the south side of Sunshine Canyon across from the Mt. Sanitas Trailhead or at Settlers Park at the west end of Pearl Street, where a plaque lists the nineteen original Boulder settlers. Red Rocks Trail, less than a mile in length, connects Pearl Street and Sunshine Canyon. There are also several unnamed trails in the vicinity.

ROCK CREEK FARM

This working farm is part of Boulder County's Open Space and dates back to 1864 when Lafayette and Mary Miller ran a stage station and a roadhouse here as well as a farm. Many of the buildings date to 1933, when W. S. Stearns operated a dairy farm. Most of the 1,128 acres are leased, but 3.5 miles of trails are fenced off from the agricultural pastures. The trails meander past grazing cattle and prairie dogs, along the creek, and across the Stearns Lake dam. The lake is stocked with tiger muskie and channel catfish and is a good place to see waterbirds, including early avocets. Great horned owls and Swainson's hawks often nest in the cottonwoods, and hawks and eagles soar overhead. The cilantro-like fragrance of blue mustard pervades this pastoral scene.

The farm is located northwest of Broomfield at the intersection of Dillon Road and South 104th Street. There are two parking areas and trailheads: one on Dillon Road, 0.3-mile east of the intersection; the other on 104th Street, adjacent to Stearns Lake. A trail connects the two roads, and there are two loop trails along old farm roads with panoramic views of snow-covered mountains. Extensions of these trails are planned for the future.

UNION RESERVOIR AND HAMM'S NATURE AREA

Just across East County Line Road in Weld County is a place frequently cited on rare-bird hotlines: Union Reservoir. Scores of white pelicans and western grebes often congregate here in the summer, and the increasingly rare Lewis's woodpeckers are sometimes seen in the cottonwood groves. In recent summers, a peregrine falcon has been seen swooping down on the numerous gulls. Most of the 736-acre reservoir is surrounded by private land, but the city of Longmont operates a park (fees charged) on the southwest end that gives access to boating, fishing, picnicking, and birding.

Hamm's Nature Area, a small pond also good for white pelicans and wading birds, is bordered by a cattail marsh on one end and cottonwoods and Russian olives on the other.

Take East County Line Road to 17th Avenue east of Longmont. Hamm's Nature Area is west of the intersection; Union Reservoir is east.

BUTTON ROCK PRESERVE

The North St. Vrain Creek shoots out from beneath Button Rock dam in a thundering display of the power of water. Behind the dam is the Ralph Price Reservoir, part of Longmont's water supply. Because vehicle access is limited, this reservoir, surrounded by red rock formations and ponderosa pine forest, provides an oasis of peace. Many spring wildflowers bloom along the trail.

Brown and rainbow trout populate the cascading creek and Longmont Reservoir, the lower of the two reservoirs. Dippers are abundant, and pygmy owls and golden eagles nest in the vicinity. A dozen or more bald eagles roost around the reservoir in winter. Look for swallow nests along the cliffs and evidence of beaver along the bank.

From Lyons, drive west 4 miles on SR 36, turn left on CR 80, continue for 3 miles to a barricade, and park along the road. A short distance from Longmont Reservoir, the Sleepy Lion Trail takes off to the left. You may either hike the trail (with some elevation gain and loss) to the reservoir, or continue for 2 miles along the road. Many hikers like to go up one way and come back the other.

BEACH PARK

At the end of the month or early in May, go to this "handkerchief park" at 12th and Euclid in Boulder to see masses of crabapples in bloom, and walk around the neighborhood to enjoy the pink fantasyland created by these ornamental trees. If conditions are just right, a white deciduous magnolia may bloom at the south end of the park.

The Harbeck House, built in 1899 and now home of the Boulder Historical Society and the Boulder Museum of History, is located here and is worth a visit. A few blocks away, the University of Colorado campus with its many south-facing stone walls is a good place to see bulbs and trees blooming earlier than elsewhere. Varsity Pond yields the added bonus of newly emerged turtles and goldfish and is a good spot for warblers.

APRIL OUT-OF-COUNTY EXCURSIONS

In April, booming prairie chickens shuffle and strut in eastern Colorado on dancing grounds called "leks." The best time to see them is before sunrise. To avoid disturbing the birds, it's important to be in place while it's still dark.

Greater prairie chickens, an endangered species, are concentrated in Yuma County around Wray. In recent years their population has increased to about ten thousand birds, and they are being considered for downlisting from endangered to threatened. The leks are on private land, but trips to observe them can be arranged through the Colorado Division of Wildlife by calling 484-2836.

Lesser prairie chickens, a threatened species, inhabit the southeastern part of the state. Comanche National Grassland is the best place to see their courtship rituals. There is a public viewing blind near Campo. Phone (719) 852-4382 for details and a map.

APRIL AT A GLANCE

MAMMALS

- Mink mate in midwinter, and after delayed embryo implantation, the young are born in April and May.
- Long-tailed weasels also undergo delayed implantation. They mate in summer and the young are born the following spring.
- Beaver, raccoon, and porcupine young are born in April or May.
- Baby prairie dogs appear above ground.

BIRDS

- Golden eagle chicks hatch. (They fledge in late June or early July.)
- Burrowing owls return and mate.
- Great blue herons start to nest, with the peak of activity occurring in May.
- Broad-tailed hummingbirds return.
- Goldfinches transmute drab winter plumage into gold.

OTHER CRITTERS

- Bull snakes mate in April and May.
- More butterflies appear: cabbage whites, sulphurs, skippers, Melissa blues, red admirals, and painted ladies.

PLANTS

- Mouse-ear chickweed, mertensia, and various species of milk-vetch and mustard join the wildflower display.
- Fruit trees bloom, and rhubarb is harvested in towns.
- Ferns unfurl.

SPECIAL EVENTS

- Arbor Day and Earth Day are celebrated.

A P R I L   A T   A   G L A N C E
(Continued)

IN THE SKY

- The Lyrid meteor shower, which features spectacular fireballs scattering cinders across the sky, occurs around April 20. Look to the northeast.
- The Gemini twins (Castor and Pollux) are high in the western sky around 9:00 P.M. Look along the ecliptic about halfway between Orion and Ursa Major (the Big Dipper). The ancient Egyptians referred to these stars as "The Two Sprouting Plants," and Hindus called them "The Twin Deities."

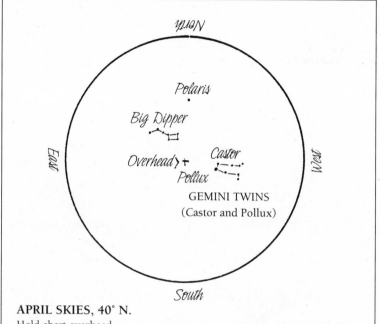

North

Polaris

Big Dipper

Overhead〉✚   Caster

Pollux

GEMINI TWINS
(Castor and Pollux)

East

West

South

APRIL SKIES, 40° N.
Hold chart overhead

9 PM MST - Early April
8 PM MST - Late April

April

"*Green Grass Moon*"
—*Pawnee*

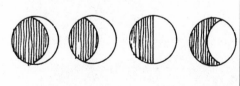

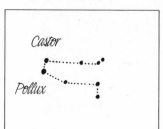

Caster

Pollux

GEMINI TWINS (Castor and Pollux)

103

American avocet, Walden Ponds

MAY

May can be as capricious as a chickadee choosing the perfect nest cavity, as colorful as a field of golden banner, and as clamorous as a cattail marsh full of yellow-headed blackbirds.

One year a broad-tailed hummingbird arrived at our feeder on May 1. On the fourth a record-breaking snowstorm began. Throughout the storm, the tiny bird fed on sugar water as three feet of wet snow flattened the daffodils. Crabapple trees heavy with pink blossoms broke in the storm, but the hummingbird triumphed. An ounce of spring won out over a ton of winter.

This wasn't quite what Tennyson meant when he wrote "The world is white with May." Normally, the words "white" and "May" conjure up visions of flowering plum, cherries, apples, and hawthorns.

Actually, May is a many-colored month. Western tanagers, bright yellow birds with heads as red as maraschino cherries, linger in town on their way to breeding areas in the foothills. Orange-and-black orioles return and start to construct their pendulous nests. Migrating flocks of warblers sing from greening treetops. Lazuli buntings glitter from the tops of shrubs, rivaling the gemstone for which they are named.

Imagining colors helps to combat terminal boredom in meetings when you'd rather be outdoors. Think of a color and where to find it in nature: pink – in the V-shaped vest of the rose-breasted grosbeak, in the satiny blooms of ball cactus, in the first wild geraniums, shootingstars, and fairy-slippers; yellow – goldfinches, swallow-tailed butterflies, clove-scented

Butterfly Irruptions

For reasons shrouded in mystery, butterfly and moth populations sometimes skyrocket. In May 1991, Miller moths invaded Boulder in enormous numbers; in May 1973 and (in lesser numbers) in 1992, it was painted ladies. A mild winter preceding the population explosion may be one reason for these gentle invasions.

golden currant, and the "eyebrow" of evening grosbeaks; blue–indigo buntings, larkspur, chiming bells, penstemon, and little blue butterflies. Around Memorial Day, bearded irises–named for Iris, the Greek goddess of the rainbow and the messenger of the gods–burst into colors as varied and vibrant as their namesake.

During May, the most concentrated chorus of the year occurs. It's a time of establishing territories, courting, and mating. Robins start singing before first light. From rock walls, canyon wrens let fall a downward cascade of notes 'ending in a soft Bronx cheer. House wrens bubble a cadenza of ecstasy. Blackbirds and frogs create a cacophony in the wetlands.

May is a month for surprises and paradox. Statistically, it's the wettest month of the year. It may begin with a snowstorm and end with a thunderstorm–or temperatures in the nineties. In 1894 it ended with a hundred-year flood. And someday it will happen again.

So much happens in May that it's impossible to keep track of all the "firsts." There's a new flower or a new bird on every walk. The warbler migration is in flood; baby owls fledge as robins start to nest; and successive waves of wildflowers paint the hills.

Beware of sensory overload in May. How can you not be overwhelmed by the heavy scent of blue mustard, wild plum, lilac, and apple blossom? Or the taste of the first wild asparagus picked from fencerows east of town?

FLORA

ALMOST ANYTHING CAN HAPPEN

Just when everyone is more than ready for spring, May can throw in some really rude surprises. It is almost always hotter, drier, colder, or windier than the so-called average. With this in mind, beware when local weather prognosticators expound that it is much warmer than it "should" be, or that it is thirty degrees below what it "ought" to be.

There are lessons in these fluctuations for local gardeners trying to use the USDA plant hardiness zones, which are based on average minimum winter temperatures. In Boulder County, cold winter temperatures are rarely as detrimental to plants as are spring and fall freezes. Ill-adapted plants may respond to alternating warm and cold periods by initiating growth too early, only to lose their blossoms during spring freezes. Saucer magnolia (*Magnolia X soulangiana*), for example, seems to be fully winter hardy, but May freezes often destroy the flowers just as they are about to put on a showy display.

Knowledge of local blooming sequences can help gardeners. Research from several regions suggests correlations between spring development of indicator plants and local insect pests. The precision and regularity of these associations offers the opportunity to target pests more effectively, thus reducing pesticide applications. For example, hawthorn mealy bugs are most vulnerable to insecticides when the bugs disperse onto branches. This dispersal usually occurs as juneberries (*Amelanchier* spp.) are blooming and redbuds (*Cercis canadensis*) are about to bloom.

MAY WEATHER

MAY 1

Sunrise: 5:01 AM MST
Sunset: 6:54 PM MST

	Boulder	Allens Park	Niwot Ridge
	5,445'	8,500'	11,565'
Ave. Max.	65°F	59°F Ave. May high	38°F Ave. May high
Ave. Min.	39°F	32°F Ave. May low	23°F Ave. May low

MAY 31

Sunrise: 4:34 AM MST
Sunset: 7:21 PM MST

Ave. Max.	73°F	59°F Ave. May high	38°F Ave. May high
Ave. Min.	48°F	32°F Ave. May low	23°F Ave. May low

MAY CHANGES (May 1–May 31)

Day Length: 13 hours, 53 minutes to 14 hours, 47 minutes=change of +1 hour 34 minutes

Change: Max.	+8°F	+11°F	+10°F
Change: Min.	+9°F	+8°F	+9°F

MAY EXTREMES

Max. Temp.	93°F	78°F	See note
Min. Temp.	20°F	+6°F	See note
Max. Wind	110 mph	211 mph	Not available
Ave. Precip.	3.07 in.	2.8 in.	4.44 in.
Max. Precip.	9.27 in.	9 in.	7.4 in.
Min. Precip.	Trace	.4 in.	2.2 in.
Ave. Snow	2.7 in.	8.6 in.	Not available
Max. Snow	26.7 in.	30 in.	Not available
Min. Snow	00 in.	00 in.	Not available

Note. 77°F is highest for any summer and −31°F is lowest for any winter on Niwot Ridge.

MAY NOTES:

31 May 1894 is the date of the most recent "100 year flood."

Stalking the Wild Asparagus

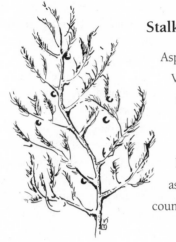

Asparagus was first planted in Boulder Valley along Farmers Ditch, which winds through North Boulder to farms northeast of town, soon after the irrigation ditch was built in 1862. Birds helped spread the seeds, and now wild asparagus can be found throughout the county along ditches and fencerows.

Mealy bugs are less vulnerable a little later, when fringe trees (*Chionanthus* sp.) and cockspur hawthorn (*Crataegus crusgalli*) start to bloom.

OLD-GROWTH FORESTS

No one knows for sure what the coniferous forests of Boulder County looked like before white settlement. During the last half of the nineteenth century, miners, loggers, and other settlers cut or burned most of the forests in the county. Cinders thrown from locomotives caused many catastrophic fires; other fires were intentionally set by miners to expose mineral-bearing rocks. By 1900, large areas of the county had been devastated, and few of the original forests remained. See Tom Veblen and Diane Lorenz's book, *The Colorado Front Range: A Century of Ecological Change*, for "then and now" photos of local forests.

A few areas of Engelmann spruce/subalpine fir forest, which were outside the mineralized belt or inaccessible to loggers, survived. You can still find pockets of old-growth spruce/fir (defined here as forest that has escaped major disturbances for at least two hundred years) on Chittenden Mountain, west of Eldora, and on the lower slopes of Niwot Ridge. These old-growth pockets display the cathedral-like qualities of ancient forests, including large trees, a multistoried canopy, vigorous green undergrowth, and numerous standing dead trees and downed logs. The sounds are distinctive as well: the flutelike songs of hermit thrushes, the shrill twitter of golden-crowned kinglets, and the soft rustling of southern red-backed voles in the blueberries on the forest floor.

Old-growth ponderosa pine/Douglas fir forests are much harder to find. There are a few side canyons to North St. Vrain Canyon, including Coulson Gulch and Rattlesnake Gulch, where the ponderosas grow 100 feet high and flammulated owls poke their heads out of holes in giant yellow-barked snags. In lower Shadow Canyon in the Boulder Mountain Park, some Douglas firs are 3 feet in diameter. But places like this are rare. Throughout the county, dense, stunted stands of second-growth ponderosa pine/Douglas fir forest predominate.

Reestablishing old-growth forests will be a challenge for future generations. Studies conducted in northern Arizona and elsewhere suggest that periodic low-intensity fires are necessary to maintain the vitality of many ponderosa pine forests. In the absence of fire, trees become stunted and crowded; litter accumulates on the forest floor, discouraging regeneration. Over time, conditions become ripe for catastrophic fires similar to those in Yellowstone National Park in 1988. Foresters have used the technique of thinning to mimic the effects of natural fires. But thinning alone may not be enough.

Why are old-growth forests so important? The common arguments are that they provide essential habitat for a variety of species and are among the last untainted ecosystems on earth. But there's a simpler, more visceral justification. Sit in lower Shadow Canyon on a May morning when the air is pungent with pine scent and hermit thrushes are singing. Or hike down Coulson Gulch on a May evening when the moon is full and flammulated owls are hooting softly from the towering ponderosas. When these sights, sounds, and smells are gone, our lives will be poorer.

FAUNA

WARBLERS AND OTHER RARE FINDS

When we hear the first yellow warblers singing in the cottonwoods along Boulder Creek, we know that spring has arrived. Warblers are perfect emblems of the season with their flashy colors, sweet songs, and frenetic foraging activity. They come from as far away as Brazil and Ecuador, and their arrival often coincides with the onset of the first long stretch of hot, sunny weather. Warblers are also sensitive indicators of environmental quality. As warblers go, so goes much of the natural world.

Though the more than fifty warbler species that nest in North America are similar in shape, size, and habits, each has evolved to fit a unique niche in the natural order. Some nest in deciduous trees, others in conifers. Some forage in the treetops, others in the shrub understory. Some glean insects mostly from the trunks and branches of trees, whereas others specialize in snatching insects from the air. Some winter in tropical rain forests, others in subtropical brushlands and savannahs. No two species combine all these attributes in the same way (see the table on page 112).

Breeding-bird censuses conducted in the United States during recent years indicate that the populations of North American warblers that winter in tropical rain forests may be declining as much as 1% per year (two rare Boulder County warblers, the ovenbird and American redstart, are included). Many local observers swear that the numbers of warblers along Boulder Creek in May have plummeted. Yet none of our most common warblers winter exclusively in rain forests.

Some studies suggest that fragmentation of warbler breeding habitat in North America may be a major cause of the observed decline in warbler numbers. Parasitism of warbler nests by brown-headed cowbirds, a native North American species that benefits from disturbance of natural ecosystems, has probably also contributed to the decline. The cowbirds lay their eggs in the warblers' nests, and the cowbird hatchlings outcompete hatchlings of the host species. University of Colorado ornithologist Alexander Cruz

May

NESTING WARBLERS OF BOULDER COUNTY

Species	Nesting Elevation (feet)	Nesting Habitat	Arrival Date	Wintering Location	Abundance
Virginia's Warbler	5,400–9,000	Dry scrub, pine understory	May 1	Mexico	Common
Chestnut-sided Warbler	5,400–7,000	Riparian understory	May 1	Central America	Rare**
Yellow-rumped Warbler	5,400–11,000	Coniferous forest	March/April*	South to Central America	Common
Yellow Warbler	5,000–8,500	Riparian overstory	May 4	Mexico south to Brazil	Common
Wilson's Warbler	8,000–11,500	Willow thickets	May 4	Mexico south to Panama	Fairly Common
MacGillivray's Warbler	5,400–10,000	Riparian understory	May 10	Mexico south to Panama	Fairly Common
Ovenbird	5,400–8,000	Riparian or forest understory	May 15	Mexico south to Venezuela	Rare**
Common Yellowthroat	5,000–8,000	Wetlands	May 7	Mexico south to Panama	Fairly Common
Yellow-breasted Chat	5,000–7,000	Dry scrub	May 10	Mexico south to Panama	Fairly Common
American Redstart	5,000–9,000	Forest edge or riparian	May 10	Mexico south to Ecuador and Brazil	Rare**

*Some individuals may stay in Boulder County throughout the winter.
**Nesting in Boulder County is poorly documented.

has reported that as many as 50% of the nests of some Front Range songbirds have been parasitized by cowbirds.

In addition to cowbirds, a number of Boulder County bird species have become more plentiful over the years. Ravens, now common, were nonexistent here around the turn of the century. European starlings, introduced into New York City's Central Park in 1890, did not appear in our area until 1945. Rock doves arrived even more recently, and the now ubiquitous Canada goose was once considered a rarity. Several of these species are generalists that thrive in a variety of environments and may benefit from human disturbance of natural habitats. Many specialists, particularly those inhabiting marshes and grasslands, have declined locally to the point of near-extinction.

Northern harriers (marsh hawks) now breed in only a few locations in Boulder County, including cattail marshes on the west side of Boulder Reservoir and the west side of Lagerman Reservoir. In May, harriers lay four to nine eggs on platform nests constructed from cattails. Adults share in the incubation, and the young leave the nest soon after hatching in July. Harriers are most conspicuous at dawn or dusk, when they swoop low over the marshes and adjacent grasslands searching for meadow voles.

Two other rare and threatened marsh birds, the American bittern and the least bittern, can be seen, or more likely heard, this month at Sawhill Ponds. Listen for the low "pumping" call of the American bittern ("oonk-a-lunk") and the high staccato chirping of the least bittern before dawn.

While hiking through the grasslands east and south of Boulder you may hear the thin, insectlike trills of male grasshopper sparrows. These small sparrows are endemic to North American prairies, and they were only recently rediscovered in Boulder County when the city began to inventory newly acquired Open Space land on the plains.

Bobolinks are among the rarest of our local grassland birds. They nest in a few remaining wet meadows along South Boulder Creek, between Arapahoe Road and South Boulder Road. Bobolinks begin courtship in late May and usually fledge their young by mid-July. From late May on, look for bobolinks as you hike the Centennial Trail near the Flatirons Country Club or the South Boulder Creek Trail south of Baseline Road.

Boulder County's coniferous forests have escaped many of the ravages of civilization, but the destruction of old-growth ponderosa pine/Douglas fir forests throughout the county has placed some specialists in jeopardy. The diminutive flammulated owl is an old-growth-dependent species found in isolated canyons along the Front Range. This migratory owl nests in woodpecker cavities in dead ponderosa pines and aspens. It subsists on moths and other insects gathered from the forest understory. In May and early June, listen for the resonant three-note hoot given by males establishing nesting territories in the foothills. After sunset, flammulated owls respond readily to any reasonable imitation of their vocalizations. Try the most remote canyons in the Boulder Mountain Park or side canyons off North St. Vrain Canyon.

While walking in the foothills, you may come upon a troupe of Abert's squirrels performing their bizarre "mating bouts" high up in the ponderosa pines. Abert's squirrels (also known as tassel-eared squirrels) live in mature ponderosa pine forests. They nest in the forest canopy, forage on pine seeds and bark, and dig into the soil to harvest truffles attached to ponderosa pine roots. Mating bouts occur in May, when males line up in single file to chase estrous females through the forest. The order of males in the chase group is determined by the proximity of each male's foraging territory to that of the estrous female's. If one male forgets his place, another male may challenge him, resulting in a spirited wrestling match on the forest floor. Abert's squirrels inhabit ponderosa pine forests throughout Boulder County.

How long can specialists such as ovenbirds, northern harriers, and flammulated owls continue to survive as their breeding habitats become islands in a sea of development and disturbance? What effect would extinction of these species have on life processes within natural ecosystems? These are questions to ponder while hiking through our fragile wetlands, grasslands, and forests listening for the songs of warblers or the exuberant clatter of amorous squirrels streaking through the pines.

INDICATOR SPECIES

What do Abert's squirrels, American bitterns, and grasshopper sparrows have in common? All are specialists with breeding ranges largely restricted to one habitat type. These birds and mammals, sometimes referred to as "indicator species," tend to be more sensitive to environmental change than are species that breed in a greater variety of habitats.

While Boulder County populations of such generalists as coyotes, mule deer, American robins, and chipping sparrows have increased or remained stable over the years, populations of many specialists have declined. Grasshopper sparrows disappeared throughout most of Boulder County as native grasslands were overgrazed or plowed under. American bitterns are now restricted to a few remaining cattail marshes. Sharp-tailed grouse (an inhabitant of tallgrass prairies) vanished entirely.

In recent years, local conservation organizations and government planners have used the indicator species concept to locate and protect critical plant and wildlife habitat. Surveys of flammulated owl populations throughout the county have helped to identify areas of relatively undisturbed ponderosa pine/Douglas fir forest. Marshlands where American bitterns, least bitterns, and northern harriers nest have been protected and buffered. Remnant tallgrass prairies supporting nesting grasshopper sparrows have been mapped and managed under the state Natural Areas Program.

Below is a list of some indicator species for selected Boulder County ecosystems:

- *Grasslands* – Black-tailed prairie dog, thirteen-lined ground squirrel, grasshopper sparrow
- *Freshwater marshes* – American bittern, yellow-headed blackbird, sora
- *Ponderosa pine forest* – Abert's squirrel, pygmy nuthatch
- *Spruce/fir forest* – Golden-crowned kinglet, boreal owl, pine grosbeak
- *Alpine tundra* – White-tailed ptarmigan, American pipit

WHERE TO GO IN MAY

WALDEN AND SAWHILL PONDS

These wetlands (west of 75th between Jay and Valmont roads) show that abandoned gravel pits can be good wildlife habitat. A network of ponds, marshes, brush, and cottonwoods was once the site of a gravel operation along the edge of Boulder Creek. Some mining still occurs along the periphery, and noisy planes from Boulder Airport roar overhead. But wildlife thrives. Dirt roads, once open to traffic, now serve as hiking trails.

Red foxes den along the banks, beaver and muskrat inhabit the ponds, and great horned owls nest in the tall cottonwoods at the west end. Young owls fledge in early to mid-May and sit near the nest looking like sulky children in fluffy white snowsuits. This grove is a good place to see migrating warblers, western tanagers, orioles, and black-headed grosbeaks. The shallow edges of the ponds attract such shorebirds as great blue herons, black-crowned night herons, killdeer, yellowlegs, and avocets, while ducks and teal feed farther out. In early May, raucous yellow-headed blackbirds return about the same time as Canada geese lead newborn goslings into the water. In June and July, fireflies, rare in Boulder County, flicker on and off.

GOLDEN PONDS

These three Longmont ponds are partially restored gravel pits similar to Walden and Sawhill. Turn west off Hover Road at the intersection of Hover Road and 3rd Street. Paved paths circle these ponds, where ducks, grebes, and geese congregate. St. Vrain Creek, west of the ponds, attracts additional wildlife, including warblers and orioles in the trees lining the creek. The view across these ponds to Mount Meeker and Longs Peak is superb.

BOULDER COUNTY FAIRGROUNDS LAKE

A trail, less than a mile in length, circles this 19-acre lake where Canada geese and mallards nest on the reedy islands. Because there are no shade trees, the trail is best in early morning or evening. Several other restored ponds and marshes are in the area north of the fairgrounds, and it's also possible to walk a short distance along St. Vrain Creek. To reach these wetlands, turn east off Hover Road at the Boulder County Fairgrounds in Longmont. Because the fairgrounds are near Golden Ponds, the two areas can be visited on a single trip.

BOULDER CREEK PATH

Stretching from Boulder Canyon to east of 55th Street, this trail *is* the heart of the city. It's loved almost to death by multitudes of users from bicyclists to bird-watchers. But at dawn the creek path belongs to nature and to naturalists. Probably more rare warblers (including golden-winged, palm, and prothonotary) have been seen along the section between Eben Fine Park and 30th Street than anywhere else in the city. However, in recent years heavy use seems to have had an adverse effect on migrating birds. Swallows, rock doves, and dippers nest under the older bridges, but the newer bridges offer nothing on which to attach a nest.

The section of the trail from Eben Fine Park to the stream observatory near the Clarion Harvest Hotel, called the "Boulder Creek Interpretive Walk," includes plaques giving information on history and natural history. In April and May a profusion of crocus, tulips, daffodils, and other naturalized bulbs burst into bloom along this section. This stretch includes a demonstration xeriscape garden and an international peace garden that were designed and built by volunteers with native plants from foreign lands.

Volunteers play a large role in the well-being of the creek and have built pools and riffles to protect breeding and feeding areas for fish. To watch fish in action, look through the windows at the stream observatory west of 28th Street. Although fly fishing is allowed, Boulder Creek is a catch-and-release stream.

From Eben Fine Park, you can continue up Boulder Canyon along the paved path or walk through the underpass to Settler's Park, where several trails diverge.

DOUDY DRAW

Many birds are attracted to water and to brushy areas such as Doudy Draw. Warblers, lazuli buntings, rufous-sided towhees, tanagers, grosbeaks, and orioles sing from the cottonwoods, willows, and plum thickets; and this is one of the few nesting sites in the county for sage thrashers.

The plums reach their blooming peak in May, and their heady fragrance attracts numerous butterflies, such as the orange, brown, and black fritillaries. The ethereal blues (gossamer-wing butterflies) are attracted by minerals in the mud along creek crossings, especially where animals have urinated. These tiny butterflies fold their sky blue wings when they alight and become almost invisible. Sometimes clusters of several dozen sparkle unexpectedly into the air as you step across the creek. The orange, brown, and gray colors are due to pigmentation in the wing scales, but the shimmering blues, greens, purples, and coppers are caused by light refraction.

As you climb out of the draw, notice the changes in vegetation. Golden banner, larkspur, mertensia, and wallflowers give way to ponderosa pines and midgrass prairie at the top. Some of the first snowball saxifrages of the year grow under the pines.

Park at either the Flatirons Vista Trailhead on the west side of SR 93, just south of SR 128, or at the Doudy Draw Trailhead about 2 miles west of 93 on Eldorado Springs Drive. This latter section provides a wheelchair-accessible trail for the first 0.3-mile, ending in a cottonwood grove picnic area. For a 6-mile-loop hike, you can connect the two ends of Doudy Draw Trail with the Greenbelt Plateau Trail and Community Ditch.

How Things Haven't Changed

"The almanac tells us it is the month of May, and, but for that timely adviser, we should certainly not know what season of the year it is. Snow, wind, and the tops of trees are amongst our instruments of entertainment. We believe summer is somewhere on the road, but whether its arrival will be celebrated this year or next, remains to be seen."

—a Caribou resident writing in *Boulder County News*, May 3, 1872; quoted in Duane Smith, *Silver Saga* (Pruett Publishing Company, 1974).

WALKER RANCH

Many miles of trails thread through this historic district, once the largest cattle ranch in this part of Colorado. Settled in 1882 by James Walker, the ranch is interesting from a historic, as well as natural, point of view. Although the original ranch house burned down on November 30, 1992, most of the outbuildings are still intact. However, they are closed to the public except on designated Living History Days, when volunteers show what daily life was like in the 1800s.

Ball cactus (*Pediocactus simpsonii*) flaunts showy flowers, ranging from pale pink to torrid fuchsia, from early to mid-May on the ridge above Crescent Meadow and along trails leading to the meadow. This cactus copes with winter by losing water and shrinking into the ground. Some plants actually disappear until spring rains plump them up again.

Late in the month another exquisite

rose-pink flower, the fairy-slipper orchid, blooms along the upper stretch of South Boulder Creek. Look for it else-where in the county at 6,000 to 9,000 feet in moist coniferous forests. The pale lavender flowers of rock clematis (*Clematis columbiana*) often signal the place.

Several trails can be combined for an 8-mile loop through a variety of foothills habitats. From the South Boulder Creek trailhead, descend to the creek, which is at its rampaging best in May, head up to Crescent Meadows with outstanding views of the Front Range, go back down to South Boulder Creek, then up again to the starting point via Eldorado Canyon and Columbine Gulch Trail.

Other trails that originate at Walker Ranch include:

• *Eldorado Canyon Trail.* Goes up and down over several ridges to Eldorado Canyon State Park in 4.5 miles.

• *Meyers Homestead Trail.* Starts across the road from Walker Ranch and con-tinues for 2.5 miles to a scenic over-look. There are several aspen groves and flower-filled meadows along this trail. In July, rare wood lilies have been found here and, in October, elk may bugle.

Some of the trails are open for bicy-cling, but check signs at the trailheads for current information.

To reach Walker Ranch, take Flagstaff Road and Gross Reservoir Road (CR 56 and CR 77) to a marked parking area about 1.5 miles south of Kossler Lake.

GREGORY CANYON

Step for step, this short (about 2 miles one way) but steep trail is one of the best wildflower hikes in the county. It begins in Baird Park just west of the spot where Baseline becomes Flagstaff Road. Starting in thickets of wild plums, chokecherries, and apple trees, you progress up through all the usual May flowers, reaching pasque flowers and wild phlox at the top. These flowers attract swarms of butterflies and broad-tailed humming-birds. Hummingbirds zoom in to the color red, so wear a red hat or bandanna to get buzzed.

In addition to the usual influx of May birds, this canyon is home to one of the sweetest singers of the avian world: the canyon wren. Look for a small russet-brown bird with uptilted tail and listen for his wrendition of springtime. Also look for rock wrens, house wrens, chipmunks, and golden-mantled ground squirrels.

At the top of the canyon, several other hiking possibilities open up. You can continue on up Green Mountain or you can cross Flagstaff Road and take either the Range View Trail or Ute Trail (about half a mile each) to the summit of Flagstaff. On summer weekends, stop to see the nature displays at the Flagstaff Summit Center, where volunteers answer questions about local natural history. If you wish to return to Baird Park via a different route, take the Flagstaff Trail; however, this trail has the disadvantage of crossing the road five times.

ANNE U. WHITE TRAIL

This 1.75-mile trail crosses Fourmile Canyon Creek twenty-two times and passes lovely pools and miniature waterfalls. About halfway up look for a small, secret garden of emerald moss and magenta shootingstars. Petals that flare backwards give this flower the look of a jewel in flight. Look for it at progressively higher elevations throughout June and July. Pink flowering cactus and purple sugarbowls (*Clematis hirsutissima*) can be found at the upper end of the

trail, and western tanagers and black-headed grosbeaks are fairly common. Mountain lions have also been seen here.

From North Broadway, turn west on Lee Hill Road and drive 1.1 miles to Wagonwheel Gap Road. Turn left and go 1 mile; turn left again onto a dirt road that dead-ends in 0.2-mile. Park alongside the road.

WALTER ORR ROBERTS NATURE TRAIL

Located behind the National Center for Atmospheric Research, this half-mile loop offers spectacular views of the Flatirons and is keyed to descriptions in a booklet available at NCAR. At the far end of this wheelchair-accessible loop, the Dakota Trail connects NCAR to the Mesa Trail. Mule deer browse in the vicinity, and pale blue wild iris bloom in the meadow below the mesa top in mid-May. The award-winning NCAR building, made from pink-tinted concrete, simulates pink sandstone and dominates the skyline like an Anasazi city. Inside are exhibits on the sun, atmospheric phenomena, climate, and the flora and fauna of the mesa.

Thunderstorms

The first major "T-storms" often occur in May. Typically, they begin over the foothills around noon and drift eastward, growing rapidly as they encounter warm updrafts from the flatlands. Eastern Colorado has one of the most active thunderstorm seasons on the planet, with sixty or so such storms in a three-month season. Several tropical and semitropical areas have more thunderstorms, but those storms are scattered over a twelve-month season.

NORTH ST. VRAIN CREEK AND MEADOW PARK

Wood ducks, Lewis's woodpeckers, cedar waxwings, dippers, and raptors nest along this creek and in the bluffs above the park at the west end of Lyons.

LONG'S IRIS GARDENS

At the end of the month visit this garden and nursery that has been selling flowers and plants to Boulder gardeners since 1905. Walk up and down the rows of bearded iris, stopping to savor their delicate scent. The garden, located at 3240 Broadway, is open to the public daily during the iris blooming season from 10:00 A.M. until 6:00 P.M.

HERON ROOKERIES

Great blue herons hatch in May. Because the adults are easily disturbed when incubating or caring for the young, it is important to observe them from a distance with binoculars. The largest rookery in the county is at Boulder Valley Farms (private property) on 95th Street, about a mile north of the intersection with Valmont Road. There is adequate parking along the road, and the birds can easily be observed from here. A few black-crowned night herons and common egrets also use the rookery, and many waterbirds, including avocets, ducks, and teal, can be seen in nearby ponds.

MAY OUT-OF-COUNTY EXCURSIONS

Late May is the perfect time with the perfect temperature for visiting the prairie at Pawnee National Grassland (near Greeley) or at Comanche National Grassland (near La Junta). Long-billed curlews, lark buntings (Colorado's state bird, rarely seen in Boulder County), and burrowing owls nest in both grasslands. Prairie wildflowers flourish from May through August. Because there's little light pollution and nothing to obstruct the sky, the grasslands are ideal for stargazing. These two places are still relatively "undiscovered," so you're likely to see more prairie falcons and pronghorns (and cows) than people. Maps, available from the Roosevelt National Forest Office, are essential for finding your way around the grasslands, which are a checkerboard of intermixed private and public lands.

If you missed the lesser prairie chickens in April, they are still active in early May at Comanche National Grassland, also noted for its petroglyphs. Picket Wire Canyonlands, located in this grassland, contains the longest set of known dinosaur tracks in the world and was opened to the public for guided tours in 1992.

Another must for May is Barr Lake State Park, a few miles east of Brighton at 13401 Picadilly Road. A pair of bald eagles has successfully raised eaglets here

Open Space Grasslands,
South Boulder

Black-footed Ferret

Former Species of
Boulder County Grasslands

Bison
"Tatonka," Lakota

Pronghorn

Sharp-tailed Grouse

for several years. (Until recently they were the only ones to nest east of the Continental Divide in Colorado.) They usually nest in a cormorant rookery on the west end of the lake. Best viewing is from a gazebo 1.5 miles from the Visitor Center. For additional information, call the Visitor Center at (303) 659-6005.

Great horned owl fledgling

MAY AT A GLANCE

MAMMALS

- Colorado chipmunks are born late May or June.
- Short-tailed weasels breed in May or June, but because of delayed embryo implantation, young are not born until the following April or May.
- Spotted skunks are born in May; striped skunks in May or June.
- White-tailed deer are born in May or June.
- Abert's squirrels engage in mating bouts.

BIRDS

- Blue grouse drum and display throughout coniferous forests.
- Many species of birds mate and nest: Swainson's hawks and great blue herons nest on the plains; robins and finches in urban areas; flammulated owls and western tanagers in the foothills.
- Migration and bird song reach peak.
- Great horned owl young fledge.

OTHER CRITTERS

- Cecropia moths hatch from cocoons spun on deciduous trees last fall.
- Miller moths pass through on their way to mountain breeding areas.
- Tent caterpillars emerge from their cobwebby tents.

PLANTS

- Wild asparagus attains perfection.
- Ball cactus, fairy-slippers, sugarbowls, larkspurs, shootingstars, and iris bloom in the foothills.
- Conifers release great clouds of golden pollen in late May and throughout June.
- Lilacs and fruit trees blossom in urban areas.

MAY AT A GLANCE
(Continued)

IN THE SKY

- The Eta Aquarid meteors peak in the southeast sky around midnight on May 3.
- May Day (May 1) traditionally marked the approximate halfway point between the vernal equinox and the summer solstice, the blossoming of flowers, and the arrival of warm days.
- The pentagon-shaped constellation Auriga (The Charioteer), though not particularly well known, is prominent in the low northwestern sky around 9:00 P.M. The first-magnitude star Capella is actually a binary system with the two suns orbiting around a common center of gravity. They complete one orbit in 104 days.

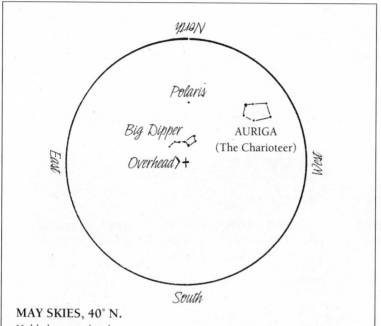

MAY SKIES, 40° N.
Hold chart overhead

9 PM MDT - Early May
8 PM MDT - Late May

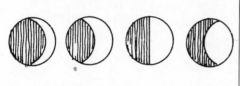

May

"Moon of the Budding Plants"
—Ojibwa

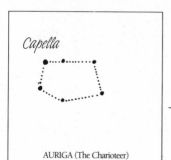

Capella

AURIGA (The Charioteer)

127

Longs Peak (photo courtesy Glenn Cushman)

JUNE

June is the month for newborns, who look at the world in astonishment as though it were newly made. Fawns, their eyes still blue, appear in the newly sprouted lettuce in some urban gardens. By the end of the month baby raccoons begin to twitter and trill, and young marmots and skunks emerge. Goslings and ducklings paddle industriously behind stately parents. Other baby birds cheep loudly, their feeding demands keeping parents so busy the males frequently sing with their mouths full.

At higher elevations, many birds are still courting and nesting. The male hermit thrush, establishing his nesting territory in the spruce/fir forest, seems to sing a duet with himself. He whistles an arpeggio high on the scale, and then he repeats it at a lower pitch. Sometimes he seems to start on a note so high he can't complete the flutelike song. Although anthropo-morphism is frowned upon by scientists, we imagine the bird pausing in embarrassment before starting again at the "proper" pitch. The louder song of the warbling vireo in nearby aspen seems to say, "Summertime, summertime, summertime. Here it comes, here it comes, here it comes."

In moist aspen groves the Colorado columbine, our state flower, begins to bloom, and if weather conditions are right, the first puffballs and meadow mushrooms appear. From the foothills to the high mountains, a tall plant with greenish white flowers shoots up. Called green gentian or monument plant, this unusual species requires twenty to sixty years to reach maturity and send up a flowering stalk; then it dies.

On the plains, white prickly poppies, evening primroses, and scarlet globe mallow (sometimes called cowboy's delight) predominate. In towns, roses reach their peak and seem to hold the essence of June in their perfume. Wild roses and various penstemons bloom in the foothills, and marsh marigolds and globeflowers carpet high mountain meadows. Higher still, glacier lilies and buttercups poke yellow flowers through melting snow.

This snowmelt feeds creeks, causing them to flow at peak levels and to cascade riotously down the mountainsides. Now is the best time of year for waterfall-watching and for finding the moss-covered domed nests of dippers behind the sheets of water.

Many high-altitude trails and roads are still blocked by deep snowdrifts, sullied by blown dirt and fallen conifer needles. These accumulations of snow are slow to melt in the shade of spruce/fir forests. However, if you climb above the dark forests onto the open tundra, a magic carpet of alpine flowers awaits you. Late in the month, alpine forget-me-nots reach their peak while the lower elevation spruce/fir zone is still barren of flowers.

If you don't mind being caught with your rump in the air, the best way to enjoy these miniature alpine flowers is on your knees with nose to ground and hand lens to eye. Otherwise, as one mountain climber said, "It's like looking at a flower through the wrong end of the binoculars." Under magnification, grains of pollen look like gold dust sprinkled on petaled jewels. The whole world looks different from this perspective. The inch-high willow becomes a giant, and the red-saddled bumblebee a monster.

It's also easier to appreciate the fragrance of rock jasmine and Parry's clover from a prone position. However, if you inadvertently lie in a clump of sky pilot, the aroma is distinctly skunk. When the leaves are not crushed, the flower smells surprisingly sweet.

Above tree line, the air itself is sweet and unpolluted. We hear life murmur and see it glisten and feel that all elements of heaven and earth are, indeed, in tune.

JUNE WEATHER

JUNE 1

Sunrise: 4:34 AM MST
Sunset: 7:22 PM MST

	Boulder	**Allens Park**	**Niwot Ridge**
	5,445'	8,500'	11,565'
Ave. Max.	73°F	69°F Ave. June high	49°F Ave. June high
Ave. Min.	48°F	39°F Ave. June low	33°F Ave. June low

JUNE 30

Sunrise: 4:35 AM MST
Sunset: 7:32 PM MST

Ave. Max.	84°F	69°F Ave. June high	49°F Ave. June high
Ave. Min.	57°F	39°F Ave. June low	33°F Ave. June low

JUNE CHANGES (June 1–June 30)

Day Length: 14 hours, 48 minutes to 14 hours, 57 minutes=change of +9 minutes

Change: Max.	+11°F	+10°F	+11°F
Change: Min.	+9°F	+7°F	+10°F

JUNE EXTREMES

Max. Temp.	104°F	94°F	See note
Min. Temp.	30°F	13°F	See note
Max. Wind	123 mph	78 mph	Not available
Ave. Precip.	1.82 in.	2.3 in.	1.98 in.
Max. Precip.	9.27 in.	6 in.	2.64 in.
Min. Precip.	Trace	.5 in.	1.12 in.
Ave. Snow	00 in.	.4 in.	Not available
Max. Snow	2.2 in.	7 in.	Not available
Min. Snow	00 in.	00 in.	Not available

Note. 77°F is highest for any summer and −31°F is lowest for any winter on Niwot Ridge.

FLORA

ALPINE GARDENS

At the top of the world, where no trees grow, fragile and diminutive flowers defy the elements to form colorful, improbable gardens from late June through August. Swept by blizzards and wind, this high, lonely country called the tundra seems a forsaken land to some and the Garden of Eden to others.

In Colorado, tree line usually occurs at about 11,500 feet, though the level varies depending on local conditions. Tree line signals the passage from a temperate to an Arctic climate, where winter air temperature rarely rises above freezing and where blizzards may occur any time of the year.

At this elevation, wind and driving snow prune the last outposts of evergreens into bonsai hedges termed "krummholz." The krummholz seems to migrate as the leeward side creeps forward while the windward side dies. These trees, toughened by the elements, provide shelter for more tender plants, such as Jacob's ladder. Above the krummholz, some willow shrubs spread into carpets only half an inch high, and tiny forget-me-nots rival the intense blue of the alpine sky. Old-man-of-the-mountains lords it over the alpine community with the showiest and largest flowers. Paradoxically, this member of the sunflower family evolved from desert species.

Tundra plants have evolved many unusual stratagems to cope with their harsh environment. By growing low to the ground they conserve moisture, escape the shearing effect of the wind, and expend less energy producing unnecessary mass. Some also benefit from a snow blanket during much of the year. In fact, one alpine plant endemic to the Rocky Mountains, snow-lover (*Chionophila jamesii*), is found *only* where there is winter snow cover.

Moss campion and many other tundra plants have deep taproots that hold the plant in place, store nutrients, and extend down to water. The fuzzy hairs on some plants protect them from dehydration and burning and at the same time hold in heat like a greenhouse. Other plants, such as stonecrop (*Sedum lanceolatum*), produce fleshy, succulent leaves to retain moisture.

It's no surprise that alpine plants are perennials. They save time and energy by not having to start from scratch each summer. Also, if they fail to reproduce one summer, there's always another chance. Many of them cope with the short growing season by utilizing runners, rhizomes, or other methods of vegetative reproduction than seeding. The only annual in the Rocky Mountain alpine region is the minuscule *Koenigia*, a member of the buckwheat family that grows in running water. Look for its red leaves, which are more conspicuous than the 1/16-inch white flower.

Cushion plants dominate the alpine region known as "fellfields" ("fell" is Norse and Gaelic for "rock"). In fellfields, frost has broken rocks into gravel, which is then colonized by the plants. Observing this process, Boulder poet Reg Saner wrote: ". . . But with outcrops insisting / the last word should be rocks, then flaking / and falling away from that, we noticed / how each tuft put them to use / improvising soil from palmfuls of grit . . ."

Many visitors marvel at the "moss" dotting this gritty, exposed ground. However, these plants are true flowering plants with all the requisite parts reduced to elfin size.

Mat plants, such as sandworts (*Arenaria*

Trees

The sun-warmed bark of ponderosa pines emits a fragrance like vanilla on a hot day. When you hug the trunk and inhale, do you smell vanilla? Or is it butterscotch or strawberry?

spp.), are similar to cushion plants but are looser and larger and can take root wherever their spreading branches touch ground. Still other plants, such as big-rooted spring beauties (*Claytonia megarhiza*), form rosettes, permitting maximum exposure to light and minimum exposure to the elements. These flowers are aptly named: only 2 to 3 inches across at the top, their roots go down 10 to 15 feet.

Tundra plants look dainty and delicate, but if they are not disturbed, many can live for centuries. Map lichen (*Rhizocarpon geographicum*) grows only three-eighths-inch in diameter during its first thousand years. Many lichens are used for dating purposes because of their slow growth.

In *Land Above the Trees* (our chief source for the information in this essay), Ann Zwinger and Bettie Willard describe many different alpine ecosystems: fell-fields, boulder fields, talus and scree slopes, alpine meadows and turfs, snow-bed communities, wet marsh communities, and gopher gardens, each with its own complement of characteristic plants. This is a book to read while stretched out in an alpine meadow, where you can match living flowers with the drawings while inhaling the minty scent of alpine sage (*Artemisia scopularum*).

The tundra also displays microclimates. In his book *Ecosystems of the East Slope of the Front Range in Colorado*, John Marr writes: "Some areas are snow-free 95% of the year, while a few meters away snow covers the ground 11 months of the year; the growing season of any one plot may be from zero to 70 days. Moss campion (*Silene acaulis*), the pinkish-flowered cushion plant, flowers in June in one area and in September in another area less than 100 feet away."

Although alpine plants are adapted to thrive in an environment where no one expects a garden, they can be killed when people repeatedly walk on them. The effects of horseback travel on routes used since about 1600 A.D. in Rocky Mountain National Park are still visible, and this alpine ecosystem will take many more generations to regenerate.

Bettie Willard has studied human impacts on alpine plants in Rocky Mountain National Park for over thirty years, observing the rates at which plants recover. When Forest Canyon Overlook on Trail Ridge Road was opened in 1958, a large patch of moss campion was quickly worn down to the ground, except for a narrow outer ring. Willard established an exclosure designed to protect the plant from unnatural contact, and it started to fill in the barren circle. Growing at about ¼-inch per year, the campion, truly a "champion" survivor, had almost filled in the circle twenty years later. (This particular plant's luck ran out, however, when a pocket gopher consumed it in the twenty-first year.)

Other plants, such as "superturf" sedge (*Kobresia*) require five hundred years or more to revegetate. Because of the cumulative effect of hundreds of thousands of feet in the park, people are now urged to stay on paved paths in heavily used areas, such as those along Trail Ridge Road.

Alpine wildflowers can be seen almost anywhere above the tree line. Niwot Ridge, Mt. Audubon, Arapaho Pass, and Pawnee Pass in the Indian Peaks Wilderness offer choice examples but require somewhat strenuous hiking. Paved roads lead to Mt. Evans and Loveland Pass, where alpine gardens also flourish.

Tundra flowers are remarkably similar the world over. The tundra in Colorado resembles the tundra of Switzerland, Siberia, Alaska, and the Andes; a hiker in the Himalayas may see mountain dryad (*Dryas octopetala*) and other species also found in the Rockies.

Whether you're on the Matterhorn in Switzerland or Mt. Audubon in Colorado, this high mountain world is not the moonscape it appears from a distance. It's a mosaic of colors, shapes, textures, and smells that brings flower lovers to their knees.

FAUNA

MOUNTAIN BIRD COMMUNITIES

In the mountains, bird-watching is often a matter of listening. Birds are difficult to see in dense forests, so most identification is by ear. Experienced bird-watchers, even when blindfolded, can determine bird population, type of forest, and its condition by listening to characteristic songs in a particular location.

In mature aspen groves, the "dee-dee-dee" of chickadees, the bubbly chatter of house wrens, and the rhapsodies of warbling vireos blend with the soft tapping of nuthatches and woodpeckers. Aspen groves support a diversity of cavity-nesting birds. Williamson's and red-naped sapsuckers, downy and hairy woodpeckers, and common flickers excavate nest holes in the trunks of live or dead trees. These holes are later used by flammulated and saw-whet owls, tree swallows, and mountain bluebirds, as well as the chickadees and house wrens. Sometimes three or more species inhabit the same tree as if it were a high-rise apartment building.

Montane and subalpine willow thickets (also known as willow carrs) are among the most productive breeding-bird habitats in the county. A morning walk around one of the larger willow thickets, such as the one in Copeland Meadow near Allens Park, may turn up as many as fifty species. A 1984–85 study conducted by Dave Hallock and Mike Figgs of the Boulder County Nature Association determined that montane willow carrs support two to three times the number of breeding birds found in ponderosa pine and Douglas fir forests, and about ten times the density of breeding birds in lodgepole pine forests. Characteristic species include dusky flycatchers, Swainson's thrushes, Wilson's warblers, fox sparrows, and Lincoln's sparrows. Early in the morning you can usually hear the winnowing of common snipe and the raucous "konkeree" of red-winged blackbirds, along with the more complex songs of the sparrows and the clear voices of the warblers and thrushes.

In contrast, spruce/fir forests seem more serene, and avian sounds there are easier to sort out. The distinctive songs of hermit thrushes and ruby-crowned kinglets are complemented by the melodic, rolling whistles of pine grosbeaks, the nasal calls of mountain chickadees, the raucous rasps of gray jays and Clark's nutcrackers, and the breathy whistles of yellow-rumped warblers. Some species are seldom seen or heard but can be found with effort. Golden-crowned kinglets breed in remaining stands of old-growth spruce/fir. Goshawks nest in remote areas, usually in dense conifers or aspen. Boreal owls roost in conifers and lay their eggs in tree cavities. Three-toed woodpeckers forage in burned areas. Black swifts, among the rarest of local birds, build their nests on damp cliffs protected by waterfalls.

In the alpine tundra, temperature extremes, exposure to the elements, and the shortness of the summer season limit the nesting avifauna to a handful of specialists. American pipits lay their eggs in sheltered depressions beneath overhanging banks or rocks, often by small rivulets or waterfalls. These birds often explode from the nest site only seconds before a hiker's foot descends, giving away the secret of their location. Rosy finches build their nests in rock crevices and line them with ptarmigan feathers. Horned larks are able to nest in the open because their young can tolerate extremes of heat or cold that would kill young of most other songbird species. Ptarmigan hens nest on the ground,

TYPICAL BIRDS OF MOUNTAIN ECOSYSTEMS

Ecosystem	Birds of Prey	Omnivores	Insectivores	Seed Eaters
Ponderosa Pine/ Douglas Fir Forest	Sharp-shinned Hawk	Steller's Jay	Hairy Wood-pecker*	Black-headed Grosbeak
	Red-tailed Hawk	American Crow	Cordilleran Flycatcher	Chipping Sparrow
	Great Horned Owl		Pygmy Nut-hatch*	Pine Siskin
	Northern Pygmy Owl*		Solitary Vireo	
	Flammulated Owl*		Virginia's Warbler	
Aspen	Cooper's Hawk	Gray Jay	Red-naped Sapsucker*	Dark-eyed Junco
	Northern Goshawk	American Robin	Black-capped Chickadee*	
	Northern Saw-whet Owl*		House Wren*	
	Flammulated Owl*		Mountain Bluebird*	
			Warbling Vireo	
Lodgepole Pine Forest	Northern Saw-whet Owl*	Gray Jay	Williamson's Sapsucker*	Chipping Sparrow
		American Crow	Mountain Chickadee*	Dark-eyed Junco
			Brown Creeper*	Cassin's Finch
			White-breasted Nuthatch*	

(Continued on page 138)

TYPICAL BIRDS OF MOUNTAIN ECOSYSTEMS
(Continued)

Ecosystem	Birds of Prey	Omnivores	Insectivores	Seed Eaters
Montane Willow Carr	Osprey	American Robin	Dusky Flycatcher	Black-headed Grosbeak
			Swainson's Thrush	Fox Sparrow
			Warbling Vireo	Song Sparrow
			Macgillivray's Warbler	Lincoln's Sparrow
			Wilson's Warbler	
Spruce/Fir Forest	Northern Goshawk	Gray Jay	Three-toed Woodpecker*	Dark-eyed Junco
	Boreal Owl*	Common Raven	Golden-crowned Kinglet	Pine Grosbeak
		American Robin	Ruby-crowned Kinglet	Red Crossbill
			Hermit Thrush	Cassin's Finch
			Yellow-rumped Warbler	Pine Siskin
Tundra	Golden Eagle	Common Raven	Horned Lark	White-tailed Ptarmigan
	Prairie Falcon		Rock Wren	Rosy Finch
			American Pipit	

*Cavity Nester

where their camouflage makes them practically invisible to predators.

Except for the clear trilling of white-crowned sparrows nesting in the krummholz, most tundra species sing softly, if at all. Occasionally a raven will croak or an American pipit will protest plaintively from a rock or during its "skylarking" flight. Otherwise, the tundra is a quiet place where bird song is barely audible above the rushing of the wind.

A MIDSUMMER NIGHT'S CHORUS

No sound is more evocative of summer than the chorusing of frogs on a warm evening. In Boulder County, courtship activity of many amphibian species peaks in midsummer.

Striped chorus frogs, sometimes called "bubble-gum frogs" because of their inflatable throat patches, begin calling in March and may continue sporadically into August. These 1-inch-long inhabitants of wet meadows, bogs, marshes, and ponds range from the plains to the high mountains. Their rhythmic chirruping is particularly pronounced at places like Sawhill Ponds, Prince Lakes, and wet meadows along South Boulder Creek.

Krummholz

Beyond the subalpine forest, within the tundra, subalpine fir and Englemann spruce exist in scattered groves of picturesque knarled krummholz and "flag" trees.

Like most other frogs, chorus frogs have the annoying habit of going dead silent just when you ease within viewing range. One alternative is to sit quietly in the marsh for several minutes, but usually the mosquitoes start biting long before the frogs resume chorusing. A second possibility is to tape-record the frogs' voices and play the recording back to them. The sound of other territorial males is a powerful stimulus to male chorus frogs wishing to advertise their

Wetlands

Boulder County is blessed with
relatively few wetlands, but they
are a wonderfully rich treasure.

own location and attract a mate. Edwin Way Teale says that even airplanes may stimulate frogs into greater vocal endeavors.

Northern leopard frogs, which inhabit marshes and ponds from the plains to the high mountains, call only in early spring. Their typical vocalization has been described by Geoffrey A. Hammerson, author of *Amphibians and Reptiles in Colorado,* as "a prolonged snore lasting 2–3 seconds followed by 2–3 series of stuttering croaks each lasting no more than a second." Leopard frogs are usually abundant at Sawhill and Walden ponds. Early in the morning you can see their bulging eyes protruding from the placid surface of the ponds and hear loud "splooshes" as they bound for cover.

Bullfrogs are found in similar habitats but only on the plains. Their low, distinctive "b-rumm" resonates in prairie marshes throughout the summer, with calling activity peaking in June or July. Bullfrogs stand motionless at the water's edge, waiting for prey to pass by. According to Hammerson, they will eat "any animal that can be captured and swallowed, including each other."

In eastern Boulder County, you can hear the snorelike call of plains spadefoot toads throughout the summer. These toads breed in temporary pools, puddles, and wet meadows after rainstorms. On still nights they are audible from up to half a mile away. Grasslands around Prince Lakes and the small ponds along North 119th Street usually hold good populations. Plains spadefoots spend most of their time underground, resting, sleeping, or hibernating in winter. The "spades" are hard protuberances on the hind feet used for digging burrows. In the daytime you can sometimes find these toads resting under rocks or logs.

Three other toads inhabit Boulder County. Western toads are rare inhabitants of the middle to high mountains, mostly west of the Continental Divide. They breed in late spring or early summer. Great Plains toads have been observed in southeastern Boulder County. Their breeding call, a high staccato trill, can be heard in late spring and early summer. Woodhouse's toads frequent the plains and foothills and are often seen in urban areas. Like the plains spadefoot, they breed on warm nights following thunderstorms.

The chorusing of frogs and toads is becoming less audible in parts of Boulder County. For reasons not yet fully understood by scientists, worldwide

Bees

Boulder is the type location (a place where a new species is collected) for many bee species because Theodore Cockerell, biology professor at CU from 1906–48 and author of thousands of scientific publications, discovered so many new species here. On his way home from a collecting expedition to Siberia, he was caught in a major earthquake in Japan. He cabled home: "Bees safe, Theo." On another occasion he discovered a new species of insect on a bouquet of flowers at a banquet. His collection of insect fossils from the Florissant shale beds contains more than two hundred type specimens and is housed in the Henderson Museum at CU.

populations of some amphibians are disappearing from their historic ranges. Locally, western toads have vanished in parts of the Indian Peaks Wilderness Area, and northern leopard frog populations have declined in the mountains of southern Wyoming.

Destruction of wetlands, habitat fragmentation, acid rain, pesticides, and global warming have all been implicated as possible causes of amphibian die-off. Frogs and toads are particularly sensitive to environmental change. They live in ephemeral wetlands, ponds, rain-dampened meadows, and forests. Their thin, permeable skin absorbs pesticides and airborne pollutants.

So far, there is insufficient information to determine the exact causes or extent of the apparent decline in amphibian populations. But scientists are concerned enough to have convened several worldwide conferences during the late 1980s and early 1990s to discuss the problem. Like canaries in coal mines, frogs and toads may be sensitive indicators of environmental toxicity. As their chorusing grows fainter, our chances for survival may be ebbing as well.

AMPHIBIANS AND REPTILES
OF BOULDER COUNTY

Species	Where	Breeds
AMPHIBIANS		
Tiger Salamander	Lakes and ponds; plains, foothills, and mountains	March–August
Plains Spadefoot	Grasslands and sandhills; plains	May–August
Western Toad	Wet meadows and forests; mountains	May–June
Great Plains Toad	Grasslands and flood plains; plains	May–July
Woodhouse's Toad	River valleys and floodplains; plains and foothills	April–June
Striped Chorus Frog	Wet meadows, ponds, and marshes; plains, foothills, and mountains	March–August
Bullfrog	Ponds, marshes, and streams; plains	May–August
Northern Leopard Frog	Shallow ponds and marshes; plains, foothills, and mountains	March–June
REPTILES		
Snapping Turtle	Permanent water; plains	March–August
Painted Turtle	Permanent water; plains	March–September
Spiny Softshell	Stream pools and slow water; plains	April–July
Short-horned Lizard	Grasslands and shrublands; plains	April–August
Eastern Fence Lizard	Rocky areas; foothills	May–August
Six-lined Racerunner	Grasslands, sandhills, and floodplains; plains	April–July
Racer	Grasslands, sandhills, shrublands; plains and foothills	May–July
Milk Snake	Most habitats; plains and foothills	May–July
Northern Water Snake	Streams, lakes, and marshes; plains	July–September

(Continued on page 144)

AMPHIBIANS AND REPTILES
OF BOULDER COUNTY (Continued)

Species	Where	Breeds
REPTILES		
Smooth Green Snake	Riparian woodlands; plains and foothills	Not known
Bull Snake	Most habitats; plains and foothills	May–August
Plains Blackhead Snake	Grasslands and rocky canyons; plains and foothills	Not known
Western Terrestrial Garter Snake	Most habitats; foothills and mountains	May–September
Plains Garter Snake	Most habitats; plains and foothills	April–September
Common Garter Snake	Marshes, ponds, and riparian areas; plains	June–September
Lined Snake	Grasslands and canyon bottoms; plains	Spring–Fall
Western Rattlesnake	Most habitats; plains and foothills	Spring–Fall

Sources: Boulder County Comprehensive Plan, Environmental Resources Element, 1987. Geoffrey A. Hammerson, *Amphibians and Reptiles in Colorado*.

WHERE TO GO IN JUNE

COAL CREEK TRAIL

Eventually this riparian trail may stretch all the way from Eldorado Canyon to the east county line. Such a trail will give an unprecedented opportunity to observe streamside, foothill, and prairie habitats. At present, only a few links of the trail have been completed. For an easy walk with no elevation gain, try the sections in Lafayette (Empire Drive to US 287) and in Louisville (Empire Drive to SR 42). Because of its low elevation, this trail can be hot, so it's better early in the month and early (or late) in the day.

The trail meanders along Coal Creek and is shaded by numerous cottonwoods. Look for black-crowned night herons in the creek and great horned owls and woodpeckers in the cottonwoods. Several steep embankments provide nesting sites for bank swallows in May and June. In a seemingly impossible feat, these birds dig tunnels 2 to 4 feet long where they lay their eggs. Kingfishers, which patrol the creek for fish, also tunnel into banks for nesting.

CERAN ST. VRAIN

This trail follows South St. Vrain Creek and offers an interesting contrast to Coal Creek Trail, described above, which is about 3,000 feet lower in elevation. The South St. Vrain cascades through a moist environment of ponderosa pine, Douglas fir, and spruce. In early June we have found nesting hummingbirds, three-toed woodpeckers, goshawks, and large clusters of fairy-slippers. One contiguous patch of fairy-slippers contained forty-five blooming orchids.

From the trailhead on CR 94 between Jamestown and the Peak to Peak Highway, hike downhill 2.2 miles to an old wagon road. Turn left and continue another mile uphill (and away from the creek) to Miller Rocks, a good place for a picnic with views of the Indian Peaks.

At a slightly higher elevation, starting at 8,800 feet, the South St. Vrain Trail (see the February chapter) follows the same creek, passing through aspen and limber-pine forests and open meadows. In June listen for hermit thrushes and look for the first Colorado columbines.

CARIBOU

Some of the earliest subalpine wildflowers bloom on the dry ridges and wet meadows near this ghost town, and the northernmost bristlecone pines in the Rocky Mountains cling tenaciously to some windswept slopes above 10,000 feet. On a single day in June you can find moss campion and sandwort on top of Caribou Hill; pasque flowers, globe anemone, and paintbrushes on the hillsides; and shootingstars, globeflowers, buttercups, and marsh marigolds in the meadows. This is also a good place for mushrooms. We have found puffballs in spring and boletus mushrooms (plus raspberries) in August.

Listen and watch for bluebirds, wrens, and chipping sparrows. Chipmunks, marmots, and ground squirrels usually play around the rock outcroppings.

The ruins of a few of the cabins and larger buildings, which date from when this was a booming silver city in the 1860s and 1870s, are visible from the parking area. Caribou burned down several times and seemed to be a magnet for tragedy. Many children are buried in the historic cemetery, which has been badly vandalized over the past thirty years.

Take CR 128 west from SR 72 just northwest of Nederland. (The road is very rough.) Park at the top, where the road branches in four different directions. Trails are not marked and there are many intersecting old roads, so take a topographic map and avoid any active mines. For the best wildflowers, head southwest toward Caribou Hill (10,502 feet) and make a loop through the meadows below this high point. Climb Bald Mountain (11,340 feet) for alpine flowers late in the month. To see the cemetery, take the road that heads uphill to the northeast.

HESSIE

A waterfall throws torrential water wheels across a ledge of rock a mile above the historic town site of Hessie. Dippers almost always nest behind a rainbow here in June. Along the trails following the South Fork of Middle Boulder Creek and Jasper Creek, globe-flowers and marsh marigolds bloom at the same time hermit thrushes and ruby-crowned kinglets start to sing.

In the damp meadows and forests near Hessie, look for shootingstars and fairy-slippers. If you continue to tree line, alpine flowers carpet the slopes.

From Hessie, follow the main trail to Woodland Flats, where several trails diverge, each climbing to alpine lakes. The first trail to the left dead-ends at Lost Lake. After the main trail crosses the creek, the left fork leads to Betty, Bob, and King lakes (King is 5 miles from Hessie) and eventually to tree line at the old Corona town site on the top of Rollins Pass. The right fork leads to Jasper Lake (4.2 miles from Hessie) and Devils Thumb Lake (5 miles from Hessie) with one branch going to Woodland Lake and Skyscraper Reservoir. At the end of the month or later (depending on the snow cover), a backpacking loop can be made by hiking across Devils Thumb Pass, across the tundra to Rollins Pass, down to King Lake, and back to Hessie. This loop offers several miles of alpine gardens for flower enthusiasts. Also watch for marmots in the rocks and for nests of ptarmigan and American pipits on the tundra.

To reach the trailhead, take CR 130 past Eldora to the sign for Hessie. At this point the rough gravel road drops down. Because you must usually drive through water to reach the parking area, four-wheel-drive is helpful.

WILD BASIN

Several waterfalls and cascades highlight the trails that follow North St. Vrain Creek in Rocky Mountain National Park. In June, the runoff is at its peak and the waterfalls at their rampaging best. Fairy-slipper orchids (*Calypso bulbosa*) are so abundant that one of the falls, Calypso Cascade, is named for them. Ouzel Falls is named for nesting dippers, frequently called "water ouzels." Also look for nesting black swifts around waterfalls

and for northern three-toed woodpeckers in the burned-over areas.

Rare brownie ladyslippers (*Cypripedium fasciculatum*) have been found along the trail beyond Ouzel Falls. The trail forks beyond Ouzel Falls (3 miles from the trailhead), with the left fork leading to Ouzel, Bluebird, and Pipit lakes and the right fork to Thunder Lake and Boulder-Grand Pass, where alpine flowers bloom.

To reach the trailhead, take SR 7 to the Wild Basin sign about 2 miles north of Allens Park. Turn west and continue until the dirt road dead-ends in another 2 miles at a ranger station. Other trails in Wild Basin lead to Finch Lake and to Sandbeach Lake.

FORSYTHE CANYON CREEK

This riparian trail follows the creek downhill through lush forests, skirts a secluded waterfall, and dead-ends at an inlet of Gross Reservoir. Along the way look for shootingstars, fairy-slippers, and early Colorado columbines. Mountain lions have been sighted in the vicinity.

Take Magnolia Drive (CR 132) to CR 68. Continue on CR 68 for about 2 miles to a parking area on the right (just below where the road starts to drop). A map is essential because the trail is not well marked and the various remnants of old roads are confusing.

BOULDER FALLS

This famous landmark is at its best in June because of the runoff. It's a favorite tourist spot that is deceptively dangerous. Several people have been killed while scrambling around the falls, so viewers are urged to stay on the short paved path.

A large parking area is located halfway up Boulder Canyon (SR 119) between Boulder and Nederland.

JUNE OUT-OF-COUNTY EXCURSION

Rivers run high in June because of snowmelt in the mountains, so rafting and kayaking are at their most exciting. To combine white-water thrills with natural beauty, take a trip down the Green or Yampa rivers in the northwest corner of the state. Several outfitters offer trips through spectacular gorges in Dinosaur National Park.

River-running is one of the best ways to see wild animals, which are relatively unafraid of people in boats. In June watch for bighorns with lambs on shore, merganser families in the water, and peregrine falcons in the cliffs near Dinosaur. In the evenings, hike up the side canyons to enjoy wildflowers and waterfalls. Excellent petroglyphs adorn the walls in some of the canyons; the Deluge Site, 2 miles up Jones Creek, a tributary of the Green, is outstanding.

Be sure to visit the Quarry Visitor Center in the park to see dinosaur skeletons *in situ.*

JUNE AT A GLANCE

MAMMALS

- Black bears mate in June or July, but embryo implantation is delayed until November.
- Little brown bats, weighing 1.5 to 2 grams, are born in late June or early July, big brown bats in late June.
- Marmots are usually born in June and appear above ground in July.
- Elk calves and mule deer fawns are born.
- Bighorn lambing peaks early in June.

BIRDS

- Swallows, robins, wrens, woodpeckers, and other avian species are busy feeding their young at lower elevations.
- Common nighthawks perform aerial courtship displays, "booming" as air passes through the wings on their descent.
- Dippers nest behind waterfalls, and ptarmigan and American pipits nest in the tundra.

PLANTS

- Alpine forget-me-nots, moss campion, rock jasmine, and other alpine flowers begin to bloom.
- The first Colorado columbines appear.
- Early cherries ripen in urban gardens.

SPECIAL EVENTS

- Waterfalls flow at peak due to spring runoff.

IN THE SKY

- The summer solstice, around June 20, is the longest day of the year. In Latin, "solstice" means "the sun stands still."
- The appearance of Scorpius in the southern sky marks the beginning of summer. Look for the scorpion just above the southern horizon after 9:00 P.M. Its most prominent star is Antares, a red giant with a diameter of 504 million miles. Antares was known in classical mythology as the rival of Mars.

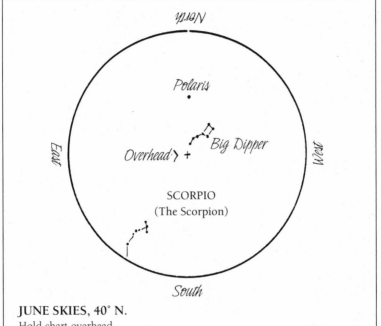

North

Polaris

Overhead ⟩ +

Big Dipper

SCORPIO
(The Scorpion)

East

West

South

JUNE SKIES, 40° N.
Hold chart overhead

9 PM MDT - Early June
8 PM MDT - Late June

June

"*Rose Moon*"
—*Pawnee*

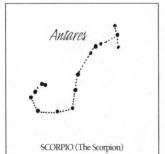

Antares

SCORPIO (The Scorpion)

Bullfrog

Salsify

JULY

The dry, crackling sound of grasshoppers characterizes this month, usually the hottest of the year. Snakes seek the shade. Lizards and some insects stand on "tiptoe" to lift their bodies away from the heated ground. In the morning, grasshoppers sit broadside to the sun to absorb radiation, but as the day gets hotter they shift their bodies parallel to the sun's rays to reduce their silhouettes. Evening primroses and lowland hikers wilt by midmorning.

In 1954, four consecutive July days simmered with temperatures above 100°F. A record high of 104°F for the city of Boulder was reached twice in that year—on June 23 and July 11.

To escape the heat, we head for tree line, where it is still spring (the temperature drops about three to five degrees for every 1,000 feet climbed), and where flowers are fresh and dewy. If we had to choose a favorite flower in July, it might be the rose-colored paintbrush that fills the moist high-elevation basins. The subtle gradations of color range from magenta to pale pink to creamy yellow to red-orange, with some unexpected combinations.

A paint palette in July's tundra would also have to include the bright fuchsia of Parry's primrose, the garnet red of king's crown, the pink and rose of rose crown, the sunny yellows of various composites, and the reddish golds of the grasses.

These plants, a feast for our eyes, are a literal feast to one of the most fascinating alpine animals—the pika. This member of the rabbit family

---

Weather Lore

There's an old Native American expression: "When the sun retires to his house (its halo) it is because it is going to rain." It's true that halos around either the sun or moon (caused by ice crystals refracting the light) may

mean rain, because high cirrus clouds are often forerunners of a low-pressure weather system.

"The northeast wind brings the ice fruit" (another weather saying, possibly of Native American origin) may also be true, because our hailstorms are often preceded by a northeast surface wind.

harvests grasses and other flowering plants, piling them into tiny hay mounds to cure in the sun, and sometimes poses – like Carmen – with a mouthful of flowers. Marmots, which range from the lower edge of the foothills to the tundra, also relish the rich mountain herbage. Both of these mammals squeak and whistle as people approach but will go on about their business if you simply sit and watch.

Short as they are, alpine plants provide cover for two ground-nesting birds: American pipits and white-tailed ptarmigan. If a bird flushes underfoot, look carefully and you may discover a nest with eggs or nestlings. But don't linger or touch, because human scent may lead a weasel or other predator to the nest.

Surprisingly, many insects thrive above tree line. Look for Parnassian butterflies (white with black markings and a red-orange dot on each hind wing), for ladybugs, for jumping wolf spiders, and for red-saddled bumblebees with pollen-coated legs.

A scorching day often precedes an afternoon thunderstorm. There's an exhilaration about being in the midst of a thunderstorm with graupel (soft hail) pelting down as lightning flickers, but it's also dangerous. When a storm approaches, get off the mountaintop and avoid seeking shelter under large boulders or tall trees. To estimate the distance in miles from a lightning strike, count the seconds between the flash and the sound of thunder and divide by five.

The light show following a late-afternoon thunderstorm on the plains is filled with drama. As dark clouds move east, double rainbows are often superimposed against them. When you stand with the low sun behind you (it must be at an angle less than 42 degrees), raindrops act as prisms refracting the light into the colors of its spectrum: red, orange, yellow, green, blue, and violet. The secondary arc reverses the order of the colors, and sometimes "supernumerary arcs" of green and pink bands appear inside the primary rainbow. When conditions are right (a rare occurrence), morning rainbows can be seen in the west. The finer and more numerous the water drops, the more brilliant the rainbow.

Near sunset, as the storm clears to the west, cumulonimbus clouds in the east transform into towering pink and gold mounds like swirls of peppermint, apricot, and vanilla ice cream. Where mountains hide the setting sun, the best color is often in the east.

Only yesterday it was spring and migrating birds were headed for breeding grounds. Now many are already returning and pause for a month or so at backyard feeders.

A Cricket Thermometer

Crickets indicate the local Fahrenheit temperature by the way they chirp. Count the chirps in fourteen seconds and add forty for the temperature (plus or minus one degree). There may be centigrade species in Europe, and there are rumors of confused crickets in Great Britain.

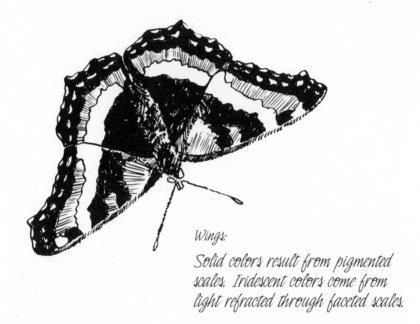

Wings:

Solid colors result from pigmented scales. Iridescent colors come from light refracted through faceted scales.

Milbert's Tortoise Shell

This colorful butterfly may be seen in mild winter weather.

Along the lower edge of the foothills, broad-tailed and rufous hummingbirds engage in fierce aerial battles, with the "red barons" usually victorious. Occasionally, a tiny calliope hummingbird appears.

July starts with alpine flowers at their peak and ends with the beginning of mushroom season. It smells of clover and tastes of sweet corn and juicy tomatoes. It buzzes with insects and hummingbirds, crashes with thunder, and is lit by lightning and rainbows.

JULY WEATHER

JULY 1

	Boulder	Allens Park	Niwot Ridge
Sunrise:	4:35 AM MST		
Sunset:	7:32 PM MST		
	5,445'	**8,500'**	**11,565'**
Ave. Max.	84°F	76°F Ave. July high	56°F Ave. July high
Ave. Min.	56°F	45°F Ave. July low	39°F Ave. July low

JULY 31

Sunrise:	4:58 AM MST		
Sunset:	7:14 PM MST		
Ave. Max.	85°F	76°F Ave. July high	56°F Ave. July high
Ave. Min.	59°F	45°F Ave. July low	39°F Ave. July low

JULY CHANGES (July 1–July 31)

Day Length: 14 hours, 57 minutes to 14 hours, 16 minutes=change of −41 minutes

Change: Max.	+1°F	+7°F	+7°F
Change: Min.	+3°F	+6°F	+6°F

JULY EXTREMES

Max. Temp.	104°F	90°F	See note
Min. Temp.	40°F	30°F	See note
Max. Wind	45 mph	63 mph	Not available
Ave. Precip.	1.85 in.	2.3 in.	3.3 in.
Max. Precip.	7.46 in.	4.1 in.	6.64 in.
Min. Precip.	Trace	.7 in.	1.4 in.
Ave. Snow	00 in.	00 in.	Not available
Max. Snow	00 in.	00 in.	Not available
Min. Snow	00 in.	00 in.	Not available

Note. 77°F is highest for any summer and −31°F is lowest for any winter on Niwot Ridge.

July

FLORA

TALLGRASS PRAIRIE

They may not be "as tall as a man on horseback," but the grasses that grow in the City of Boulder's Tallgrass Prairie Natural Area are the same species that once carpeted the eastern Great Plains. The tallgrass preserve is actually a mosaic of several small tallgrass plots (encompassing about 270 acres) and a much larger area of mixed-grass prairie along South Boulder Creek between Eldorado Springs and Baseline Reservoir. In July the tallgrass stands out as deep blue-green patches along either side of the South Boulder Creek Trail, and the "turkey foot" seed heads of the big bluestem grass are conspicuous. In autumn, when the big bluestem turns to shades of burgundy and mauve, the tallgrass areas are easy to spot from the Denver-Boulder Turnpike.

The grasslands of the Great Plains are usually categorized as being either "shortgrass" (ankle-high or less), "midgrass" (roughly knee-high), or "tallgrass" (over waist-high). Blue grama and buffalo grass dominate the relatively dry shortgrass prairie, and big bluestem,

Indian grass, and switchgrass characterize the moister tallgrass prairie. Sideoats grama, little bluestem, and western wheatgrass are typical in the transitional midgrass prairie. Because the tallgrass prairie is more common in the eastern Great Plains and the shortgrass prairie is more common in the drier western section, Boulder County's tallgrass prairies are something of an anomaly.

These stands of big bluestem, little bluestem, switchgrass, Indian grass, and other typical tallgrass species are thought to be Pleistocene relicts, remnants of a cooler, wetter time when open forests, tallgrass savannahs, and marshes covered much of the high plains. Porous soils, relatively abundant ground water, and slightly higher precipitation levels along parts of the Front Range enabled tallgrass prairies to persist while most of eastern Colorado evolved toward midgrass and shortgrass prairies. Most of the remaining tallgrass prairies were destroyed by farming, intensive grazing, and urbanization after white settlement of the Front Range.

The City of Boulder Open Space Department, in partnership with the Colorado Natural Areas Program, is currently studying the effects of grazing and fire in the Tallgrass Prairie Natural Area. Grazing and fire were integral parts of the ecosystem prior to European settlement. Herds of bison were drawn to the Front Range foothills by the relatively mild winter climate and lush vegetation. Prairie fires, many natural and some deliberately set by Plains Indians, burned periodically, protecting the fire-evolved tallgrasses from woody species, including ponderosa pines.

To simulate the effects of natural prairie fires, controlled burns have been conducted on several plots. Controlled grazing by cattle and horses during the winter and spring months is designed to suppress "cool season grasses" such as cheatgrass and smooth brome, giving the later-developing tallgrasses opportunity to grow. In controlled plots where no grazing or burning has occurred, the tallgrasses have suffered and introduced species such as Canada thistle have increased.

The prairies along South Boulder Creek consist of much more than just grass. A total of 230 flowering plants have been identified in the eight tallgrass plots alone. During July, look for common chicory (*Cichorium intybus* – an introduced species), showy milkweed

Colorado's Oldest Tree

In 1992 a bristlecone pine in South Park was estimated to be 2,435 years old, based on a growth ring count.

(*Asclepias speciosa*), white prairie-clover (*Dalea candidum*), purple prairie-clover (*Dalea purpurea*), Mexican hat coneflower (*Ratibida columnifera*), wild rose (*Rosa* sp.), prickly poppy (*Argemone* spp.), western salsify (*Tragopogon dubius* – introduced), and common sunflower (*Helianthus annuus*).

Many of these wildflowers attract butterflies, including monarchs, dark wood nymphs, and a variety of sulphurs, hairstreaks, and blues. Listen for the high thin buzz of grasshopper sparrows, the exuberant song of meadowlarks, and cries of kestrels and red-tailed hawks. Or lie down in a patch of big bluestem, gaze at the blue sky, and imagine yourself adrift in the ocean of grass that once stretched from the Missouri River to the Rocky Mountain foothills.

FAUNA

BUTTERFLY-WATCHING

Consider these butterfly facts. There are more than twenty thousand species worldwide, more than seven hundred species in North America, and around two hundred in Boulder County. So intricate is butterfly design that photographer Kjell B. Sandved has captured all the letters of the English alphabet and all the Arabic numerals on the wings of various species. Migrating butterflies fly as far as 2,000 miles and as high as 7,000 feet above the ground. Butterfly courtship behavior, as varied and complex as that of most birds and mammals, has been described for only a small minority of the world's species. Butterflies inhabit almost every ecosystem on earth and are relatively easy to observe. Yet there seem to be at least one hundred serious bird-watchers for every serious butterfly-watcher.

Why not watch butterflies? All that's required is a little patience and inquisitiveness. A pair of close-focusing binoculars, a camera with a macro or telephoto lens, and a hand lens are optional accoutrements.

Although some butterflies, including mourning cloaks and tortoise shells, overwinter as adults, most live as adults for only a few days or weeks. After emerging from the chrysalis, butterflies spend their short lives extracting nourishment from flowers, fruit, carrion, and scat; seeking out mates and breeding; and laying their eggs on a carefully selected host plant. Flight activity tends to peak in early summer, when more wildflowers are available for nectaring and host plants are well enough developed to receive eggs.

Like birds, butterflies can be divided into generalists and specialists. Painted ladies range throughout the world and are not too particular about where they lay their eggs; a variety of thistles or other composites will do. Melissa arctics are confined to the alpine tundra, where their larvae feed on alpine grasses and sedges. Because most butterflies tend to specialize, a good way to find them is to first search for host plants: milkweeds for monarchs, legumes for common sulphurs, conifers for pine whites, violets for Aphrodite fritillaries.

Host plants serve as more than food sources for larvae. Adult mourning cloaks hibernate under the bark of host aspens and willows. Adult monarchs are protected from predators by residual toxins they absorb from host milkweeds; birds get sick after eating a monarch and may never attempt it again.

Some collectors believe adult butterflies smell like their host plants: western tiger swallowtails like fennel, common sulphurs like clover, and so on. Lepidopterist Robert Pyle reports that many adult swallowtails do have a sweetish odor, but he attributes this aroma mainly to pheromones. He adds that the pheromones emitted by male Phoebus Parnassians smell like corn chips. His *Handbook for Butterfly Watchers* offers an array of such offbeat and thought-provoking observations.

Butterflies have evolved close mutualistic relationships with other insects. Some blue, metalmark, and hairstreak caterpillars have glands that secrete a clear sugary liquid savored by various ants. To protect their source of "honeydew," the ants keep watch over the caterpillars, driving potential predators away. Caterpillars of the Ross's metalmark, a small multicolored butterfly that inhabits volcanic slopes in southeastern Mexico, are actually "herded" by their carpenter ant companions. The ants construct a "corral" inside the stem of the host plant, where they hide the caterpillars by day. At dusk they carry the caterpillars out into the open, and the ants spend the night feeding on the sweet honeydew. Many of the blues seen in Boulder County are ant-symbionts.

Because they are so closely associated with individual host plants, many butterfly species are excellent indicators of environmental quality. The Karner blue butterfly of New York is a case in point. This species inhabits the Albany Pine Bush, a diverse area of swamps, woods, and sedge-covered sand dunes in upstate New York. It was placed on the state endangered species list in 1977 after populations plummeted. Scientists discovered that fire control, a result of development of the region, was threatening the blue's host plant, a fire-resistant lupine. Other fire-resistant species were disappearing as well. The decline of the Karner blue pointed to the tragic and possibly inexorable alteration of an entire ecosystem.

In Colorado, the Uncompahgre fritillary has been cited as perhaps the first example of a species succumbing to global climate change. This Arctic butterfly, now confined to one known population high in the San Juan Mountains, lives

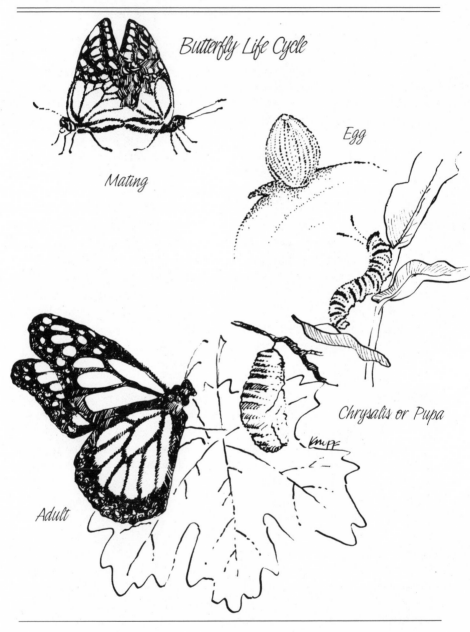

Butterfly Life Cycle

Mating

Egg

Chrysalis or Pupa

Adult

on snow-moistened, northeast-facing slopes. Larvae feed on the Rocky Mountain snow willow, a common alpine plant. Since 1982, one of two remaining colonies has completely disappeared, and the other has been reduced from around 1,000 to around 360 individuals. Researcher Peter Brussard of the University of Nevada, Reno, believes that hot, dry summers in the early 1980s and a reduction in the number of summer thunderstorms during the late 1980s are causing the decline.

A common question about butterflies is how creatures so delicate and conspicuous can survive in a world of predators. Robert Pyle estimated that one-tenth of the wood nymphs he collected on the plains east of Boulder had beak marks on their wings from bird attacks. Beak marks on this and other species are usually found around the "eyespots" on the tips of the wings. These markings divert bird attacks away from more sensitive areas of a butterfly's anatomy.

Other defenses against predation include camouflage, bluff, a bad taste, and erratic flight. Many brush-footed butterflies, a large family including mourning cloaks, tortoise shells, and monarchs, look like dried leaves hanging from a tree when they fold up their wings. Some caterpillars have false eyespots on their forward segments that make them look snakelike, possibly deterring avian attack. Anyone who has ever tried to catch a flying tiger swallowtail with a butterfly net can imagine the frustration a songbird must feel chasing these zigzagging insects.

Mimicry may be the most interesting butterfly adaptation to predation. Müllerian mimicry, named for the German naturalist Fritz Müller, describes the tendency of two or more distasteful butterflies to share color patterns. The theory is that if a bird sees two butterflies that look alike and the first one tastes bad, the bird will also avoid the second one. Batesian mimicry, after British naturalist Henry Bates, describes the tendency of some edible butterflies to resemble distasteful species.

For years the similarity in appearance of monarchs and viceroys was cited as an example of Batesian mimicry. Scientists thought willow-feeding viceroys had evolved to resemble the distasteful milkweed-feeding monarchs and thus avoid predation. However, a recent "taste test" performed by caged red-winged blackbirds suggests that some viceroys may be even *less* palatable than some monarchs. So, the similarity of these two species is probably an example of Müllerian mimicry in which each species mimics the other.

The ability of many butterfly species to elude or outfly birds has attracted the attention of lepidopterist James Marden, who studied body shapes and flight patterns of palatable and unpalatable species in Costa Rica. He found that palatable species tend to have much higher flight-muscle to body-mass ratios than do unpalatable species. Using physics to calculate acceleration potential for butterflies and birds, he concluded that almost all palatable butterflies and day-flying moths can accelerate faster than can the swiftest songbirds. The least powerful fliers are some unpalatable mimics who have "so little flight muscle that they can just barely counteract gravity and are probably incapable of any evasive maneuver other than a dive."

By staying low to the ground, moving slowly, and keeping track of your shadow, you can get within a few inches of almost any perching butterfly. This approach works especially well on cool mornings when butterflies are basking in the sun but have not yet reached threshold temperatures necessary for flight. If you rub your forefinger on your nose or other sweaty part of your body and slip it under the perching insect, the butterfly may hop aboard and begin nectaring on your hand!

Any marsh, meadow, or forest clearing where wildflowers are blooming should provide good July butterfly-watching. Our favorite spots include Sawhill Ponds, where monarchs, eastern black swallowtails, and sulphurs drink from thistles, milkweeds, and clovers; upper Gregory Canyon, with its fields of gaillardia, monarda, and thistle crowned with Aphrodite fritillaries, western tiger swallowtails, painted ladies, Weidemeyer's admirals, mourning cloaks, and many others; and Arapaho Pass, where the annual July wildflower display is heightened by a butterfly presence of equal color and intensity.

If you would like to learn more about butterflies and contribute to their conservation, join the annual Fourth of July North America Butterfly Count, patterned after the Audubon Christmas Bird Count. Beginners are welcome. For information write the Xerces Society (address in Appendix 5, page 311).

Butterfly Parts

Knowing names of the parts helps in identification.

Butterflies are important pollinators, and their caterpillars rarely compete significantly with humans for the same plants.

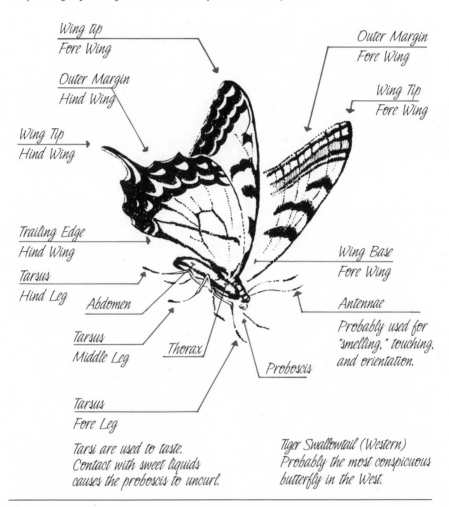

Wing tip
Fore Wing

Outer Margin
Fore Wing

Outer Margin
Hind Wing

Wing Tip
Fore Wing

Wing Tip
Hind Wing

Trailing Edge
Hind Wing

Wing Base
Fore Wing

Tarsus
Hind Leg

Abdomen

Antennae

Probably used for "smelling," touching, and orientation.

Tarsus
Middle Leg

Thorax

Proboscis

Tarsus
Fore Leg

Tarsi are used to taste. Contact with sweet liquids causes the proboscis to uncurl.

Tiger Swallowtail (Western) Probably the most conspicuous butterfly in the West.

A BOULDER COUNTY BUTTERFLY SAMPLER

Species	Host Plants	Location	Adults Fly
Common Branded Skipper *Hesperia comma*	Grasses and sedges	Open coniferous forests to 10,000 feet	July–September
Nevada Skipper *Hesperia nevada*	Bunchgrasses	Mountains to 11,000 feet	May–July
Pine White *Neophasia menapia*	Pines and firs	Coniferous forests to 10,000 feet	July–September
Cabbage White *Artogeia rapae*	Mustards, including cabbage, broccoli, and cauliflower	Cultivated areas	March–October
Western White *Pontia occidentalis*	Native mustards and bee plants	Mountain meadows to 14,000 feet	June–September
Checkered White *Pontia protodice*	Native mustards	Fields and meadows to 10,000 feet	April–October
Orange Sulphur (Alfalfa Butterfly) *Colias eurytheme*	Alfalfa and other legumes	Countywide	April–October
Common Sulphur *Colias philodice*	Clovers and other legumes	Open country, plains to high mountains	March–November
Phoebus Parnassian *Parnassius phoebus*	Sedums	Plains to 14,000 feet	May–October
Anise Swallowtail *Papilio zelicaon*	Biscuit roots and mountain parsleys	Foothills and mountains to 14,000 feet	April–July
Western Tiger Swallowtail *Pterourus rutulus*	Deciduous trees and shrubs	Moist meadows and riparian canyons, 5,000–12,000 feet	June–July
Two-tailed Tiger Swallowtail *Pterourus multicaudatus*	Wild cherry, wild plum, and green ash	Moist valley and canyon bottoms, foothills	May–August

(Continued on page 167)

A BOULDER COUNTY BUTTERFLY SAMPLER
(Continued)

Species	Host Plants	Location	Adults Fly
Common Blue *Icaricia icarioides*	Lupines	Forests and meadows to 10,000 feet	May–September
High Mountain Blue *Agriades franklinii*	Rock jasmine and shootingstars	Mountain meadows, subalpine forests, and tundra	June–August
Ruddy Copper *Chalceria rubidus*	Docks and cinque-foils	Open country in mountains to 11,000 feet	June–August
Large Wood Nymph *Cercyonis pegala*	Grasses	Meadows and wood margins to 10,500 feet	June–September
Magdalena Alpine *Erebia magdalena*	Grasses around talus slopes	Rock slides at or above timberline	June–August
Riding's Satyr *Neominois ridingsii*	Grasses	Grasslands and dry meadows to 10,000 feet	June–August
Monarch *Danaus plexippus*	Milkweeds	Plains and foothills	May–September
Titania's Fritillary *Clossiana titania*	Willows and bistorts	Willow bogs and moist meadows in high mountains	June–August
Edwards' Fritillary *Speyeria edwardsii*	Violets	Plains and foothills canyons to 9,000 feet	May–September
Atlantis Fritillary *Speyeria atlantis*	Violets	Clearings and streams, foothills and mountains	June–September

(Continued on page 168)

A BOULDER COUNTY BUTTERFLY SAMPLER
(Continued)

Species	Host Plants	Location	Adults Fly
Aphrodite Fritillary *Speyeria aphrodite*	Violets	Open meadows, foothills to 8,000 feet	June–August
Field Crescentspot *Phyciodes campestris*	Asters	Grasslands, meadows, and fields, all elevations	May–August
Mourning Cloak *Nymphalis antiopa*	Willows, elms, aspens, cottonwoods, roses, and others	Plains, foothills, and mountains	February–November
Milbert's Tortoise Shell *Aglais milberti*	Nettles	Plains, foothills, and mountains	February–November
Weidemeyer's Admiral *Basilarchia weidemeyerii*	Willows, aspens, cottonwoods, juneberries	Canyons, foothills, and mountains	May–September
Red Admiral *Vanessa atalanta*	Nettles	Forest margins, meadows, fields, and clearings to tree line	May–October
Painted Lady *Vanessa cardui*	Thistles and other composites	All habitats and all elevations	April–October

Sources: Robert Michael Pyle, *The Audubon Society Field Guide to North American Butterflies*; Clifford Ferris and Martin Brown, *Butterflies of the Rocky Mountain States*.

July

COUNTING BATS

With bird counts and butterfly counts flourishing, it shouldn't be too surprising that there is also a bat count. The Colorado Summer Bat Trend Survey, initiated in 1991 and modeled after a similar survey in Pennsylvania, is held the last week in June and the first week in July. Participants sit by a body of water on two successive evenings and count "bat passes" – the number of times individuals descend from the sky to drink.

University of Colorado mammalogists David Armstrong and Rick Adams have helped to organize the survey. Armstrong believes the data collected will help scientists to chart bat population trends and locate areas with high bat concentrations. "It's also a consciousness-raising experience," he says. "We now have a hundred or more people out counting bats in the summer when we didn't used to have any."

This trend survey and others like it may help scientists understand the causes and extent of a perceived decline in bat numbers throughout the United States. Numbers of cavern-dwelling bats, such as the gray bat, Indiana myotis, and Mexican free-tailed bat, have dropped dramatically as roost sites have been disturbed by cavers. Because many bat species hibernate in large aggregations (entire populations of some species may hibernate in a single cave), hibernating bats are particularly sensitive to human disturbance.

Insecticide poisoning has also contributed to the decrease in populations of some species. Bat numbers have declined noticeably in the irrigated valleys of central California and Arizona and in the tobacco-raising region of Connecticut, all places where pesticide use is particularly heavy.

In Colorado, disturbance and closure of caves and mines, which serve as bat roosting and hibernating areas, may be affecting bat populations. In 1991, the Colorado Division of Wildlife initiated a program to protect bat habitat in inactive mines scheduled for closure as a safety measure. A bat detector that converts bat echolocation to audible sound is used to locate bat roosts. Biologists then install "bat gates," which allow the bats to come and go freely after the mine is closed to the public. "A mine is a terrible thing to waste," says Connie Knapp, former project coordinator.

Fear and misunderstanding of bats has

also contributed to the decline. Bat conservation efforts have been hindered by the misapprehension that most or all bats carry rabies. Adams says the actual rate is about one-half of 1%, less than the rate in striped skunk or red fox populations. As a frequent handler of bats he takes preventive shots, but he says the threat to the average person is minimal. Nevertheless, both Adams and Armstrong advise people not to handle bats because any bat that allows itself to be handled is likely to be sick.

About ten bat species inhabit Boulder County. Telling them apart while they are zipping through the air at dusk is extremely difficult, so participants in bat surveys tally total numbers, not individual species. Local bats can be identified, however, by size and behavior. Some common characteristics are given in the following table. For more information on local bat counts or bat conservation efforts, write the Colorado Bat Society (address in Appendix 5, page 311).

BOULDER COUNTY BATS

Species/ Wing Spread	Habitat	Roost Site	Behavior
Little Brown Myotis (*Myotis lucifugus*) 9–11 inches	Urban forests or urban areas near water; plains, foothills, mountains	Buildings, bridges, caves, rock crevices	Emerges late dusk; follows set hunting route over water, meadows, trees
Long-eared Myotis (*Myotis evotis*) 11 inches	Open coniferous forests; foothills and mountains	Buildings or tree hollows (day); caves and tunnels (night)	Emerges late in the evening; forages in forests and over woodland ponds
Fringed Myotis (*Myotis thysanodes*) 9–11 inches	Open forests; plains, mesas, and foothills	Caves, mines, rock crevices, and buildings	Forages in open areas for moths and other insects
Long-legged Myotis (*Myotis volans*) 10–11 inches	Forested areas; foothills and mountains	Buildings, rock crevices, trees (day); caves and mines (night)	Emerges early evening; flies relatively slowly 10–15 feet high over water and forest openings

(Continued on page 171)

BOULDER COUNTY BATS
(Continued)

Species/Wing Spread	Habitat	Roost Site	Behavior
Western Small-footed Myotis (*Myotis ciliolabrum*) 8–10 inches	Rocky, open country; plains and foothills	Caves, mines, rock crevices; hibernates singly in caves and mines	Emerges early evening; slow, fluttering flight over open water
Silver-haired Bat (*Lasionycteris noctivagans*) 11–13 inches	Coniferous forests; foothills and mountains	Behind loose bark or in a woodpecker hole (summer); migrates south in winter	Emerges early; slow, leisurely flight over woodland ponds and streams
Big Brown Bat (*Eptesicus fuscus*) 13–14 inches	All habitats; plains, foothills, and mountains	Hollow trees, caves, mines, beneath bridges (summer); hibernates in attics, mines, caves, and cellars	Emerges at dusk; steady, nearly straight flight; may forage in same location night after night
Hoary Bat (*Lasiurus cinereus*) 15–17 inches	Wooded areas; foothills and mountains	Leafy area of tree, 10–15 feet above the ground (summer); migrates south in winter	Emerges late in evening; swift, direct flight; audible chattering sound
Red Bat (*Lasiurus borealis*) 12–14 inches	Deciduous woods and fencerows; plains	Leaves and bark of deciduous trees	Emerges early in the evening and engages in slow, erratic flight; after 15–30 minutes, flight becomes swift and straight near ground
Western Big-eared Bat (*Plecotus townsendii*) 12–13 inches	Rough, broken country; foothills and mountains	Caves and mine tunnels (summer and winter)	Emerges after dark; acrobatic flight, feeding on moths; most often seen around cave entrances

Sources: David Armstrong, *Rocky Mountain Mammals*; Roger Barbour and Wayne Davis, *Bats of America*.

WHERE TO GO IN JULY

ARAPAHO GLACIER, SOUTH ARAPAHO PEAK, ARAPAHO PASS, DOROTHY LAKE, DIAMOND LAKE

The basin below Arapaho Pass presents a changing wildflower show starting with glacier lilies in June and climaxing with multicolored paintbrush in July. Colorado columbine dot aspen groves; monkshood, mertensia, and larkspur mass along streamsides; bog orchids, lady's-tresses, monkey flowers, and grass-of-Parnassus grow on moist banks along the trails; elephantheads fill the marshes; alpine flowers carpet the tundra. Above tree line, listen and look for ptarmigan, pipits, pikas, and Parnassian butterflies.

Arapaho Glacier (the largest in Colorado) is the only glacier in the world owned by a city and is one of the sources for the city of Boulder's water supply. It covers about 100 acres and is 400 feet deep in places. Look for rosy finches dining on frozen insects and for the rosy tint of "watermelon snow." From the saddle at the top of the glacier, a short, steep climb brings you to the top of South Arapaho Peak (13,397 feet). Strong climbers can continue another 0.75-mile along the ridge to North Arapaho Peak (13,502 feet).

The trail starts at Buckingham Campground (sometimes called Fourth of July Campground), 10 miles northwest of Nederland, at the end of CR 111. The trail to Diamond Lake, where Indian paintbrush and mushrooms abound, veers to the left in about a mile. At the Fourth of July Mine the trail divides again, with the left fork going to Arapaho Pass and Dorothy Lake and the right fork to the glacier and South Arapaho Peak. Both the pass and the glacier are about 6 miles round-trip.

BRAINARD LAKE AREA

Brainard Lake is the hub for many trails leading into the Indian Peaks

Rosy Finches

If you want to thrill out-of-state bird-watchers, take them to the tundra to look for rosy finches, nicknamed "refrigerator birds" for their habit of picking frozen insect dinners out of permanent snowfields. All three rosy finch subspecies (gray-crowned, brown-capped, and black) are found in  Colorado, and the brown-capped is endemic to the southern Rockies. In winter they descend to lower elevations, where flocks of more than three hundred are sometimes seen.

Wilderness and up to the tundra. (Permits are needed for backpacking trips into this heavily used wilderness.) This entire area is superb for wildflowers and for mushrooming. To reach Brainard Lake, take CR 102, which heads west off the Peak to Peak Highway just above Ward. Here are some of our favorite trails originating near Brainard Lake.

• *Lake Isabelle, Isabelle Glacier, and Pawnee Pass.* Starting at the Long Lake trailhead, this trail climbs through spruce/fir forests, skirts Long Lake, and reaches Lake Isabelle in 2 miles. At the lake the trail splits, with the left branch going to the glacier (another 1.7 miles) and the right branch going to the pass (another 2 miles). On both branches you hike through subalpine and alpine terrain. The views looking down into Lake Isabelle from the Pawnee Pass Trail are dramatic, and the craggy gendarmes on the west side of Pawnee Pass are spectacular. From the pass, you can climb Pawnee Peak (12,943 feet) or Shoshone

Peak (12,967 feet) or drop down to Pawnee, Crater, and Monarch lakes on the western side.

It's also possible to climb several other Indian Peaks from this point or to make a loop trip, crossing Pawnee Peak and dropping down between Pawnee Peak and Mount Toll to Blue and Mitchell lakes and then back to the Long Lake trailhead. There are no marked trails to most of the peaks, so a topographic map is essential.
• *Mitchell Lake, Blue Lake, Mount Toll.* Starting at the Mitchell Lake trailhead, this trail passes Mitchell Lake in 1 mile and reaches Blue Lake in 2.5 miles. The Parry's primrose and mertensia at the creek crossing just beyond Mitchell are especially luxuriant. Blue Lake is one of the gems of the Indian Peaks Wilderness Area. Mount Toll (12,979 feet) rises majestically above it; a waterfall cascades into its upper end and wildflowers surround it. A steep climb (no trail) involving talus-scrambling brings you to the top of Mount Toll.
• *Mount Audubon.* Starting at the Mitchell Lake parking area , this trail reaches the top of Mount Audubon (13,223 feet) in 3.5 miles, most of which is above tree line with abundant alpine flowers and views of the Indian Peaks and of the plains.

BUCHANAN PASS, SAWTOOTH AND ELK TOOTH MOUNTAINS, RED DEER LAKE, AND ST. VRAIN GLACIERS

Sawtooth (12,304 feet) and Elk Tooth (12,848 feet) are aptly named peaks that stick up from the skyline like snaggled teeth. In addition to the customary sensational flowers and mushrooms, this area is rich in archaeological remains. Archaeologist Jim Benedict has identified many hunting blinds and low stone walls used by prehistoric people for communal hunting on the tundra. Bighorn sheep, formerly plentiful here, have been reintroduced into the North St. Vrain area and are returning to this region.

Various pack trails start from the Mitchell Lake parking area, Beaver Reservoir, and Camp Dick. The most straightforward route to Buchanan Pass and nearby attractions is from Camp Dick along the Middle St. Vrain Creek. Turn west off the Peak to Peak Highway at the community of Peaceful Valley and park just west of Camp Dick Campground. Take the Buchanan Pass Trail along the creek to the wilderness boundary. Continue to follow the trail, which forks several times. Each junction is well marked with forest service signs. A USGS topo map is useful; however, it is out of date and shows several trails that have been closed or re-routed.

ST. VRAIN AND MEADOW MOUNTAINS

Starting in pine and aspen, the trail follows a cascading creek, zigzags through an old burn area, and culminates in the tundra on St. Vrain Mountain. Take this trail early in the month; it goes up a south-facing bowl that can be very hot but is good for early flowers. In mid-August mushrooms are usually plentiful along the lower portion of the trail.

From Ferncliff, take CR 107 or the "Ski Road" (good ski-touring in winter) west to where it forks in 2.2 miles. The right fork deadends in about a quarter-mile at the parking area. When the trail reaches a saddle on the tundra, it divides, with the right fork going to Meadow Mountain (11,612 feet) and the left fork to St. Vrain Mountain (12,162 feet). It's also possible to reach this area from Middle St. Vrain Creek.

SOUTH BOULDER CREEK TRAIL

This 3-mile trail follows South Boulder Creek through the Tallgrass Prairie Natural Area, where many species of native tallgrasses flourish. Much of the trail is shaded by old cottonwoods and willows, so it's comfortable early or late in the day, even in midsummer. A rare bog orchid, Ute lady's-tresses (*Spiranthes diluvialis*), begins to bloom in late July and continues into August in the wetlands between South Boulder Road and the turnpike. Its tiny white blossoms pinwheel around the stalk and are similar to the more common hooded lady's-tresses (*Spiranthes romanzoffiana*) found in the mountains. Be careful not to crush it underfoot, and avoid flagged study plots. Virginia rails and common snipe can be seen here, and at night there is a chance of seeing fireflies in the wetlands.

Park at the Bobolink trailhead 0.1-mile west of the intersection of Baseline and Cherryvale. The trail, which will probably be extended in the near future, passes underneath both South Boulder Road and the turnpike.

July

PLACES TO SEE PELICANS AND FIREFLIES

White pelicans can be seen at Panama Reservoir (see the February chapter), Teller Lakes (see the November chapter), and Union Reservoir (see the April chapter). These large birds with their improbable bills and throat pouches are regular summer residents on prairie lakes in the eastern half of the state, and breeding colonies have become established at Riverside Reservoir, a private reservoir east of Greeley, and at Antero Reservoir in South Park.

After sunset following a hot day, check the wetlands around Sawhill Ponds, Centennial Trail, Boulder Valley Ranch, and Twin Lakes in Gunbarrel for fireflies, which are rarely seen in Boulder County. Each species of firefly has its own unique light signal, which is used to find a mate. Males fly several feet off the ground flashing a greenish yellow light at regular intervals, while the females perch on grass, flashing a response with different timing. These small beetles with the romantic glimmer continue blinking until they find one another and mate. The warmer the evening, the more rapid the signaling.

JULY OUT-OF-COUNTY EXCURSION

Mount Evans, 14,264 feet high, is the place to take out-of-state guests to see a fourteener because a paved road, highest in the U.S., reaches the summit. It's also a joy to go alone and find a quiet place to "meadowtate" among alpine wildflowers and resident mountain goats or bighorn sheep.

The goats were introduced here in 1961 and have increased dramatically. However, there is some fear they may be adversely affecting the native bighorn sheep and native vegetation. Both goats and sheep are relatively tame and easily photographed. Pikas, chipmunks, and golden-mantled ground squirrels scamper around the rocks in a comical contrast to the larger, lumbering marmots. Horned larks, American pipits, and white-tailed ptarmigan nest on the ground, expertly camouflaging their nests in the diminutive vegetation.

We walk carefully to avoid crushing the nests or the alpine flowers. Some unusual color varieties, such as magenta wallflowers, and rare species, such as *Koenigia*, occur on Mount Evans. Half-way between Echo Lake and the summit, the Mount Goliath Alpine Garden Trail loops for half a mile through alpine flowers and connects with the Long Trail, which descends into a bristlecone pine forest. Although some Nevada and California bristlecones have weathered more than four thousand years, most of Colorado's bristlecones are only fifteen to sixteen hundred years old and may be a different subspecies. Still, their gnarled, contorted shapes are mute witness to the harsh conditions at the top of the world.

Elk, Rocky Mountain National Park

July

JULY AT A GLANCE

MAMMALS

- Pikas start making hay piles and continue until snow covers the ground.
- Least chipmunks are born by early July and leave the nest about four weeks later.
- Mountain lion kittens are born throughout the year but the birth rate peaks in July.

BIRDS

- American pipit and horned lark young hatch above tree line.
- Ptarmigan chicks, under parental supervision, hunt for insects.
- American and lesser goldfinches nest in the foothills.
- Hummingbirds start to return to lower elevations, and fierce battles take place at feeders.
- Franklin's gulls begin to arrive from the north.

OTHER CRITTERS

- Grasshoppers swarm on the plains and in the foothills.
- Butterfly populations peak in July and August.

PLANTS

- Paintbrush and Parry's primrose bloom in alpine meadows, larkspur and monkshood lower down on the mountains, and prickly poppy and sunflowers on the prairie.
- Mushroom season begins.
- Sweet corn and Colorado peaches hit the fruit stands.

IN THE SKY

- The Aquarid meteors are visible during the last week. Look to the east-southeast.
- Ursa Major (The Great Bear, or the Big Dipper) is almost straight overhead around 9:00 P.M. This is the most distinctive of all constellations, although its resemblance to a bear is questionable. How the Iroquois in North America and the ancient Greeks both came to give it the same name is one of the mysteries of stellar mythology. To locate Polaris, the North Star, extend a straight line from the last two stars of the bowl of the dipper.

July

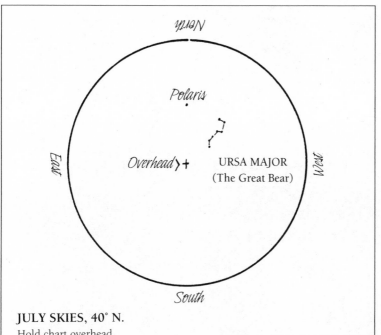

Polaris

Overhead〉+

URSA MAJOR
(The Great Bear)

North

East

West

South

JULY SKIES, 40° N.
Hold chart overhead

9 PM MDT - Early July
8 PM MDT - Late July

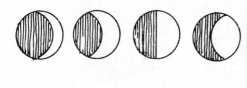

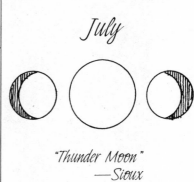

July

"*Thunder Moon*"
—*Sioux*

Double Star

URSA MAJOR (The Great Bear)

179

Bighorn sheep on Specimen Mountain

AUGUST

Seasons collide in August with an explosion of color that is like the climax of a fireworks show. In midmonth the tundra takes on an autumnal hue at the same time petunias, zinnias, marigolds, and other urban annuals reach their peaks.

Above tree line, many alpine flowers continue blooming as their foliage turns russet and crimson. Big-rooted spring beauties flaunt a rosette of translucent ruby leaves as they continue to bloom. Rose crown and king's crown, still flowering, turn an incandescent red. Alpine willows and mountain dryads form yellow-and-orange mats. Entire slopes glow a dull red from the foliage of mountain avens, with an occasional yellow spark from its flower.

The handkerchief gardens in the city of Boulder soothe irritable drivers from early spring to first frost, but in August these splashes of color stop traffic. Approximately 125,000 annuals, 35,000 bulbs, plus perennials are planted each year. The City of Boulder Parks and Recreation Department keeps records each year of what is planted where so that a pattern is seldom repeated.

Along roadsides and on the prairie, sunflowers emulate their counterpart in the sky. Between the plains and peaks this is the time for fireweed, shy wood nymphs, grass-of-Parnassus, monkey flowers, and many varieties of gentian. Finding the first fringed gentian always brings a touch of sadness: It means that summer is shifting into autumn.

Even snowfields have a tinge of red, color that is concentrated when you step on the patch. It's called "watermelon snow" and is caused by a green algae enclosed in a red gelatinous substance. Some people think it smells and tastes like watermelon, a sort of wilderness Sno-cone. However, it can cause diarrhea and is best avoided.

An abundance of food overwhelms us in August. Sweet corn and peaches from the Western Slope and Rocky Ford cantaloupe appear at roadside stands. Hikers compete with local animal populations to find succulent wild raspberries, strawberries, and (when they are *very* lucky) blueberries. Pikas continue to harvest the sweet-smelling mountain grasses, and robins gorge on chokecherries. And mushrooms – those magical, mystical fruits of the earth – suddenly emerge from the forest floor.

The earth seems ready to burst with good things, but something is missing. Almost without our realizing it, most birds have stopped singing. Occasionally a bird "whispers" a subdued song as though remembering earlier courtship exuberance, but – except for jays and other members of the loquacious Corvidae family – most birds now twitter and chat in conversational tones.

The sounds we still hear – the buzzing and whirring of insects and the crackling of seared grass underfoot – seem the essence of hot, dry August heat that still reaches into the nineties. At night, however, there's a chill, and midnight watchers of the Perseid shower snuggle into down sleeping bags to enjoy the annual sky show of meteors – an appropriate way to celebrate an explosive month.

FLORA

MUSHROOMS

The surreal shapes and colors of these strange growths conjure up images of elves sitting under umbrellas, of fairies dancing in a ring, of witches munching malevolent red toadstools flecked with warts. The truth is almost as strange.

Mushrooms don't produce chlorophyll or seeds and have no roots. They are usually classified into a kingdom of their own: the fungi. The mushroom is actually just the fruit of an underground

AUGUST WEATHER

AUGUST 1

Sunrise:	4:58 AM MST
Sunset:	7:13 PM MST

	Boulder	**Allens Park**	**Niwot Ridge**
	5,445'	8,500'	11,565'
Ave. Max.	85°F	73°F Ave. August high	55°F Ave. August high
Ave. Min.	60°F	44°F Ave. August low	39°F Ave. August low

AUGUST 31

Sunrise:	5:27 AM MST
Sunset:	6:33 PM MST

Ave. Max.	82°F	73°F Ave. August high	55°F Ave. August high
Ave. Min.	55°F	44°F Ave. August low	39°F Ave. August low

AUGUST CHANGES (August 1–August 31)

Day Length: 14 hours, 15 minutes to 13 hours, 6 minutes=change of −1 hour 9 minutes

Change: Max.	−3°F	−3°F	−1°F
Change: Min.	−5°F	−1°F	0°F

AUGUST EXTREMES

Max. Temp.	102°F	87°F	See note
Min. Temp.	35.6°F	27°F	See note
Max. Wind	88 mph	78 mph	Not available
Ave. Precip.	1.52 in.	2.3 in.	2 in.
Max. Precip.	7.49 in.	4.1 in.	3.24 in.
Min. Precip.	.03 in.	.7 in.	.4 in.
Ave. Snow	00 in.	00 in.	Not available
Max. Snow	00 in.	00 in.	Not available
Min. Snow	00 in.	00 in.	Not available

Note. 77°F is highest for any summer and −31°F is lowest for any winter on Niwot Ridge.

COLD SUMMERS

Coldest Summers (June, July, August):

1915	65.5°F
1992	65.8°F
Ave.	70.2°F

Cool and Dry 1992: Days of rain 48 (ave. amount per storm .05″!)
Record 49 in 1967

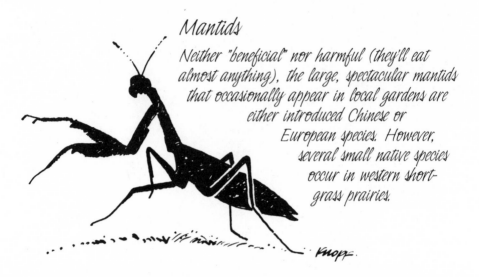

Mantids

Neither "beneficial" nor harmful (they'll eat almost anything), the large, spectacular mantids that occasionally appear in local gardens are either introduced Chinese or European species. However, several small native species occur in western short-grass prairies.

Knopf

growth called the "mycelium." The mycelium spreads underground (or in wood or a host organism) in an ever-growing network of interconnecting strands, usually white, which draw nourishment from organic matter in the substrate. Species (called saprophytes) that depend on dead material are valuable in recycling dead trees and other organic materials. Other species parasitize living hosts and can be destructive.

Some mushrooms form a symbiotic relationship, called a "mycorrhiza," with other plants. Boletus mushrooms, for instance, grow in symbiosis with conifers. The fungus obtains moisture and nutrients from the tree and, in turn, helps

the tree absorb nitrogen, phosphorous, and other nutrients.

Reproduction takes place through tiny spores that fall to the ground where, if conditions are suitable, they start a new mycelium that spreads out in filaments from the center. The underground mycelium can live for many centuries, expanding into a weblike growth larger than a blue whale or a giant sequoia.

Monster-mushroom mania started in Michigan in 1992, when the mycelium (estimated to weigh 220,000 pounds) of an *Armillaria bulbosa* was found spreading under 38 acres of ground. A few months later a 1,500-acre *Armillaria ostoyae*, thought to be between four hundred and one thousand years old, was reported near Mount Adams in Washington. Scientists suspect there are even larger ones yet undiscovered.

The forms taken by mushrooms are bizarre. They may look like coral, or blobs of jelly, or dead men's fingers, or brains, or phallic symbols, or the prototypical parasols. Many mushrooms produce caps with gills; others have caps with a spongelike or a toothed material underneath. Puffballs, or "stomach" mushrooms, are homogeneous throughout. Although the majority of mushrooms come in shades of brown, gray, or white, they can also be red, pink, salmon, orange, yellow, green, violet, or black.

Mushrooms vary in flavor as much as do different varieties of fruits and vegetables. The taste of a succulent wild mushroom as compared to the supermarket variety is comparable to the taste of tree-ripened peaches versus canned ones. However, some mushrooms, such as *Amanita verna* (nicknamed the "destroying angel"), are deadly. The rule is: Never eat a mushroom unless you know it well enough to call it by its scientific name. Also, be sure it has no lookalike, and don't trust old adages such as the one about poisonous mushrooms tarnishing a silver spoon.

There are no shortcuts. Identify the mushroom by carefully checking its description in a good field guide and taking a spore print. If possible, get a knowledgeable person to confirm its identity. Take a class or join the Colorado Mycological Society (address in Appendix 5, page 311) and go on forays with experienced people who know what to look for and where. A good way to get started is at the Annual Mushroom Fair, sponsored by the Colorado Mycological Society every August at the Denver Botanic Gardens.

Different species of mushrooms grow in different habitats, ranging from the prairie to the tundra. Look for *Boletus edulis* (steinpilz) near spruce and fir, *Agaricus campestris* (meadow mushrooms) in meadows, and *Hydnum imbricatum* (scaly urchin) in conifer forests. Various species of *Calvatia* and *Lycoperdon* (puffballs) grow just about anywhere. Different species fruit at different times of year, but August is when you find the most species and the greatest number.

Good mushrooming spots are located near Caribou, Brainard Lake, Forest Lakes, Beaver Reservoir, and Diamond Lake. Hot, wet summers provide the best conditions for a bountiful mushroom

Blueberries

Wild blueberries (*Vaccinium spp.*) flourish from 8,000 to 12,000 feet in Colorado but are erratic about producing fruit. Although they form healthy mats of foliage, many plants fail to get enough sun to bear berries. When they do produce a crop, the fruit is small but delectable. Look for blue scat stains where chipmunks and birds have feasted. In September, look for the bright red leaves of the low-growing blueberry plant.

crop. The summer of 1984 was an especially good season; eight years later, we were still eating dried mushrooms picked then.

Some mushroom species thrive on dead wood and proliferate after a forest fire. There were rumors of abundant morels during the 1970s following the Finch Lake fire near Allens Park, but don't expect anyone to tell you specific locations for these prize delicacies. A mystique has grown up around morels, which are not as common in Colorado as in the Midwest. However, the species listed above are, in our opinion, just as delectable and are relatively easy to find.

Picking mushrooms, like picking blueberries, is not believed to harm the plant because the part we eat is simply the fruit produced by the mycelium. However, be careful to avoid disturbing the mycelium and to firm the soil back into the hole. Also, use discretion in harvesting; many animals, such as squirrels, depend on mushrooms as survival food.

To enjoy their subtle flavor, sauté mushrooms in butter and refrain from adding other ingredients. Some people are sensitive to even the most palatable varieties, so follow these steps the first time you eat a new species: Eat only a spoonful or two and wait for twenty-four hours before eating more; don't mix with other species; and save some uncooked fresh whole specimens in waxed paper in the refrigerator for twenty-four hours so their identification can be checked if you do become ill.

Don't let these commonsense precautions scare you. Treated with caution, mushrooms can be delicious. However, it's not the feasting but the search and discovery of something strange, beautiful, and slightly mysterious that provides the thrill of mushrooming.

FAUNA

SHOREBIRDS HEADING SOUTH

In late July or early August the mornings begin to feel a little crisper, the sky grows noticeably bluer, and migrating shorebirds appear around prairie lakes and ponds. They come in bunches. Least sandpipers skitter nervously across the mud flats at Sombrero Marsh. Long-billed dowitchers, lesser and greater yellowlegs, and avocets probe for invertebrates at Walden Ponds. Solitary sandpipers wade gracefully in the shallows of Prince Lakes. Farther east, at places like Union Reservoir and Barr Lake, you can find a complete assortment of shorebirds encompassing a variety of shapes, sizes, and feeding habits.

Shorebirds always seem to be ahead of

schedule. In early spring they pass through long before the first leaves appear on the cottonwoods. They come again in midsummer, when the days are hot and other birds are still incubating eggs or feeding young.

For many shorebird species, the timing of migration is largely determined by the availability of food along the migration route. A few, such as Hudsonian godwits, may complete migrations of up to 8,000 miles in a single uninterrupted flight; but most undertake a series of shorter flights, stopping to refuel along the way. "Staging areas," like Cheyenne Bottoms in Kansas, Gray's Harbor in Washington, and Delaware Bay, serve as critical feeding and rest stops. These shallows and wetlands may attract as many as one million shorebirds at a time

American Avocet

This eye-appealing shorebird feeds by moving briskly forward while sweeping its distinctive curved bill from side to side through shallow water.

during migration. Some staging areas support almost the entire North American population of a few individual species, such as western sandpipers at Alaska's Copper River Delta. Destruction of staging areas by commercial development, removal of water for irrigation, and pesticide or sewage infiltration currently pose the greatest threat to North American shorebird populations.

Although it would be presumptuous to call Boulder County a shorebird staging area, our aquatic resources provide migrants with important foraging habitat as they move south. Numbers and species vary depending on water levels in lakes and ponds. Higher water favors waders such as long-billed dowitchers. Exposed mud flats attract least and Baird's sandpipers, willets, and an occasional black-bellied plover. Migrating shore-birds begin to arrive in late July and are usually gone by mid-September.

Five species nest in Boulder County and are present throughout the summer. Killdeer lay their eggs in shallow depres-sions in disturbed areas – gravel bars, sand flats, and parking lots. American avocets and Wilson's phalaropes prefer grassy shores of prairie lakes and marshes. Common snipe nest in fresh-water marshes from the plains to the high mountains. Spotted sandpipers lay their eggs in depressions on the muddy edges of lakes and streams, primarily in the mountains.

Long-billed curlews may once have nested in Boulder County, but destruc-tion of native midgrass and tallgrass prairies has eliminated potential nesting habitat. On the other hand, some migrants such as long-billed dowitchers and willets may have benefited from alteration of our prairie landscape. These species were locally rare around the turn of the century, before reservoir construc-tion and flooding of abandoned gravel mines expanded their foraging habitat.

Shorebird-watching is a good way to get a jump on the fall season. To hear the shrill call of a sandpiper, yellowlegs, or avocet on a warm summer day is invigorating and energizing, bringing memories of cool, windswept places. Peter Matthiessen captured this feeling when he wrote, in *The Wind Birds* (New York: Viking, 1981), "The restlessness of shorebirds, their kinship with the dis-tance and swift seasons, the wistful sig-nal of their voices down the long coast-lines of the world makes them, for me, the most affecting of wild creatures. I think of them as birds of wind . . ."

ALPINE UNGULATE-WATCHING

As the summer progresses and the tundra turns golden, elk, bighorn sheep, and mountain goats may become more approachable. The half-grown young are less in need of parental supervision and less vulnerable to predators. Young and old alike are intent on consuming as much food as possible before autumn snowstorms arrive.

The mountain goat, a rarity in Boul-der County, is the only hoofed animal, or ungulate, that typically spends the entire year above tree line. Bighorn sheep and elk usually winter in meadows and forest clearings lower down; prior to white settlement, both species frequented the plains of eastern Colorado.

Boulder County's elk herds generally arrive in the high country in late June. Calves are born in forested areas along the migration route and then accompany their parents up into the high meadows and alpine tundra, where they spend the summer fattening on grasses and other plants.

Bighorn sheep also give birth to their young in June. Lambing grounds are located in remote, cliffy areas inaccessible to predators. Bighorn sheep were extirpated from Boulder County during the early part of this century and have only recently been reintroduced. The largest herd winters in North St. Vrain Canyon and summers in the upper canyon and the high meadows west of the Peak to Peak Highway. Bighorns occasionally wander down into lower Boulder Canyon, and a few have even been seen on Flagstaff Mountain.

Mule deer also make their way up into the tundra during the summer months. They browse on willows and other shrubs growing at the upper limits of the subalpine forest. Look for them around dawn and dusk.

The most popular ungulate-watching spots along the northern Front Range are Mount Evans, where the road passes within touching distance of herds of mountain goats and bighorn sheep, and Trail Ridge Road, where elk herds graze in lush meadows above tree line. Specimen Mountain, on the west side of Rocky Mountain National Park, supports one of the largest bighorn sheep herds in our area. However, much of the mountain is closed to visitors in summer to protect lambing grounds.

For many visitors to these areas, the "wildlife experience" consists of jumping out of an idling automobile long enough to snap a few pictures of goats, sheep, and tourists milling about on the asphalt. To avoid this zoo-like scene, walk a mile or two away from the road, locate a herd of elk, sheep, or goats, and observe them at a discreet distance. Within a few hours they usually accept your presence, and you can get to know them close up, with only the tundra and snowcapped peaks as distractions.

WHERE TO GO IN AUGUST

LONGS PEAK

Longs Peak (14,255 feet) is the only fourteener in Boulder County. The 8-mile trail starts at 9,400 feet and passes through many vegetation zones to culminate in the alpine tundra. The first recorded ascent was made in August 1868 by explorer John Wesley Powell, five of his students, and newspaperman William Byers. However, Native Americans had climbed it earlier. In his book *Longs Peak Tales* (Boulder: Stonehenge Books, 1981), Glenn Randall relates how Old Man Gun, an Arapaho warrior, was told in a vision to build an eagle trap on the peak and to catch an eagle with his bare hands. After four days of enduring snow and other hardships, he succeeded in grabbing and holding onto a bald eagle. Powell is said to have found the remains of an eagle trap on the summit. Now, approximately ten thousand people climb the peak each year, so don't expect solitude.

For those who don't feel the need to climb a mountain, a more leisurely 5.5-mile hike can be made to rock-rimmed Chasm Lake. Peak-baggers sometimes climb Mount Meeker (13,911 feet) on the same trip as to Longs. A 2-mile offshoot of the Longs Peak Trail goes to Eugenia Mine and makes a pleasant short summer hike or winter ski tour.

To reach the Longs Peak trailhead, drive 10 miles south of Estes Park on SR 7, turn west at the sign, and continue 1 mile to the Ranger Station.

RAINBOW LAKES AND GLACIER RIM TRAILS

Both trails begin at Rainbow Lakes Campground and head up through a spruce/fir forest, with several stands of limber pine twisted into shapes like lyres and candelabras. Rainbow Lakes Trail passes numerous small lakes and peters out above a double lake in less than 2 miles.

Glacier Rim Trail skirts Boulder's watershed, which is closed to the public. Above tree line the tundra is now putting on autumnal colors, and there are good views down into the forbidden

191

Climbers

In 1887, Frank Hornbaker began leading trips from Boulder to the top of Longs Peak, according to Paul Nesbit, author of *Paul Nesbit's Longs Peak: Its Story and a Climbing Guide* (Mills Publishing Company, 1990). The climbers took a train to Ward, a stage to Meeker, and horses to the boulder field below the summit. Nesbit also writes that in 1926 William Butler of Longmont became the oldest person to reach the top when he climbed the peak on his eighty-fifth birthday.

lush basin that contains Goose Lake and Silver Lake, part of the watershed closure. This 6-mile trail continues up to the saddle above Arapaho Glacier. When conditions are right, mushrooms are abundant on both trails, and patches of blueberries, strawberries, and wintergreen berries can be found.

From the Peak to Peak Highway halfway between Nederland and Ward, turn west onto CR 116 at the CU Mountain Research Station sign. This rough gravel road dead-ends in 5 miles at the Rainbow Lakes Campground. If one party parks at Rainbow Lakes Campground and another party at Buckingham Campground, a 9-mile one-way hike with key exchange can be made.

FOREST LAKES, ARAPAHO LAKES, CRATER LAKES, AND HEART LAKE

Although this area was described in February for skiing and showshoeing, we're including it again for summer hiking because the mushrooms and wildflowers are especially profuse in August.

The main access to these lakes is from the East Portal of Moffat Tunnel. This 6-mile tunnel, which opened in 1928, goes under the Continental Divide and was built to avoid the hazardous route over Rollins Pass where Corona, the train station at 11,600 feet, lay under

Mosquitoes

Mosquitoes belong to the same family as the common housefly.
Approximately fifty species flourish in Colorado wherever there is standing
water for the larvae. Since some species go from egg to adult in three to four
days, even a mud puddle will do. Only the female, who uses blood for egg
development, whines and bites. Mosquitoes are active from late May to the
end of August and can sometimes be controlled by a small
mosquito-eating fish called gambusia. The
Boulder County Health Department gives
these fish to pond owners on request.

snow from October to June. See the February chapter for trail descriptions.

An alternative summer route to Forest Lakes is to drive the Rollins Pass road for 7 miles beyond the East Portal fork. Yankee Doodle and Jenny lakes are passed en route and are worth a stop. The parking area for Forest Lakes is on a hairpin curve just above Jenny Lake. The trail drops down in less than a mile to one of the upper lakes. From there you can descend to the others or climb up (no trail) to the highest lake near tree line. Paintbrush flourishes in this area. Above tree line the road itself is good hiking, with colorful autumn tundra to either side. Look for ripe raspberries in the road cuts.

BALD MOUNTAIN SCENIC AREA

Light pollution in urban areas makes stargazing there a frustrating business, so astronomy buffs frequently head for the mountains. Although the summit of Bald Mountain (not the same peak as the one near Caribou) is only 7,161 feet high, it's a convenient spot to see the stars and the Perseid meteor shower. Just 4.5 miles west of Boulder along Sunshine Canyon

Raccoons

Chiefly nocturnal, these extraordinarily crafty critters are active year-round, eating a wide range of meat and vegetables and averaging about 15lbs. A monster of 62lbs.-6oz; (55" tongue to tail) was reported in Wisconsin in 1955.

(a continuation of Mapleton Avenue), the area is handy for after-work picnicking. The 1-mile loop, called "Pines to Peak Trail," goes through meadows and ponderosa pines to Bald Mountain, a bare, windswept knob where you can listen for owls and watch for bats and common nighthawks as well as the Perseids. Viewpoints along the trail offer vistas of the plains and the foothills to the east and the Continental Divide to the west. Because of its intermediate elevation, this area is also good for off-season hikes.

AUGUST OUT-OF-COUNTY EXCURSIONS

August, the month of garden bounty,is a time for tasting. What better way to celebrate the burgeoning mushroom season than to head for the San Juan Mountains and the mushroom festival at Telluride, where experts teach the mysteries of mushrooms? Because this part of the state receives more than its share of precipitation, both the mushrooms and the wildflowers are profuse. Precipitous mountains are just a bonus.

Other tasting excursions are to Rocky Ford in eastern Colorado for cantaloupe (and to enjoy the late-summer prairie flowers and grasses) or to Palisade and Grand Junction in western Colorado for the peach harvest. Roadside stands offer crateloads of just-picked tree-ripened peaches, apples, and grapes, and five area wineries offer tours and tasting rooms. At Palisade, a Peach Festival is held in August and a Winefest in September.

Near Grand Junction you can also visit the Cross Orchards Living History Farm; Dinosaur Valley, with displays of dinosaur bones and other fossils; the Museum of Western Colorado; and Colorado National Monument, with red and buff sandstone formations rivaling those of Utah.

AUGUST AT A GLANCE

MAMMALS

- Colorado chipmunks, born late in May or in June, appear above ground.
- Fawns begin to lose their spots and their gawkiness.

BIRDS

- Mountain chickadees, pine siskins, and nuthatches begin their vertical migration.
- Migrating shorebirds feed at lakes and ponds on the plains.
- Common nighthawks congregate and swoop erratically after flying insects.

OTHER CRITTERS

- In spite of the nighthawks, mosquitoes still abound and bite.

PLANTS

- Mushrooms "mushroom."
- Blue chicory blooms on the plains and blue gentian in the tundra.
- Blazing-stars bloom at night along the edge of the foothills and on the plains.
- Tundra foliage takes on an autumnal hue.
- Wild blueberries, raspberries, wintergreen berries, and chokecherries ripen.

IN THE SKY

- The Perseid meteor shower, possibly the best of the year, peaks around August 12. If you get away from the city lights (Flagstaff Mountain is a popular viewing spot) and look to the north, you may see as many as sixty meteors per hour.
- Lammas, the time of hot weather, the beginning of the harvest, and the approximate halfway point between the summer solstice and the autumn equinox, was traditionally celebrated on August 1.
- The loosely organized constellation Sagittarius (The Archer) is visible above the southern horizon just to the right of Scorpius at around 9:00 P.M. This group of second- and third-magnitude stars is said to represent an archer aiming his arrow at the scorpion.

August

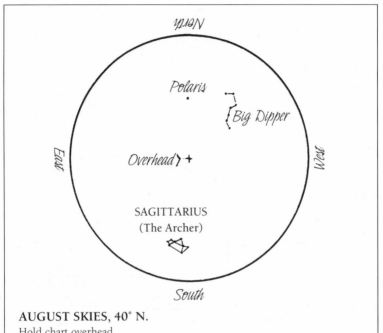

AUGUST SKIES, 40° N.
Hold chart overhead

9 PM MDT - Early Aug.
8 PM MDT - Late Aug.

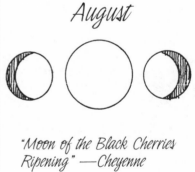

August

"*Moon of the Black Cherries Ripening*" —*Cheyenne*

SAGITTARIUS (The Archer)

196

Ripening chokecherries

Yawning marmot

SEPTEMBER

Tundra colors fade to tan, hummingbirds leave, snow dusts the mountains, and the most incandescent show of the year begins. It's aspen time. Early in the month an occasional branch or tree turns into a golden candle, and usually by the fourth weekend high-country colors peak. Leaves glitter and glow in luminous tones of yellow, sometimes shading into salmon and red. By the end of the month, when many groves are half-bare, the individual leaves – like yellow dots of paint – create pointillist art.

Native Americans called aspen "the tree that whispers to itself." It's usually called quaking aspen (*Populus tremuloides*) because the leaves tremble and murmur in the slightest breeze. This shimmy and shake is caused by a thin, flat petiole attached to the leaf at right angles, creating a hinge that is sensitive to any movement. Aspen not only delight our eyes and ears, they also emit a spicy scent as the fallen leaves decay, and the creamy bark feels like suede.

Aspen usually colonize disturbed areas, such as roadsides or sites of forest fires or avalanches. In the absence of fires or other disturbances, conifers eventually replace them. Look for groves at altitudes of 7,000 to 10,000 feet.

Although they occasionally reproduce through seeds, their primary method is to clone by root-suckering. Aspen are the most widespread tree species in the world, and they may also be among the oldest because of this ability to clone. Although the tree trunk dies, new ones spring from the original root stock. Some cloned clumps are estimated to be 10,000 years old. In fact, a few researchers say some clones predate the Ice Age.

199

In 1992, botanists reported an aspen clone that may be the world's largest living organism—outweighing even the monster mushroom mentioned in the August chapter. Covering 106 acres in the Wasatch Mountains of Utah, this clone weighs more than 6,000 tons and consists of some 47,000 connected stems from the root of a single individual.

The splendor of the aspen overshadows other fall colors, but the understory of shrubs and small leafy plants is also suffused with color. Smooth sumac, three-leaf sumac, redtwig dogwood, fireweed, strawberry, wild geranium, and wild rose turn crimson, magenta, and vermilion. Jamesia flaunts gradations of rose-red, orange, yellow, and green all on the same leaf. Miniature forests of yellow dogbane with bright red stalks flourish under the real forest. And poison ivy forms glorious, fiery bouquets that tempt the unwary to pick them.

Berries continue to ripen. Some, such as raspberries and blueberries, are delectable. Others, such as the translucent orange squaw currant, the Christmas red kinnikinnick, and the blue creeping mahonia berries, are edible but hardly worth it. Still others, such as the lacquer red or china white baneberry, are

Aspens

Many taxonomists consider the North Ameriican and Eurasian aspens to be the same, making this the most widely distributed tree species on earth. Some aspen ecologists have estimated most colonies in the Great Basin to be at least 8,000 years old, and speculate that a few groves in Utah and Colorado may exceed 1 million years!

Are they "Four-pointers" or "Eight-pointers"?

Is a buck deer with eight prongs to a set of antlers called a four-point or an eight-point? West of the Mississippi only the prongs on one side are counted, whereas east of the river both sides are counted. So in Colorado we must go with the understated four-point designation.

poisonous but beautiful. Harder to see are the berries of the secretive twisted-stalk (*Streptopus amplexifolius*), which dangles orange-red beads over mountain streams. Also look for the berries of its relatives: false Solomon's-seal and fairybells. As with mushrooms, eat only those you can positively identify.

Until a hard freeze sets in, asters, wild white yarrow, pearly everlasting, harebells, Arctic gentian, and various yellow composites continue to bloom at higher elevations, while annuals in urban yards are almost as abundant as in August. Along many roads, bluestem grasses in tones of pink and burgundy form the perfect backdrop for sky blue chicory. In the plains, harvest reaches its zenith. The last of the sweet corn is savored, and apples, pears, plums, grapes, and various wild fruits tempt both people and wild animals into feasting frenzies.

At night, listen for raccoons in the crabapple trees, and during the day watch squirrels bury their booty in heaps of duff called "middens." Most fawns have now lost their spots, and bucks are losing the velvet from their antlers. Four-point bucks, well aware of their machismo status, strut about with scraggly ropes of velvet hanging from antlers dotted with blood. We sometimes see two of these magnificent males, buddies until now, sparring in the backyard—a prelude to the serious jousts of October and November. And in the high country, elk start to bugle.

Other fall phenomena to watch for include flocks of Franklin's gulls wheeling over urban areas and young spiders ballooning through the air using a single strand called a "dragline."

FLORA

SEASON OF GREAT CHANGE, ROUND TWO

September marks the start of the second season of great change and transition. Like spring, it's a period of extremes, with weather that is rarely average. According to local weather wizard Bill Callahan, there were just two days in the 1980s when both highs and lows matched the average for the dates. He also points out that extremes do tend to average out—sometimes dramatically. On September 29, 1921, the high temperature was a torrid 89°F, and the low was an improbable 35°F; the mean temperature for that day was within a few degrees of the ninety-three-year average. This kind of meteorological juggling is especially common during fall and spring. For local flora and fauna it's

rather like the old saying, "One foot is in ice water, the other in boiling water, and on the average it's comfortable."

As in spring, survival of flora and fauna depends on the timing of many things. September is like spring in reverse, as things prepare to shut down rather than start up, but the factors initiating change are different.

Most deciduous plants anticipate the need for winter dormancy by reacting more to shortening days (or lengthening nights, according to recent research) than to cooler temperature. This reaction is why the onset of fall color is more predictable than is the timing of leaf development and flowering in spring.

However, cooler weather also contributes to the onset of fall color and dormancy. The earlier coloring of aspen at higher elevations illustrates the effect of cooler temperatures. Moisture is another

SEPTEMBER WEATHER

SEPTEMBER 1

Sunrise: 5:28 AM MST
Sunset: 6:32 PM MST

	Boulder	*Allens Park*	*Niwot Ridge*
	5,445'	8,500'	11,565'
Ave. Max.	83°F	66°F Ave. September high	48°F Ave. September high
Ave. Min.	55°F	38°F Ave. September low	27°F Ave. September low

SEPTEMBER 30

Sunrise: 5:55 AM MST
Sunset: 5:45 PM MST

Ave. Max.	72°F	66°F Ave. September high	48°F Ave. September high
Ave. Min.	45°F	38°F Ave. September low	27°F Ave. September low

SEPTEMBER CHANGES (September 1–September 30)

Day Length: 13 hours, 4 minutes to 11 hours, 50 minutes=change of −1 hour 54 minutes

Change: Max.	−11°F	−7°F	−7°F
Change: Min.	−10°F	−6°F	−12°F

SEPTEMBER EXTREMES

Max. Temp.	100°F	81°F	See note
Min. Temp.	15°F	7°F	See note
Max. Wind	131 mph	128 mph	Not available
Ave. Precip.	1.5 in.	1.5 in.	2 in.
Max. Precip.	5.5 in.	4.5 in.	3.7 in.
Min. Precip.	Trace	.1 in.	.84 in.
Ave. Snow	.9 in.	2.3 in.	Not available
Max. Snow	21 in.	17 in.	Not available
Min. Snow	00 in.	00 in.	Not available

Note. 77°F is highest for any summer and −31°F is lowest for any winter on Niwot Ridge.

FALL NOTES:

	Boulder
Frost: Earliest fall killing frost:	9 September 1929, 1941
Ave. first killing frost:	12 October
Latest fall killing frost:	10 November 1907
Snow: Earliest first fall snow:	2 September 1961, 1973
Latest first fall snow:	26 November 1978

important factor. Heavier than normal fall precipitation or excessive irrigation may extend the active growing period for native plants, making them more susceptible to damage from sudden early freezes.

Fall, like spring, is a time to watch and wonder about the effects of unusual and extreme conditions. The sudden freezes of October/November 1991, and mid-October 1984, when temperatures dropped to near 0°F after extended periods of summery weather, caught many plants totally unprepared. The leaves of many deciduous plants did not develop the usual fall color following the 1984 freeze, and buds and twigs were severely damaged.

Most northern European species of plants used in local landscaping change color and lose their leaves later than do their North American counterparts. European beech (*Fagus sylvatica*), European mountain ash (*Sorbus aucuparia*), and Norway maple (*Acer platanoides*) develop fall color much later than do American beech (*Fagus grandifolia*), western mountain ash (*Sorbus scopulina*), and bigtooth maple (*Acer grandidentatum*). The slower development of color change in European plants may result from their having evolved in a more northerly latitude where maritime influences delay severe cold until day length is short.

The formula for estimating seasonal changes, based on latitude and altitude, also applies at this time of year (see page 66).

FALL COLOR CHANGE

One autumn long ago, according to several Native American legends, three hunters and a dog chased a bear who led them faster and faster in all directions. Finally the bear ran high into the sky, where the hunters killed and butchered him on a stack of maple and sumac branches. The leaves, stained by his blood, still turn blood red every fall, and the Great Bear, followed by three hunters and their dog, can still be seen in the sky at any time of the year. These eight stars (also called the Big Dipper) can never rest until the hunters and the dog again catch the bear.

The scientific explanation for fall color change is less romantic but more complex. Interactions of shortening day length, cooler temperatures, drier conditions, brilliant sunlight, and soil chemistry all contribute to color change in deciduous trees.

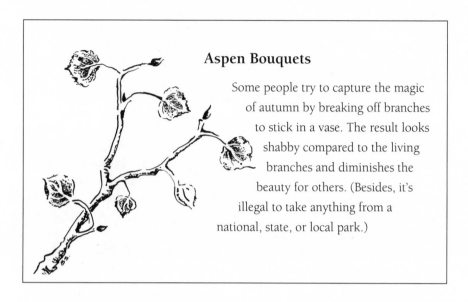

Aspen Bouquets

Some people try to capture the magic of autumn by breaking off branches to stick in a vase. The result looks shabby compared to the living branches and diminishes the beauty for others. (Besides, it's illegal to take anything from a national, state, or local park.)

The process begins long before there is any visible evidence of change in the leaves, as shorter day lengths, together with cooler temperatures and drier conditions, cause the development of a thin-walled breakaway layer of cells (abscission layer) at the base of the leaf stem. This is the point where the leaf stem will break away from the twig. At the same time, a corky layer develops between the abscission layer and the twig. This layer will prevent an open wound when the leaf falls, and it prevents sugars from moving from the leaf to the trunk.

If there is a hard freeze at the wrong time the process is interrupted, and leaves may hang on until winter winds finally sweep them away. A few trees, like pin oaks (*Quercus palustris*), develop no abscission layer and normally hold their leaves well into winter.

Leaves appear green during summer because chlorophyll, the dominant pigment, masks the yellow pigments carotin and xanthophyll. The green chlorophyll is continually destroyed and replenished during photosynthesis. However, in fall the vital activities of leaves decline in response to less favorable growing conditions and to the developing restrictions between the leaf and the rest of the plant. As a result, chlorophyll is no longer replenished, and the yellow pigments dominate.

Red or purple color is caused by chemical substances called anthocyanins. Cold temperatures (below 45°F) and shorter daylight hours cause a buildup of sugars in the leaves, which in turn leads to the manufacture of more anthocyanins at the same time the chlorophyll level is decreasing. The leaves need sunny days to manufacture sugars but cool nights to form the corky layer that keeps the sugar in the leaf. High acidity in the soil and in the sap contributes to the reddest reds. Alkaline soil and sap produce a bluish red.

With aspen, just the right degree of frost, at just the right time, traps sugars in the leaf and contributes to a red-orange color. However, many botanists believe some aspen are also genetically inclined to display this attractive variation on the typical clear yellow. Because the ability to produce anthocyanins is genetic (as in a human family of redheads), all the trees in a reddish clump are probably part of the same clone and thus genetically identical. Some nurseries are attempting to propagate trees with a tendency toward red.

FAUNA

FALL GATHERINGS

As the days grow shorter and the nights grow colder, the foraging activity of many wildlife species increases. During fall months, black bears may feed sixteen to twenty hours per day, accumulating the fat necessary to see them through winter. Pikas (also known as "rock rabbits") spend a similar amount of time constructing their winter hay piles, and chickarees scamper across the forest floor stashing fir cones. Other species gather in large aggregations as they prepare for migration or hibernation.

Perhaps the most curious of these gatherings is the early fall assemblage of ladybird beetles (popularly called "ladybugs") on the summits of Green Mountain, Bear Peak, and South Boulder Peak.

By mid-September most years, rocks and tree trunks on these summits are coated orange with tens of thousands of ladybugs. By November, many of the beetles will have crawled into cracks and crevices in the tree bark to overwinter. Others will have died, their desiccated exoskeletons lying scattered among the rocks. In spring, the survivors will emerge to mate and lay eggs.

No one knows for sure why ladybugs "choose" mountain peaks as overwintering sites. The same phenomenon occurs in the Sierra Nevada, the Swiss Alps, and other parts of the world. Assuming natural selection is at work, ladybugs wintering on mountaintops must somehow be more successful than those wintering elsewhere. Perhaps a relative lack of predators in these locations compensates for the effects of more severe weather conditions.

Unfortunately, overwintering sites in the Boulder Mountain Park are readily accessible to humans, who sometimes gather handfuls of the beetles for use in gardens. This practice disrupts the ladybugs' life cycle and may threaten the viability of some sites. In addition, ladybugs transported to gardens at this time of year are likely to disperse or head back up to the mountains.

The ladybug aggregation on Green Mountain often coincides with the appearance of large flocks of songbirds on Green Mountain West Ridge. Red crossbills and Clark's nutcrackers converge on this area to feed on ponderosa pine seeds. Thistle and mullein seed attract pine siskins, Cassin's finches, and American goldfinches. Williamson's sapsuckers, hairy woodpeckers, and pygmy nuthatches work the dead ponderosa pines and Douglas firs for insect larvae. Western bluebirds, a rarity in Boulder County, forage in forest clearings and meadows along the ridge.

The fall hawk migration soars into full swing by late September. From the summit of Green Mountain, you can look down on the hawks as they fly southward. Numbers are usually highest around midmorning on warm, clear days. See April Fauna for details.

In September and October, black bears descend into lower foothills canyons to eat wild plums, sumac, apples, raspberries, and other fruits and berries. About 70% of black bear sightings within the Boulder Mountain Park occur in these two months. During one fall, six individual bears were sighted within the park: a sow with two cubs, a solitary boar, and two yearlings. Home ranges for

Green Mountain

The summit of Green Mountain is the site of an extraordinary congregation of ladybugs each year.

black bears may exceed 200 square miles, so it is likely that these and other bears roam over a good part of Boulder County.

Bears are most active at dawn and dusk. Places to look include Bear Canyon, Skunk Canyon, and Bluebell Canyon in the Boulder Mountain Park; and North St. Vrain and Middle St. Vrain canyons in northern Boulder County. Use caution: Black bears, even when appearing curious or friendly, are always dangerous and unpredictable. Some

foothills canyons may be closed in the fall to protect foraging bears. Obeying these closures may preserve a bear's life as well as your own.

Foothills fruits, berries, and seeds entice a variety of other mammals, including porcupines, raccoons, Abert's squirrels, coyotes, and red foxes. In early evening, porcupines descend from their roosts high in ponderosa pines to forage in the forest or in nearby riparian woodlands. Stripped bark on ponderosas often reveals their presence.

As some birds and mammals move down into foothills canyons, others migrate up into the alpine tundra. Mountain bluebirds, flickers, and western meadowlarks can be seen in the tundra in September, when insects are still abundant. They stay only a few weeks, moving back down when temperatures fall. Northern harriers and prairie falcons also migrate to the tundra in September to hunt rodents.

Early fall is a great time to observe and photograph pikas and marmots because most of their attention seems focused on gathering and consuming food for winter. Look for pika and marmot colonies in rock piles and talus slopes near and above timberline. While sitting quietly in a pika colony, we've watched these small creatures scurry over our feet or through our legs carrying grass to hay piles located under sheltering rocks. We've also seen weasels dipping and diving among the boulders looking for a pika lunch. Returning in winter, we've heard the muffled chirps of the pikas underneath the snow as they scampered about in their snug quarters, safe (except from weasels), warm, and well provisioned.

Marmots may double their weight in summer as they munch grasses and other plants. In fall they enter their burrows for the winter. During hibernation their body temperature drops to around 40°F, and their pulse slows to four to five beats per minute. Although often associated with the alpine tundra, marmots are also found throughout the foothills and mountains of Boulder County. They are sometimes seen along the Walter Orr Roberts Nature Trail behind the National Center for Atmospheric Research and along the south end of the Mesa Trail.

Our yellow-bellied marmots (*Marmota flaviventris*) are close relatives of the eastern marmot, or woodchuck (*Marmota monax*). Neither of these species is likely to appear above ground on Groundhog Day in February. Yellow-bellied marmots usually wait until March or April, when grasses are beginning to green up, to emerge from hibernation.

THE SAD SAGA OF BEAR NUMBER NINE

Nearly every year, a few black bears wander down into residential areas of Boulder, Lyons, or even Longmont. Usually these bears return to the mountains and are never seen again. Bear Number Nine was an exception.

FALL BIRD MIGRATION

Species	August	September	October	November
Loons & Grebes				
Ducks & Geese				
Hawks & Eagles				
Shorebirds				
Warblers				
Sparrows				

This yearling male, weighing about 175 pounds, first appeared in the Chautauqua Park area of Boulder in July 1990. He soon gained the reputation as an unusually friendly bear. After he followed a CU graduate student down the Enchanted Mesa Trail, he was live-trapped, equipped with a pink ear tag marked "9," and removed to the Cameron Pass area north of Rocky Mountain National Park. Illustrating a strong homing instinct, Bear Number Nine reappeared in the Boulder Mountain Park two weeks later.

During ensuing weeks, the young bear's antics became front-page news in the local papers (one photo in the *Colorado Daily* bore the caption, "Coming Soon to a Backyard Near You"). He fell asleep under a grape arbor at Eighth and University, joined a family picnic in Chautauqua Park, dispersed a group of illegal campers at Bluebell Shelter, and became an unwanted companion to several hikers and joggers. In September he was trapped again and relocated to Walker Ranch, west of the Mountain Park. He returned two days later.

Wildlife officials fretted over what to do next. Finally they decided to leave Number Nine alone, hoping he would

RARE AND UNCOMMON MIGRANTS
(Selected Species)

Species	Where	When
Common Loon	Valmont Reservoir, Lagerman Reservoir, Sawhill Ponds, Baseline Reservoir	October–November
Eared Grebe	Baseline Reservoir, Sawhill Ponds, Boulder Reservoir	September–November
Tundra Swan	Baseline Reservoir, Walden Ponds	November–December
Osprey	Baseline Reservoir, Sawhill Ponds, Boulder Reservoir	August–October
Sandhill Crane	Plains	October
Broad-winged Hawk	Green Mountain, Dakota Hogback	September
Pinyon Jay	Doudy Draw, Rabbit Mountain, Green Mountain	August–October
Marsh Wren	Sawhill/Walden Ponds, Lagerman Reservoir, Boulder Reservoir	October–November
Sage Thrasher*	Doudy Draw, Rabbit Mountain, Boulder Valley Ranch	August–September
Townsend's Warbler	Mountains, middle elevations	August–September
Clay-colored Sparrow	Rabbit Mountain, Boulder Valley Ranch	September

*They sometimes nest in Doudy Draw.

Source: Boulder County Audubon Society, Monthly Wildlife Inventories 1975–92.

soon hibernate and emerge the following spring a reformed bear.

In April 1991, garbage cans at Chautauqua Park clattered with the sound of a ravenous bruin foraging through the night. Number Nine was back in town. After he followed another jogger down the McClintock Nature Trail, helping her establish a record time for her daily run, the Division of Wildlife acted decisively. Bear Number Nine was trapped and removed to a remote area west of Walsenberg.

In June 1991, a hog farmer shot and killed a young bear he believed had been carrying off his piglets. Wildlife officials later concluded that Bear Number Nine had come down from the mountains not to eat pork but to dine on his favorite fare, human garbage.

Was the death of Bear Number Nine avoidable? Boulder Mountain Park ranger Ann Wichmann, who developed a fondness for Number Nine while spending hours monitoring his activities, believes the bear's demise may have stemmed from easy access to garbage and other human food sources. "His behavior was so different from that of other bears in the park. He must have learned to associate humans with food," Wichmann says. Shortly after Number Nine's death, the Parks and Recreation Department received a substantial donation from a concerned citizen for purchase of bearproof garbage cans.

For those who came to know this bear on a personal basis, the moral of the story was clear: When large predators become tame, there is no place for them in our world. "We have to learn to tolerate and live with wildlife, or we will lose them," Wichmann says.

WHERE TO GO IN SEPTEMBER

PEAK TO PEAK HIGHWAY

From Central City to Estes Park, this road (SR 119, 72, and 7) is noted for aspen vistas. We like to stop at some of the groves on public land, sit with our backs against the trunks, and look up through backlit yellow leaves to the deep blue autumn sky.

There are several very short (mile or less) unmarked trails through the aspen leading off this highway:

• *James Creek.* Crosses under the road 1 mile north of the Brainard Lake turn-off. Park here and follow the creek up to an old beaver pond. (This is also good for columbine in July.)

• Turn onto Rainbow Lakes Road and drive 1 mile to the intersection with the road to the University of Colorado Mountain Research Station. Park at the intersection and follow an overgrown fisherman's trail downhill along an un-named creek.

SWITZERLAND TRAIL

Formerly a narrow-gauge railroad, this rough gravel road is only one lane wide in places, giving drivers the illusion of bouncing through a golden tunnel. There are several access points to this historic road. The easiest route is to take Boulder Canyon to Four-Mile Canyon to Salina; turn left and continue through Wallstreet (note the picturesque depot, now a private home) to Sunset. Many aspen brighten this latter stretch. The original railroad veered right from Sunset and went through the resort of Alto (now a picnic area with only a chimney as a reminder of past glory) to Ward. Later a spur was built, curving left to privately owned Glacier Lake and to Eldora. This branch now joins the Peak to Peak Highway.

Four-wheel-drive or high clearance will help on some sections of the road beyond Sunset. Because aspen flourish along road cuts, hiking old roads can be rewarding. For hiking or biking we especially recommend the stretch between Sugarloaf Mountain and Glacier Lake and the stretch beyond the intersection with CR 52. The latter section dead-ends in a rock fall above Left Hand Canyon. Several unmarked side trails also lead through aspen and through meadows starred with asters and colorful grasses.

For a loop drive through still more aspen, continue on CR 52. A left turn leads to SR 72 (Peak to Peak Highway); a right turn to Gold Hill and Boulder via Sunshine Canyon.

SOUTH ST. VRAIN TRAIL AND BEAVER RESERVOIR ROAD

The lower section of this trail goes through aspen, which give way to conifers in about 2 miles. The distance to the Baptist Camp is 3 miles; to Brainard Lake 6 miles.

Turn off the Peak to Peak Highway (SR 72) at the Tahosa Boy Scout sign about

2 miles northwest of Ward. Park at the trailhead sign just beyond the turnoff. A few miles farther along on the road (which dead-ends at Beaver Reservoir), you can see the effects of the big forest fire of 1988, which burned 757 acres of lodgepole pine. Within a few years, aspen saplings and wildflowers began to soften the denuded slopes. It will be interesting to check on the progress of these aspen in future years.

GREEN MOUNTAIN

At the top of this mountain, which backs the Flatirons, ladybugs by the thousands usually cluster together in autumn. These bright red beetles also favor Bear Peak and South Boulder Peak, described in the November chapter. Views of the snowcapped peaks to the west and the plains to the east make this a good hike any time of year. Several unusual plants, including rare orchids, grow on the north slopes of this mountain.

Drive up Flagstaff Road 3 miles to a three-way intersection and park in the area to the left. Follow the Greenman Trail 2 miles to the top. Or, continue on the road toward Gross Reservoir and take the Green Mountain West Ridge Trail (1.5 miles).

GOLDEN GATE CANYON STATE PARK

Although this park is located in Jefferson County, we are including it here because it is the best nearby area for immersing yourself in aspen. More than 60 miles of trails loop throughout the park; most of these trails eventually lead to Frazer Meadow, a grassy opening surrounded by aspen and containing the ruins of an old homestead.

Take SR 93 to Golden Gate Canyon Road; turn west and continue to the Visitor Center, where a map and a required state parks pass can be obtained.

PLACES TO REVISIT IN SEPTEMBER

Hessie, described in the June chapter, is rich in aspen at the lower elevations, as is the nearby town of Eldora. Stroll through Eldora and along Bryan Avenue, lined with overarching aspen.

Walker Ranch Trails, described in the May chapter, pass through some aspen groves where you may hear elk bugling. Almost all foothills trails up to 7,000 feet are spotted with flaming stands of sumac by the end of the month.

Walden and Sawhill ponds, described in the May chapter, or the first two pull-outs on Flagstaff Road give unobstructed views of the rising harvest moon.

SEPTEMBER OUT-OF-COUNTY EXCURSIONS

Most of the preceding suggestions involve places to see fall color, but aspen stands in the central and southwestern mountains are much more massive than in the Front Range. The Maroon Bells–Snowmass Wilderness and the San Juan Mountains are especially spectacular because they combine golden trees and maroon rock. For a different way to see aspen, take the Durango & Silverton narrow-gauge train. Call the railroad at (303) 247-2733 for details.

The peak of color varies with changes in altitude or latitude, and it varies from year to year because of temperature and moisture differences. Watch local newspapers or call the forest service or the Chamber of Commerce in the area to be visited.

SEPTEMBER AT A GLANCE

MAMMALS

- Mule deer bucks begin to lose velvet from antlers and start playful sparring.
- Elk start to bugle in the high country and continue through late October.

BIRDS

- Hummingbirds usually leave by second week.
- Hawk migration peaks by last week.
- Sage thrashers and pinyon jays are sometimes seen in Doudy Draw.

OTHER CRITTERS

- Ladybugs concentrate in vast numbers on top of Green Mountain, Bear Mountain, and South Boulder Peak.
- Praying mantises and crickets become more active and conspicuous.

PLANTS

- Aspen color reaches peak, usually by the fourth week of September in the high country.
- Shrubs, leafy plants, and grasses in the foothills start to change color.
- Wild plums, grapes, and "escaped" apples ripen.

SPECIAL EVENTS

- Upslope (or upslop) storms become dominant form of precipitation.

IN THE SKY

- Harvest moon, the full moon nearest the autumnal equinox, occurs in late September or early October. For several successive days the moon rises soon after sunset, giving farmers additional light for harvesting crops.
- The autumnal equinox, when the sun is directly over the equator, occurs around September 22. Day and night lengths are approximately equal all over the earth.
- Look for Cassiopeia (The Lady in the Chair) in the high northeastern sky around 8:00 P.M.

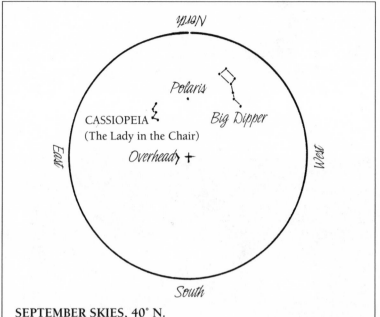

North

Polaris

Big Dipper

CASSIOPEIA
(The Lady in the Chair)

Overhead +

East

West

South

SEPTEMBER SKIES, 40° N.

Hold chart overhead

9 PM MDT - Early Sep.
8 PM MDT - Late Sep.

September

*"Moon When the Deer Paw
the Earth"* —Ogallala

CASSIOPEIA (The Lady in the Chair)

217

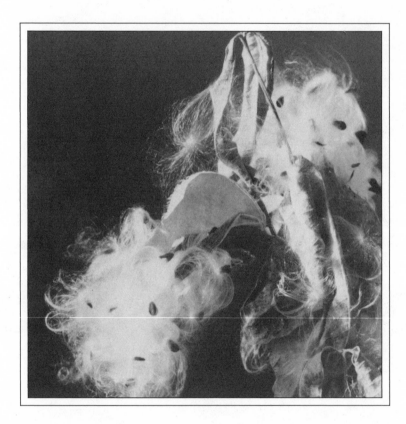

Milkweed seeds

OCTOBER

Cottonwoods, prairie grasses, and "urban forests" are swept by autumn as the season moves to lower elevations. Yellow cottonwoods delineate streambeds, and red sumac paints the foothills. Burgundy grasses turn ordinary fields into seas of wine. Orange pumpkins splotch brown farmlands. Along fencerows wild asparagus is transformed into frothy golden trees hung with ruby fruit. Silver milkweed seeds drift into the air, and some wild fruits are still to be had for the picking.

In towns, sugar maples steal the show. But other trees also take on a spectrum of colors, ranging from the rich russets of oak to the rose pink of burning bush, from the clear yellow of green ash (one of the earliest trees to change) to the subtle tones of 'Autumn Purple' ash. In recent years several landscaping designs have alternated these two ash species, and the effect is surprising and charming.

Snow is likely to frost the pumpkins and turn the red leaves into out-of-season valentines. But we're just as likely to be blessed with a week of warmth. In his book *Autumn Across America*, Edwin Way Teale credits the poet Richard Jefferies with writing, "broken bits of summer can be found scattered far into the shortening days of fall." Teale then says, "Only on calendars and in almanacs are the lines of division sharply defined." But in this almanac and in this state we are constantly leaping from one season to the next and back again. It's why living here is so exciting.

One of the most electrifying sounds of the year reverberates through the mountains in October—the bugling of the elk. They start sporadically in

Grass

To tell a member of the grass family from a rush or a sedge, here's a mnemonic: Rushes are round, sedges have edges, and grass comes in joints.

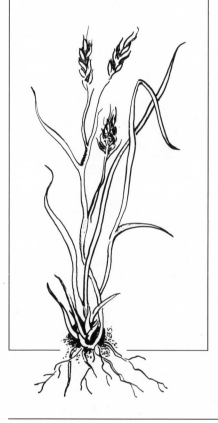

late September and continue through October. Sometimes they sound off during the day, but they are most active at dawn and dusk. Listen for an eerie high-pitched whinny ending in a snort. It's the sort of sound an indignant pig might make, not a majestic elk. A rutting elk is not something to antagonize; keep a respectful distance.

Fall bird migration is in full swing, and each week brings new arrivals to the feeders. We welcome juncos and mountain chickadees, both of which make a vertical migration down from higher elevations. In some years, pine siskins flutter from the trees to the feeder like falling brown leaves, and in other years they are as scarce as Easter daisies at Halloween.

Ducks have completed their late-summer molt and are decked out in new fall finery. Wigeons and ring-necked ducks arrive at local ponds from the north to spend the winter here, and other waterfowl (such as buffleheads, hooded mergansers, and eared and horned grebes) pause on their southward migrations.

October begins with red and yellow leaves and ends with orange pumpkins carved into grins and grimaces—a final rush of color before the muted month of November.

OCTOBER WEATHER

OCTOBER 1

Sunrise: 5:56 AM MST
Sunset: 5:43 PM MST

	Boulder	**Allens Park**	**Niwot Ridge**
	5,445'	8,500'	11,565'
Ave. Max.	72°F	56°F Ave. October high	35°F Ave. October high
Ave. Min.	45°F	30°F Ave. October low	22°F Ave. October low

OCTOBER 31

Sunrise: 6:27 AM MST
Sunset: 5:00 PM MST

Ave. Max.	58°F	56°F Ave. October high	35°F Ave. October high
Ave. Min.	33°F	30°F Ave. October low	22°F Ave. October low

OCTOBER CHANGES (October 1–October 31)

Day Length: 11 hours, 47 minutes to 10 hours, 33 minutes=change of −1 hour 14 minutes

Change: Max.	−14°F	−10°F	−13°F
Change: Min.	−2°F	−8°F	−5°F

OCTOBER EXTREMES

Max. Temp.	90°F	75°F	See note
Min. Temp.	−2°F	0°F	See note
Max. Wind	100 mph	92 mph	Not available
Ave. Precip.	1.47 in.	1.1 in.	1.6 in.
Max. Precip.	6.04 in.	4.0 in.	3.2 in.
Min. Precip.	00 in.	.1 in.	.66 in.
Ave. Snow	4.9 in.	20.7 in.	Not available
Max. Snow	49 in.	81 in.	Not available
Min. Snow	00 in.	00 in.	Not available

Note. 77°F is highest for any summer and −31°F is lowest for any winter on Niwot Ridge.

OCTOBER NOTES

At the end of October 1991 a remarkable temperature drop of 30 degrees in 24 hours (it dropped 21 degrees in 4 minutes in Boulder at one point) caused extensive damage in trees all along the Front Range from Wyoming to central New Mexico. Minimum temperatures were roughly −5°F to +5°F. The episode was preceded by continuous summer weather, offering no transition to winter conditions. Tree damage appeared worst in plantings that were being irrigated heavily and in trees of foreign origin. Native plants are often better able to withstand such events than many familiar introduced plants. Damage was especially common in Siberian elms, cottonwoods that were hybridized with Asiatic species, and peach trees. Damage in Denver public rights-of-way alone was estimated to be $11.6 million.

FLORA

SUMMER ON BORROWED TIME

October is notorious for sudden weather changes. It's possible to see temperatures in the eighties, thunderstorms, and snowfall in a twenty-four-hour period as an Arctic front sweeps across the eastern plains.

Extended periods of warm weather followed by sudden severe freezes are defining events for some plants. However, most Arctic episodes also produce significant snowfall, at least along the foothills, and the snow cover often protects low-growing plants from direct exposure to the full fury of the cold. This blanket, together with frequent mild and sunny spells throughout the winter, explains why so many herbaceous garden plants do far better here than the USDA hardiness zones would suggest.

Aspen II

In *Aspen: Blazon of the High Country*, Ann Zwinger writes: "Northeasterners may praise their massive maples and grandiose oaks, all those russets and reds, but none of those leaves ignite light as aspen do. No one has ever penned an essay on aspen, no one ever composed an aspen string quartet or an aspen rhapsody, nobody ever sprinkled aspen seeds across the country. But a sonnet in their praise is being written, even as I watch, by a breeze and a slant of October sunshine, floating into twilight."

GREENMAN'S APPLES

Hikers in the Boulder Mountain Park are often astonished to find apple trees, pear trees, and other introduced species growing in the steep canyons that cut through the Flatirons. Many, if not most, of these trees were planted by Ernest Greenman, an early Boulder business owner and naturalist.

Ernest Greenman came to Boulder in the 1890s to join his brother, Alfred A. Greenman, who had purchased a bookstore on Pearl Street. Between 1892 and 1945, the two Greenmans, along with Alfred's daughter Dorothy, managed the original store and a second store on University Hill. The University Hill store, known as Greenman's Drugs, featured the Hill's first lunch counter, a popular hangout for CU students.

While Alfred's interests turned toward civic affairs (he served as Boulder's mayor from 1909–11 and as president of the Chautauqua Association during the 1920s and 1930s), Ernest developed a passion for nature. "He loved the outdoors. It was his life," says his niece, Dorothy Greenman, who still lives in Boulder. "When we went on walks in the mountains, he would carry seeds of all kinds in his pockets and scatter them around the springs."

Ernest Greenman was one of the founders of the Rocky Mountain Climbers Club. This group has been continuously active in Boulder since 1898 and still meets monthly in the old Chautauqua Community Building. An avid rock climber, Ernest completed more than one hundred climbs of the Third Flatiron. His photographic collection, now stored in the Carnegie Library in Boulder, shows club members standing atop Longs and other local peaks and picnicking in the Flatirons.

He delighted in taking out-of-town visitors on walking tours of the Indian Peaks. A brochure he published in 1924, titled "Greenman's Arapahoe Glacier Tours," proclaimed that he had led thirty-four trips to Arapaho Peak.* The brochure described sights along the way, including Eagle Rock near Boulder Falls (this golden eagle nest site is still active today), Castle Rock, Nederland Dam, Eldora, Diamond Cascade, and another golden eagle nest on "the crags" of Arapaho Peak. The brochure continued:

*The usual spelling of the name of the glacier, the peak, and the Indian tribe is "Arapaho," whereas the road in Boulder is spelled "Arapahoe."

"Tiny rock rabbits, portly marmots and big horn sheep are frequently seen. Glacial action is evident in all of these high valleys. Beautiful lakes mirror polished rock walls and corniced snowbanks that rise above them."

When Ernest Greenman died in 1960, the Climbers Club placed a commemorative plaque on the Third Flatiron, and a trail up the North Ridge of Green Mountain was named for him. (The plaque was later removed by vandals.) On the way up to Green Mountain summit you can still see apple trees growing along Gregory Creek. At dusk Abert's squirrels, raccoons, porcupines, and black bears climb up into the tangled, overgrown branches to harvest the ripe fruits. These mammals scatter the seed around in their own way, ensuring that descendants of Greenman's original trees will continue to grow for many generations.

FAUNA

TRUMPETS OF AUTUMN

When snow begins to accumulate in Front Range subalpine forests, elk herds move down the mountains to pass the winter at lower elevations. The bugling of bull elk, a sound as eerie and penetrating as the howl of a wolf or the cry of a loon, sends a shiver of wildness and urgency through the cold autumn nights.

Elk (also known as wapiti) begin to gather in mountain meadows in late September. Bugling usually climaxes in mid-October as mature males let off steam while nervously supervising harems of five to fifteen cows. Sparring bulls lock antlers to establish dominance. Cows and calves mill about restlessly. It's a chaotic scene. The outcome, apparent by mid-November, when mating occurs, is the sorting out of the herd into discrete groups, ensuring that only the most dominant and fit males pass on their genes to ensuing generations.

Scientists are unsure about the purpose of bugling. Some believe it serves mainly to warn away other bulls. Others, including University of Colorado mammologist David Armstrong, dispute the notion that bugling is primarily a threat

Wapiti or Elk

During winter these large animals supplement their main diet of grasses and forbs with twigs and bark. Their population is so large in Rocky Mountain National Park that they are seriously affecting the park's aspen forests.

behavior. In his book *Rocky Mountain Mammals*, he says: "In part, at least, (bugling) is a sort of 'safety valve' to release the tension or excitement of seasonal physiological changes in the bull."

Whatever its impact on other elk, bugling has an almost mystical attraction to humans. In October, thousands of people converge on Horseshoe and Moraine parks in Rocky Mountain National Park to watch and listen to the elk. Disconcerting traffic jams develop along Trail Ridge Road, and often the most audible sounds are the clatter of cameras and the rumbling of automobile engines. Somehow the wapiti survive the tourist crush, but for all parties concerned, the experience is less than optimal.

To avoid the crowds, visit one of many more remote meadows where elk congregate in northern Boulder County, southern Larimer County, or Rocky Mountain National Park. Look for meadows or broad valleys between 7,500 and 10,000 feet (a 7½-minute topographic map is useful). Plan to arrive an hour or two before sunset, and consider spending the night. There's nothing more stimulating or soul-renewing than awakening on a crisp autumn morning to the bansheelike squeals of an enraptured bull elk.

The storms of October bring sounds of wildness and restlessness to the plains as well. While hiking on the plains during the first two weeks of the month you might hear a haunting, pulsating rattle overhead as a sandhill crane flock streams southward. Most of the half-million or so sandhill cranes that inhabit North America migrate through central Nebraska. A smaller group flies southward from the Gray's Lake area in Idaho to the San Luis Valley in Colorado and on to Bosque del Apache Wildlife Refuge in New Mexico. Almost every year a few strays from one of these flocks pass through Boulder County. On October 11, 1986, about ten thousand cranes stopped in a cornfield near Haystack Mountain during a snowstorm. The following day, crane sightings (some in the thousands) were reported from Flagstaff Mountain to Broomfield.

A metallic honking high overhead indicates the passing of a flock of snow geese. Look for strings of white pearls against the blue sky. Many of the infrequent snow geese sightings in Boulder County occur in late fall as the geese fly through on their way from breeding grounds north of the Arctic Circle to wintering areas in the southern United States and Mexico.

The honking of Canada geese and the quacking of ducks resonate toward the end of October as lakes and rivers to the north freeze. The first hooded mergansers appear on Baseline Reservoir, and the first buffleheads and common goldeneyes arrive at Walden Ponds. Blue-winged and cinnamon teal, eschewing the cold, leave for Argentina and other points south.

Waterfowl-watching improves as the month progresses, since this is the time of year when most duck species molt, exchanging their drab summer plumage for colorful mating plumage. Once the males are properly decked out, courtship can begin.

To an optimist, the soft quacking and head-bobbing of a pair of mallards on a half-frozen pond is a harbinger of spring. The same could be said for the restless coming together of an elk herd in a mountain meadow. Even as winter darkness approaches, the process of renewal has begun.

ELK MIGRATION CORRIDORS

How can parks and conservation areas be designed to provide sufficient habitat for wildlife? One approach is to make park boundaries encompass home ranges of large mammals such as elk, mountain

OCTOBER WATERFOWL-WATCHING

Species	Walden Ponds	Baseline Reservoir	Valmont Reservoir	Union Reservoir	Gaynor Lakes
Common Loon	*	*	*	*	
Pied-billed Grebe	**	**	*	**	*
Horned Grebe	*	**	*	**	*
Eared Grebe	*	**	*	**	
Western Grebe	*	*	**	**	
Clark's Grebe		*	*	*	
White Pelican				*	
Canada Goose	**	**	**	**	*
Wood Duck	*				
Green-winged Teal	**	**	**	*	**
Mallard	**	**	**	**	**
Northern Pintail	**	**	**	*	**
Blue-winged Teal	*	*	*		*
Cinnamon Teal	*	*	*		*
Northern Shoveler	**	**	**		**
Gadwall	**	**	**	*	**
American Wigeon	**	**	**	*	**
Canvasback	*	*	*	*	*
Redhead	**	**	*	*	*
Ring-necked Duck	**	**	*	*	*
Lesser Scaup	**	*	*	*	*
Common Goldeneye	*	*			
Bufflehead	*	*	*		*
Hooded Merganser	*	**			
Common Merganser	*	*	*		
Red-breasted Merganser				*	
Ruddy Duck	*	*		*	*

*—Possible   **—Likely

Note: Species vary from week to week and year to year. As a general rule, dabblers, such as mallards and pintails, are more common on shallow lakes; diving ducks, mergansers, and grebes are more abundant on deeper lakes.

Source: Boulder County Audubon Society, Monthly Wildlife Inventories 1975–92.

lions, and black bears. Unfortunately, none of the existing national parks and wilderness areas within the lower forty-eight states are large enough to do this. A second approach, long advocated by landscape ecologists, is to preserve islands of relatively pristine habitat, called core areas, and connect them with migration corridors.

In Boulder County, core areas might include the Indian Peaks Wilderness, North St. Vrain Canyon, and Boulder Mountain Park. Migration corridors might include undisturbed riparian ecosystems and other known migration routes of large mammals.

Since 1987, the Boulder County Nature Association (BCNA) has cooperated with the U.S. Forest Service and the Colorado Division of Wildlife to study elk migration patterns throughout the County. Elk are radio-collared and tracked on foot or by vehicle and helicopter. One goal is to locate migration corridors and divert development away from them. Dave Hallock, a Boulder County Parks planner and BCNA volunteer, believes that information gathered from this study may lead to preservation of essential habitat for a variety of wildlife species: "Casual observations suggest that the elk migration routes are also

being used by mountain lions, bears, and other species that have large territories. It's easiest to study elk. In essence, we're using elk as an indicator species for where the main movement corridors remain."

Wapiti once ranged over all of Boulder County. In fact, their historic range encompassed much of North America, including the Eastern Seaboard. By the early twentieth century most, if not all, of the elk in Boulder County had been exterminated by hunters. Hallock says elk were reintroduced in Boulder County by federal agencies around 1915: "They brought them down from the Grand Teton region in trucks, and some were even shipped in by train."

Today elk are relatively abundant along the Colorado Front Range. Overpopulation of elk in Rocky Mountain National Park has led to a significant decline in the number of aspen (the wapiti rub against the trees, eat the bark in winter, and destroy young trees in summer) and prompted some biologists to advocate reintroducing wolves to help control elk numbers.

Elk migration patterns within Boulder County are complex. Some individuals may move as far as 20 miles from summer range in the high country to winter range in the foothills. Older bulls may remain in the same general area throughout the year. In winter you can sometimes see wapiti grazing east of the Foothills Highway near Lyons. In summer some wapiti range into the alpine tundra and have been seen crossing the Continental Divide.

Hallock has carefully monitored the movements of the Winiger Ridge herd, which summers in the high country west of Eldora and winters in the Walker Ranch area just west of the Boulder Mountain Park. This herd's movements are threatened by housing developments along Magnolia Road. Hallock believes the Winiger Ridge herd sometimes makes its spring trek through this developed region on a single night, under the full moon. "On the movement corridors through developed areas, it almost seems like they're picking nighttime to get through these areas. They're showing an ability to get through, but also showing a preference to avoid some of these areas entirely."

Boulder County government and BCNA are working to protect elk migration corridors. The corridors are designated as "critical wildlife habitat" in the Boulder County Comprehensive Plan. New subdivisions must locate their units in areas where there is minimal impact on the movement corridors. Both BCNA and the county have been successful in working with property owners to establish conservation easements that prohibit or limit future development of their land. Success of this program will affect a variety of species that need room to roam in our increasingly urbanized environment.

WHERE TO GO IN OCTOBER

MAPLETON HISTORIC DISTRICT

Take a zigzag walk along Mapleton, Highland, Spruce, and Pine streets in the older section of Boulder between 9th and Sunshine Canyon. In the 1890s, James P. Maxwell (member of the Colorado Legislature, surveyor, and engineer) planted two hundred silver maples along Mapleton with wooden boxes to protect them from being devoured by horses. Evidently deer were not such a menace

in those days. A few years later the city council decided to grade the street and ordered the trees removed. Then, as now, Boulderites came to the defense of trees, and the order was rescinded.

Since many of these relatively brittle trees are reaching the end of their life spans, the Boulder Parks and Recreation Department began replacing them with sugar and Schwedler maples in 1970.

Start your walk near Mapleton School (built in 1888) at 9th Street, paying special homage to the red maple, *Acer rubrum*, planted in honor of Susan Lovelace, the school's first principal. At each corner, turn in the direction where the color is most irresistible. Crunch through the crispy leaves in the gutters and sit to enjoy the scenery at Campbell Robertson Park (5th and Mountain View), dedicated to a man who knew every tree in the city and shared his knowledge generously. A "Walking Tour" brochure describing many of the historic houses is available at Historic Boulder (18th and Canyon).

Northern Flicker

In the fall these birds peck at wood siding looking for insects that are seeking shelter from increasingly cold weather. In the spring they "drum" on metal vents to claim territory, and may even peck nest holes in siding. Bitter-tasting repellents can discourage nest-hole pecking.

UNIVERSITY OF COLORADO CAMPUS

Stately American elms once dominated the campus. About fifty elms still thrive, but most have succumbed to Dutch elm disease and have been replaced with a variety of trees and shrubs. This trend toward diversity is a healthy reaction to diseases such as Dutch elm and chestnut blight. These diseases can wipe a campus or a town clean if only one tree species is planted. One of the unusual trees to look for on campus is the ginkgo (*Ginkgo biloba*) at the southeast corner of Macky Auditorium. This species is sometimes called a living fossil because it dates back to the Triassic period (195–225 million years ago) and is considered the oldest living species of tree. Although it looks like other deciduous trees, which are grouped among the angiosperms, the ginkgo is a gymnosperm, as are spruces, firs, and pines.

A noteworthy shrub now fairly widespread both on campus and in town is the aptly named burning bush (*Euonymus alata*). It turns a singular shade of rose pink, almost the same shade as the inside of prickly pear fruit, when grown in a sunny location. Bright red Virginia creeper climbs many buildings and contrasts with the rosy sandstone, quarried near the town of Lyons and on Sanitas Mountain. Wander around Varsity Pond and down the path behind Sewall Hall to Boulder Creek, or just wander. "Tree walks" are occasionally held on campus, and self-guided tree-walk pamphlets are available at the Henderson Museum.

ANDREWS ARBORETUM

A few blocks north of the CU campus, at the intersection of Broadway and Marine, the Andrews Arboretum contains close to a hundred varieties of trees and shrubs. The three-block pedestrian walkway (wheelchair accessible) follows part of the route of the railroad trolley that once linked Boulder to Denver. This plant preserve is named for Darwin Andrews (1878–1938), a Boulder horticulturist who traveled widely, exchanging seeds with botanists in Europe, Russia, and Asia.

COTTONWOOD TRAIL

Cottonwoods and an understory of chokecherry, plum, golden currants, and wild roses paint a small streamside in October. The path follows a creek for about 2 miles round-trip. Park at the trailhead near Hayden Lake, adjacent to the Boulder municipal airport, on Independence Road east of SR 119.

CENTENNIAL TRAIL

East of 55th Street in Boulder, this trail skirts Flatirons Municipal Golf Course, where dignified Canada geese patrol the grounds. Farther on, the trail passes a llama farm, where the long-lashed, big-eyed creatures watch walkers curiously. The willows and cottonwoods put on a good show in October, and in May baby screech owls sometimes peer from cavities in the trees. West of 55th, the trail follows sidewalks through a residential area.

You can park at the Centennial Trailhead along 55th Street halfway between Arapahoe and Baseline. However, there is better parking at the Bobolink Trailhead, 0.1-mile west of the intersection of Baseline and Cherryvale. Cross Baseline and walk one block along Dimmit Drive to catch the Centennial Trail. The distance from Dimmit to 55th is 1 mile. South Boulder Creek Trail (see the July chapter) also originates here and is a beautiful October hike because of the

yellow cottonwoods and pink and gold grasses in the adjacent prairies.

BLUEBELL-BAIRD TRAIL

A particularly photogenic smooth sumac stand, with views of the Flatirons beyond, is halfway along this 1-mile trail that connects Baird Park and the Bluebell Shelter House. Several access trails to the Flatirons branch off from the trail.

Turn left at the point where Baseline Road starts up Flagstaff and continue about a block to the trailhead and a small parking area at Baird Park. When you reach the Bluebell Shelter, you can continue south on the Mesa Trail (see the April chapter) or take one of the other trails that radiate from this point. Another extensive smooth sumac patch at the south end of the Mesa Trail just north of the Dunn House also turns crimson early in the month. Adjacent to the Dunn House is a very old orchard that still yields succulent apples.

FARMLANDS IN EASTERN BOULDER COUNTY

Drive through the farm country to admire pumpkin patches and to watch for ring-necked pheasants. You might want to stop at Nishida's, west of Longmont on Ute Road, Munson's at 75th and Valmont, or Dexter's at 95th and Valmont, where pumpkin art abounds. Also stop at the Gaynor Lakes (on Oxford Road between 95th and US 287) for waterfowl-watching.

Sugar beets, raised in the fields east of Longmont, often fall from trucks and can be picked up from the edges of dirt roads around Union Reservoir in mid- to late October. Somewhat woody in texture, they can be sliced and boiled with a bit of vinegar to add zing. Some people even make sugar beet wine.

Crane Hollow Road, between St. Vrain and Hygiene roads, is a particularly inviting country lane. The record-holding largest cottonwood tree in the United States can be seen from the road but is on private property. The National Register of Big Trees lists it as 432 inches in circumference and 105 feet in height.

OCTOBER OUT-OF-COUNTY EXCURSIONS

Early in October, aspen usually peak at Grand Mesa east of Grand Junction. The cottonwoods along the Colorado River west of Grand Junction peak around the middle of the month, when a canoe trip through Ruby and Horsethief canyons is glorious. Just an hour's drive west of Grand Junction is Moab, a mecca for mountain bicyclists and hikers who enjoy isolated canyons, arches, and petroglyphs. Crisp October weather is perfect for canyon exploration.

OCTOBER AT A GLANCE

MAMMALS

- Elk bugling and sparring reaches peak.
- White-tailed deer mate in October and November.
- Marmots hibernate, sometimes starting as early as September.

BIRDS

- Unusual migrants, such as sandhill cranes and snow geese, pass through.
- Flicker pecking increases as critters crawl into crevices.
- Hooded mergansers, buffleheads, and common goldeneyes arrive at ponds. Juncos and mountain chickadees move to lower elevations.

OTHER CRITTERS

- Rattlesnakes converge on communal hibernating sites in rocky hillsides and prairie dog towns.
- Brown trout spawn.

PLANTS

- Cottonwoods, maples, various species of ash, and variegated shrubs reach peak color at lower elevations.
- Pumpkins ripen.
- Chrysanthemums and other late flowers continue to bloom in gardens.
- It's time to plant bulbs for next spring.

SPECIAL EVENTS

- Big-game hunting season is in progress. Check with the Colorado Division of Wildlife for specific dates, and wear bright colors if you go where there are hunters.

OCTOBER AT A GLANCE
(Continued)

IN THE SKY

- The Orionid meteor shower appears in the southeast sky around October 19–22.
- Pegasus (The Winged Horse) is high in the southern sky around 9:00 P.M. This constellation can be located by drawing a line from the North Star (Polaris) through Cassiopeia and extending the line an equivalent distance. Pegasus is said to look like the head, neck, and forelegs of an upside-down horse. The Great Square, which might be interpreted as the horse's chest, contains three second-magnitude stars.

WHY IS THE SKY BLUE
AND WHY IS IT BLUER IN OCTOBER?

Atmospheric scattering of light is responsible for both the blue color of the sky during the day and the red color of sunrise and sunset. The constituents and pollutants of our atmosphere scatter short (blue) wavelengths of light more readily than they do long (red) wavelengths. When we gaze along a line of sight away from the sun, we see blue light that has been scattered away from its original direction. At sunset we can view lines of sight closer to the sun, and so we see the unscattered red light. The additional column length of atmosphere traversed at sunrise and sunset amplifies the red effect because there are more molecules to scatter the light. Fine particulates from forest fires and volcanoes also contribute to the reddening of sunlight. Sunrises and sunsets were unusually spectacular during the year following the eruption of Pinatubo.

Excessive water vapor gives the sky a whitish cast. The relative lack of water vapor in Colorado's October skies lets them appear an even deeper blue than usual.

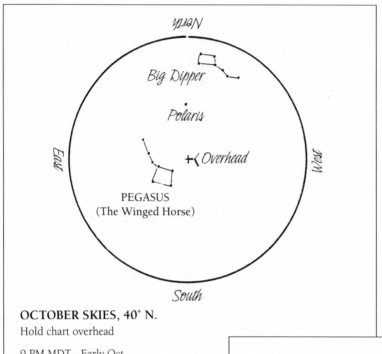

North

Big Dipper

Polaris

+< *Overhead*

East

West

PEGASUS
(The Winged Horse)

South

OCTOBER SKIES, 40° N.

Hold chart overhead

9 PM MDT - Early Oct.
8 PM MDT - Late Oct.

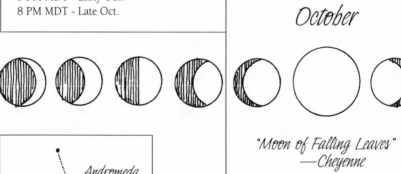

October

*"Moon of Falling Leaves"
—Cheyenne*

Andromeda

PEGASUS (The Winged Horse)

236

Common goldeneye in breeding plumage

Ferruginous hawk, Marshall Mesa

NOVEMBER

There's a poignancy to finding the last flower, the last gleaning from the garden, the last fading yellow leaf. But there is joy in the bittersweetness of the year's end as well as in the exuberance of its beginning.

In mild years we have picked the last mustard greens on November 11, the last raspberry on the fourteenth (when the forsythia ill-advisedly burst into bloom), and the last rose during the winter solstice. In other years we have skied around Sawhill Ponds and shivered, listening to the dry poplar leaves applauding the tune of the wind.

The wind provides updrafts that raptors use to effortlessly ascend so high we can no longer see them. The changing of the guard is now complete, as wintering ferruginous and rough-legged hawks take over niches vacated by Swainson's hawks long since departed to Argentina. But the big event of the month is the arrival of the bald eagles, who spend winter here feeding on fish and prairie dogs.

How can a month be dull that includes bald eagles? Or the sparring and mating of mule deer? Bucks that usually move off when chased from a garden become belligerent during November. They are unpredictable and have been known to gore pets and turn on humans.

November has been called "the pewter month" because of its soft silver light. It can also be a diamond-and-sapphire month when hoarfrost coats each twig and each blade of grass and is then splintered into multiple facets by the rising sun. This phenomenon is especially pronounced in riparian areas and happens after a cold, clear, windless night when

Goldfinches

American goldfinches have exchanged their dazzling yellow coats for drab feathers of brown and buff. It's easy now to confuse them with pine siskins (whose yellow patches have also faded), especially since goldfinches and siskins are frequently found in mixed flocks. Look for goldfinches and siskins feeding on dried common teasel flower heads at the edges of wetlands.

moisture crystallizes on every surface in a pattern suggestive of fern fronds. Rime frost, a similar creation, occurs when fog or supercooled water droplets freeze on contact. However, these granular needlelike spikes lack the crystalline detail found in hoar frost.

Red-and-black box elder bugs also brighten the muted landscape. These small harmless beetles, as well as spiders and still-chirruping crickets, are out looking for a winter home—which may be yours! In the foothills, a brown, inch-long insect locally called the "ponderosa bug" invades houses by the hundreds and is said to smell like cinnamon when crushed.

Because insects are more visible when leaves are gone, now is a good time to observe them. It's also a good time to find empty bird nests, such as the pendulous baskets woven by orioles, that were invisible in June.

Color persists in many plants. Red continues to deepen in creeping mahonia leaves that are exposed to the sun, and the color lasts throughout the winter. Also red are leaves of the matlike sulphur flower and the hips of wild rose. Prairie grasses retain

Boulder's Three Nuthatches
and their distinctive calls.

White-Breasted
"Yank, Yank, Yank"

Red-Breasted
"Ink, Ink, Ink"

Pygmy
"Peep, Peep, Peep"

traces of pink and yellow. Bracken ferns, the color of spice, also smell like spice when you walk through them. Deciduous mountain mahogany, milkweed pods, common teasel, and cattails in shades of tan and brown decorate the edges of trails and ponds. Kinnikinnick berries could be called Colorado's version of holly – they presage the spirit of Christmas.

These gifts of nature all contradict Thomas Hood's lines: "No sun – no morn! No noon . . . No shade, no shine, no butterflies, no bees, no fruits, no flowers, no leaves, no birds, November!"

However, nature does seem to be wrapping up the show during this in-between month. So festive Thanksgiving is welcome. As usual, the weather can be unusual. There was a year when a heavy snowstorm brought traffic to a halt for several days, and one determined celebrant skied nine miles round-trip to bring home the turkey.

NOVEMBER WEATHER

NOVEMBER 1

Sunrise:	6:28 AM MST		
Sunset:	4:58 PM MST		

	Boulder	**Allens Park**	**Niwot Ridge**
	5,445'	8,500'	11,565'
Ave. Max.	57°F	44°F Ave. November high	24°F Ave. November high
Ave. Min.	34°F	21°F Ave. November low	12°F Ave. November low

NOVEMBER 30

Sunrise:	7:01 AM MST		
Sunset:	4:36 PM MST		
Ave. Max.	50°F	44°F Ave. November high	24°F Ave. November high
Ave. Min.	26°F	21°F Ave. November low	12°F Ave. November low

NOVEMBER CHANGES (November 1–November 30)

Day Length: 10 hours, 30 minutes to 9 hours, 35 minutes=change of −55 minutes

Change: Max.	−7°F	−12°F	−11°F
Change: Min.	−8°F	−9°F	−10°F

NOVEMBER EXTREMES

Max. Temp.	79°F	63°F	See note
Min. Temp.	−12°F	−16°F	See note
Max. Wind	125 mph	96 mph	Not available
Ave. Precip.	.89 in.	1 in.	6 in.
Max. Precip.	3.7 in.	2.2 in.	10.9 in.
Min. Precip.	00 in.	.2 in.	2.52 in.
Ave. Snow	10 in.	17 in.	Not available
Max. Snow	47 in.	38 in.	Not available
Min. Snow	00 in.	2 in.	Not available

Note. 77°F is highest for any summer and −31°F is lowest for any winter on Niwot Ridge.

FLORA

ENDINGS AND BEGINNINGS

In late fall, when the leaves and flowers of summer are gone, seeds become more conspicuous. "There is not that profusion and consequent confusion of events which belongs to a summer's walk," wrote Thoreau, "what does occur affects us as more simple and significant." Because nature has been reduced to essentials, it's a good time to marvel at the amazing strategies for seed dispersal, dormancy, and germination that have evolved in response to our rigorous climate.

Seed dispersal strategies involve wind, water, coiling tails, mammals and birds, explosions, and sticky coatings. By dispersing seeds, plants avoid the problem of too many offspring germinating in the same place and becoming vulnerable to the same disasters. Dispersal also limits competition among siblings and with parents and expands the range of the plant.

One of the most fascinating methods of seed dispersal is used by various mountain mahogany species (*Cercocarpus* spp.). The seeds' feathery "tails" coil up when wet and straighten out when dry. Time-lapse photography reveals that these self-propelled spirals actually drill the seeds into the ground. Wild geranium seeds (*Geranium* spp.) explode when ripe, traveling outward away from the parent plant. Rabbitbrush (*Chrysothamnus* spp.) seeds have dandelionlike plumes that aid in wind dispersal. The variety is limitless.

Seed dormancy helps assure that seeds remain viable until conditions are right for successful germination and initial growth. Recent research suggests that the inert appearance of seeds in dormancy is misleading. Often a considerable amount of metabolic activity takes place.

Before germination can occur, a combination of conditions that vary with individual species must be met. The papery seed husks of saltbush (*Atriplex* spp.) contain inhibitors that must be soaked away. Early blooming penstemons (*Penstemon* spp.) often disperse seed during the heat of summer and require a period of cold, damp conditions before germinating. The seed of many penstemon species seems to germinate best after aging, sometimes for years. A few seeds, like those of creeping mahonia

Wild Plants

Clandestine collection of wild plants is rather like shoplifting—it doesn't work very well, and you might get caught. In addition, the roots of wild plants are often so extensive that successful transplanting is very difficult.

(*Mahonia repens*), germinate best after repeated periods of coldness and warmth. The seeds of the mountain common juniper (*Juniperus communis saxatilis*) appear to do best after being digested by birds. The variations are probably equal to the vagaries of the local climate and help assure that most seeds germinate only when conditions are favorable, thus perpetuating the species.

Growing your own wild plants is a good way to gain an appreciation of the complexities of seed germination. Success depends on having sunny windows or artificial lights. Some seeds require a period of cold-and-damp treatment (stratification) in the fridge. An increasing number of regional seed companies offer seeds of native plants along with helpful hints on unlocking the mysteries of germinating and growing them.

DORMANCY: MORE THAN LOSS OF LEAVES

Even hardy evergreens vary seasonally in their ability to withstand cold. When extended summerlike weather in fall is followed by a sudden Arctic cold snap, needles of ponderosa pines or other

THE ETHICS OF COLLECTING PLANTS, SEEDS, FRUIT, AND FLOWERS

Because of the perennial lack of commercially available seed for wild plants, the Colorado Native Plant Society somewhat reluctantly supports the ethical and judicious collecting of seeds and cuttings from plants in their native habitat, but only subject to the following abbreviated guidelines. Consult the society (see Appendix 5, page 311) when in doubt, and remember that collecting wild plants is totally prohibited on most of the public open land in Boulder County and elsewhere.

1. Know which plant species are threatened, endangered, sensitive, or of special concern, and do not collect such plants. However, if special circumstances exist, such as imminent destruction of habitat, contact the Colorado Native Plant Society.

2. On public lands, obtain necessary permits for collecting. Know all regulations and report any illegal collecting.

3. On private lands, obtain permission from the landowner.

4. Collect only the minimum amount of plant material necessary, and never collect the only plant at a given site. Consider the cumulative effects of multiple collecting on the survival of the plant population.

5. Do not collect whole plants when seeds or cuttings are adequate.

6. Care properly for the specimens collected. Collect discreetly so as not to encourage others to collect indiscriminately. Be prepared to explain what you are doing.

7. Respect and protect the immediate habitat. Avoid trampling nearby vegetation.

8. Conduct salvage (rescue) projects only on sites that are facing destruction.

9. Don't purchase wild-collected plants or plant parts of rare or protected plants.

Residents of Boulder County have a unique opportunity to protect our pre-European botanical heritage. The native flora of most other regions on earth has been altered more significantly by human activity than has that of Boulder County.

conifers may turn brown. Excessive irrigation or precipitation during extended summerlike fall weather may increase needle discoloration.

Plants generally suffer less from freezing conditions if they are gradually exposed to cooler weather. This preconditioning (called "hardening") of plants to withstand freezing can occur within a few days or may require a period of several weeks. During hardening, physiological changes take place in the plant. Sugars and amino acids accumulate in the cells, and the spaces surrounding the cells and in the conducting tissues change. These adaptations lower the temperature at which water in the plant cells freezes, thus reducing damage to cell structure.

The chilling requirements for hardening are met by accumulating hours of exposure below about 40°F. Once the process has been initiated, it is virtually irreversible. However, an unseasonable heat wave can sometimes shock plants, forcing an early break of dormancy—yet another hazard of the local climate.

All this serves to show that it is not how cold it gets but how it gets cold that really counts in assessing how plants will perform in our "exciting" climate.

FAUNA

HAWKS, EAGLES, AND PRAIRIE DOGS

In October and November, birds of prey stream in from the north to pass the winter in Boulder County. For many of these hawks, eagles, and falcons, the principal attraction is the county's more than 150 active black-tailed prairie dog colonies.

Black-tailed prairie dogs have long been an important food source for hawks and other predators. Francis Parkman, who visited eastern Colorado in 1846, marveled at the abundance of wildlife found in black-tailed prairie dog colonies, including hawks, rattlesnakes, burrowing owls, and badgers. Historically, prairie dog colonies were huge. Parkman described one colony that was ten miles across. These colonies dotted

BOULDER COUNTY RAPTORS
(Excluding Owls)

Species	Local Status	Nesting in Boulder County
Turkey Vulture	Fairly common summer resident	Yes. Remote caves and crevices; foothills, mountains
Osprey	Uncommon migrant	No. A few pairs in north-central and western Colorado
Bald Eagle	Fairly common winter resident, November–March	No. One pair at Barr Lake; others in western Colorado
Northern Harrier	Fairly common in winter; uncommon in summer	Yes. 1–2 pairs at Boulder Reservoir and Lagerman Reservoir
Sharp-shinned Hawk	Uncommon year-round resident	Yes. Dense coniferous forest; foothills, mountains
Cooper's Hawk	Uncommon year-round resident	Yes. Dense coniferous forest; foothills, mountains
Northern Goshawk	Uncommon year-round resident	Yes. Aspen and dense conifers; mountains
Broad-winged Hawk	Rare migrant	No. Nests primarily in eastern deciduous forest
Swainson's Hawk	Common summer resident on plains	Yes. Cottonwoods on plains; winters in South America
Red-tailed Hawk	Common year-round resident	Yes. Trees and cliffs; plains to mountains
Ferruginous Hawk	Common winter resident	No. Great basin and high plains, including eastern Colorado

(Continued on page 248)

BOULDER COUNTY RAPTORS
(Excluding Owls) (Continued)

Species	Local Status	Nesting in Boulder County
Rough-legged Hawk	Fairly common winter resident	No. Nests on tundra north of Arctic Circle
Golden Eagle	Fairly common year-round resident	Yes. Cliffs in foothills and mountains
American Kestrel	Common year-round resident	Yes. Tree cavities; plains to mountains
Merlin	Uncommon-to-rare winter resident	No. North-central U.S., Canada, and Alaska
Prairie Falcon	Uncommon year-round resident	Yes. Cliffs in foothills
Peregrine Falcon	Rare year-round resident	Yes. Cliffs in foothills

Sources: Boulder County Audubon Society, Monthly Wildlife Inventories, 1975–91. Boulder County Nature Association, occasional publications, 1982–91. National Geographic Society, *Field Guide to the Birds of North America.*

the high plains from southern Canada to Texas and contained billions of inhabitants.

The eradication of most prairie dog colonies during the late nineteenth and early twentieth centuries threatened other species. Black-footed ferrets, which lived in the colonies and preyed on the rodents, nearly became extinct. Burrowing owls, once considered common,

disappeared from much of eastern Colorado. Ferruginous hawk numbers declined, along with those of swift foxes and badgers.

When prairie dog colonies began to return to the Colorado Front Range during the 1960s and 1970s, other wildlife returned as well. Most notable was a dramatic increase in birds of prey, including ferruginous hawks, red-tailed hawks, golden eagles, and surprisingly, bald eagles.

By the mid-1980s, wintering bald eagles, once a rarity in our area, had become almost common. Eagles soared over the Boulder-Denver Turnpike, perched on telephone poles along the Foothills Highway, or huddled in cottonwoods along St. Vrain Creek and Left Hand Creek.

The local bald eagle population explosion coincided with an increase in the numbers of bald eagles throughout North America after the ban of DDT and other pesticides. But it was still difficult to understand why there were so many bald eagles in Boulder County. After all, they were thought to prey primarily on fish and waterfowl, which are relatively scarce here in winter. When local observers began to notice bald eagles carrying prairie dogs in their talons, it became apparent that a pattern of predation previously unreported in the scientific literature was occurring in Boulder County. The eagles were following red-tailed hawks and ferruginous hawks and snatching prey from them.

During the winter of 1985–1986, about forty bald eagles roosted each night in a cottonwood grove along Left Hand Creek just east of 47th Street. Each

morning these eagles would fan out to neighboring prairie dog colonies to hunt and scavenge. When a bubonic plague outbreak the following winter killed almost all the prairie dogs in the vicinity, the eagles abandoned the roost. Since then, bald eagles have roosted in smaller groups throughout the county.

Winter eagle- and hawk-watching hot spots include the Dowe Flats/Rabbit Mountain area east of Lyons, Boulder Reservoir, White Rocks/Sawhill Ponds, and Rock Creek Farm Open Space. Raptor-watching is best on cold, cloudy days, when perching raptors are reluctant to fly. Look for bald eagles and rough-legged hawks from early November to late February. Golden eagles, ferruginous hawks, and red-tailed hawks are present throughout the fall and winter months.

Our wintering rough-legged hawks nest north of the Arctic Circle. A few bald eagles nest in Colorado, and a pair has nested for several years at Barr Lake, near Brighton, but most of our wintering bald eagles probably nest in Montana, Washington, British Columbia, and southeast Alaska.

Some incredible interactions occur in prairie dog colonies in winter. One snowy November morning along Rock

Eagles

About half of the bald eagles seen in Boulder County each winter do not have white heads. "Immatures" are dark brown all over with white splotches under the wings and on the breast and tail. They assume full breeding plumage in their fifth year.

Creek, volunteers from a Boulder County Nature Association raptor study saw ten ferruginous hawks and two bald eagles battling over a single prairie dog carcass. Fifty-five participants in a Boulder County Audubon Society field trip to Haystack Mountain watched an immature bald eagle fly up to a soaring golden eagle, roll over onto its back, and snatch a prairie dog from the golden's talons.

In addition to being entertaining, these interactions point out the importance of prairie dogs in the high plains food chain. It's intriguing that prior to 1985 no one had ever written about bald eagle predation upon prairie dogs. Perhaps prairie dogs were eliminated so quickly from the high plains that no scientist had the opportunity to observe this phenomenon. Or perhaps once the prairie dog became known as a "pest," settlers and scientists became oblivious to its role in natural ecosystems.

Fortunately, there are still a few prairie remnants in Boulder County where it's possible to observe, contemplate, and become reeducated. Although the city and county of Boulder continue to poison prairie dogs, they have set aside prairie dog preserves at places like Boulder Reservoir, Rabbit Mountain, and Rock Creek Farm. If you stand in these grasslands as prairie dogs bark out warnings and raptors wheel overhead, you can begin to appreciate Parkman's description of a prairie "teeming with wildlife."

TURKEYS ON THE HOOF

There may be more wild turkeys in Colorado now than were here when the Pilgrims celebrated the first Thanksgiving. Research conducted by the Colorado Division of Wildlife suggests that wild turkeys were native to the scrub oak and piñon-juniper woodlands of southern Colorado but not to the northern half of the state. They may first have appeared in Boulder County as a result of nationwide reintroduction programs in the 1940s and 1950s.

During the 1930s the entire U.S. wild turkey population had dropped to around twenty thousand due to overhunting, habitat loss, and importation of European diseases. For several decades scientists tried to augment native turkey populations by breeding turkeys in captivity and releasing them into the wild. These efforts failed. Turkeys captured from the wild could not survive in captivity. Crossbreeding of domesticated and wild turkeys produced birds that lacked the hardiness and wariness needed to survive in the wild.

The turkey's reputation for stupidity may stem in part from the antics of crossbred turkeys released into the wild. Ted Williams, in the January 1984 *Audubon Magazine*, wrote: "The written word cannot convey the absurdity of their behavior. They strut along the yellow stripes on highways, eat tomatoes from backyard gardens, defecate copiously on car tops and housetops, attack children and motorcycles." Williams goes on to cite an instance where a flock of privately stocked game-farm turkeys "burned down a barn by shorting out the electrical wires upon which [the flock] roosted each night."

Wild-turkey populations began to increase throughout the United States when turkey hunting was severely restricted and when biologists began to use only wild birds in restocking programs. Now the National Wild Turkey Federation estimates there are over 4 million wild turkeys in the United States, and turkeys are found in every state except Alaska. Several thousand reside in Colorado's grasslands, deciduous woodlands, and coniferous forests.

In Boulder County, wild turkeys are

Wild Turkeys

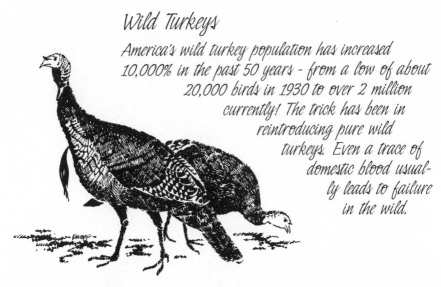

America's wild turkey population has increased 10,000% in the past 50 years - from a low of about 20,000 birds in 1930 to over 2 million currently! The trick has been in reintroducing pure wild turkeys. Even a trace of domestic blood usually leads to failure in the wild.

found mostly in foothills ponderosa pine forests. They forage for seeds, fruits, and insects by day and roost in the pines at night. Look for them at Walker Ranch, Lower Lefthand Canyon, and North St. Vrain Canyon. We've heard turkeys gobbling in remote areas of the Boulder Mountain Park in May and seen them with young in midsummer. By November turkeys will usually have gathered into their winter flocks, which may contain as many as fifty birds.

The wild turkey of the U.S. and Canada (*Meleagris gallopavo*) is one of two species found in the world. The smaller and more colorful *Meleagris ocellata* inhabits southern Mexico and central America. Wild turkeys were domesticated by North American Indians long before Columbus, so the ones we see racing through the woods and the ones we eat on Thanksgiving are the same species. But there's little resemblance between the slow-moving, fat, usually white birds found on turkey farms and their elusive cousins of the forest. Wild turkeys are tough, wily birds that have adapted to a remarkable variety of environments, from the tropical lowlands of Hawaii and the searing deserts of Arizona to the cool pine forests of Boulder County.

WHERE TO GO IN NOVEMBER

RABBIT MOUNTAIN

Bald eagles, golden eagles, and other raptors favor the ridges and updrafts of this county park, where the view stretches from the infinity of the plains to Pikes Peak and Longs Peak. The raptors dine on numerous prairie dogs, which also attract badgers and coyotes. Both white-tailed and mule deer browse on the plentiful shrubs and junipers.

Rabbit Mountain is a mountain that "walks." It lies along two major faults and over eons of time has moved three miles east of the main foothills where it originated. Careful searching of the flatter areas will reveal tepee rings, large circles outlined by partially buried stones, where the Arapaho once camped. More than eighty rings have been found in the vicinity, according to Resource Specialist Randy Coombs. A large prairie dog colony now inhabits one encampment.

Turn north on 53rd Street from Ute Highway (SR 66) between Lyons and Longmont and continue about 4 miles to a marked trailhead. In about half a mile you reach a low saddle where several trails (actually old roads) diverge.

WHITE ROCKS

Another spot to look for bald eagles and other raptors, this area also supports white-tailed and mule deer. Restored gravel pits provide habitat for many water birds, and great horned owls perch in the cottonwoods. (This is also a good place to visit in mid-October, when the cottonwoods turn to gold.)

The buff-colored sandstone formation northwest of the ponds is home to rare miner bees, to black-spleenwort (*Asplenium adiantum-nigrum*), a fern found nowhere else in Colorado, and (in spring) to nesting barn owls.

To protect this unusual ecosystem, the city of Boulder admits only a limited number of researchers with special permits to these rocks. However, a trail skirts the ponds, climbs a small ridge, and in 2.4 miles comes to a T junction. Turn west and continue to the crest of Gunbarrel Hill, a site that was farmed until the mid-1980s. After it was purchased by the City of Boulder Open Space Department, the eroded land was reseeded and allowed to revert to native grasses. Now sideoats grama, blue grama, and little bluestem flaunt distinctive seed heads, and ring-necked pheasants are sometimes seen.

Take Valmont Road to the Teller Farm North trailhead, about 1 mile west of 95th. The trail goes west for a short distance, crosses Valmont Road, and heads north. The White Rocks Trail can also be reached from the White Rocks trailhead, about a mile north of the intersection of Valmont and 95th.

TELLER LAKES

A 2.2-mile trail winds through farmland connecting Valmont and Arapahoe, with a short spur leading to these two lakes, which are good habitats for water birds. Park either at the Teller Farm North trailhead on Valmont (see above) or at the Teller Farm South trailhead on Arapahoe, 1 mile east of 75th.

BIG BLUESTEM TRAIL

To appreciate tallgrass prairie, take this trail through fields of big bluestem, a grass that is blue only in spring. Its color in autumn is both rich and subtle, and it's impossible to achieve unanimity in

describing it. Mauve? Dusky rose? Burgundy diluted with white zinfandel? (One hiker suggested renaming the grass "winestem.") Other native grasses include switchgrass, Indian grass, and muhly. A boggy area is filled with prairie cordgrass, also called sloughgrass (*Spartina pectinata*) – a material used by early settlers for roofing sod houses.

Migrating western and mountain bluebirds and an occasional eastern bluebird have been spotted along this trail, as have hawks and golden eagles.

It's possible to make a 4.3-mile loop by connecting to the Mesa Trail and returning via the South Boulder Creek Trail. Park at the pond west of SR 93 at Thomas Lane (about half a mile north of the Eldorado Springs turnoff).

RATTLESNAKE GULCH

The chance of seeing wild turkeys at the higher elevations makes this trail in Eldorado Springs State Park an apt November choice. The first switchback gives good views of rock climbers. From this point the trail heads up rather steeply and culminates in about 2 miles just below the railroad at the ruins of an old lodge. Built shortly after the turn of the century, this lodge was reached from the railroad and by tramway from the canyon. Look for golden eagles and listen for the mournful train whistle and for the gobble of turkeys.

Take Eldorado Springs Drive to the state park (a park pass is required) just beyond the town of Eldorado Springs. In winter the road is sometimes closed beyond this point. Walk or drive a short distance up the road to the trailhead.

BEAR AND SOUTH BOULDER PEAKS

Bear Peak (8,461 feet) is separated from South Boulder Peak (8,550 feet) by a saddle, so both can be climbed in a single outing. This saddle is unique because six species of conifers can be found here: lodgepole, ponderosa, and limber pine; Douglas fir; and two species of juniper.

The trail is fairly steep, with good views of the plains to the east and snow-capped mountains to the west. Try to time your climb before these peaks, too, become snowcapped and the trail covered with drifts. The usual access is from the Mesa Trail, but there are several routes, so consult a map or climbing guide for mileage and details.

LAGERMAN RESERVOIR

This 116-acre reservoir, treeless and surrounded by open fields, looks barren and often is devoid of wildlife. At other times, especially on a foggy November day, it teems with birds. We have watched common loons and a variety of grebes and ducks on the water, ring-necked pheasants and horned larks in the fields, and on one memorable day a pair of snow buntings.

Because there's nothing higher than fence posts for birds to perch on, the Boulder County Parks and Open Space Department has erected nesting platforms for raptors both here and at Rabbit Mountain. Osprey have been seen fishing at Lagerman; someday soon, perhaps, they will nest here.

The trail around the lake, located at Pike Road and North 73rd, 4 miles southwest of Longmont, is about a mile long.

WANEKA LAKE

Wood ducks, buffleheads, grebes, mergansers, and other water birds have been spotted here during autumn migration. Check around the marina and in the smaller pond just over the low ridge north of Waneka. The level walk around the lake is less than a mile long.

From US 287 in downtown Lafayette, turn onto West Emma and park in the lot where the street dead-ends.

NOVEMBER OUT-OF-COUNTY EXCURSIONS

Head South! Thanksgiving seems an appropriate time to explore Native American ruins of the Southwest in comfortable weather. A four-day weekend is ideal for Mesa Verde or Hovenweep in Colorado, or for Bandelier, Chaco Canyon, or Petroglyphs National Monument in New Mexico. But beware of slick muddy roads if the weather is wet. Bosque del Apache, the destination for many migrating water birds, is a superb wildlife refuge south of Albuquerque.

November

NOVEMBER AT A GLANCE

MAMMALS

- Mule and white-tailed deer spar and mate.
- Black bears go into a deep sleep in late November or early December.

BIRDS

- Ducks put on their brightest nuptial plumage.
- Bald eagles and rough-legged hawks arrive.
- Tundra swans and common loons pause on lakes in eastern Boulder County.
- Snow geese sometimes join large flocks of Canada geese.

OTHER CRITTERS

- Box elder bugs, spiders, and crickets try to move indoors.

PLANTS

- Some plants, such as creeping mahonia, sulphur flower, and prairie grasses retain fall color.
- Seed pods, cattails, and mountain ash berries remain decorative.

SPECIAL EVENTS

- First ski-touring and snowshoeing of the year.

IN THE SKY

- The Leonid meteor shower (look toward Leo) peaks around the fourteenth; the Andromedid (look toward Andromeda and Pegasus) between the seventeenth and the twenty-seventh; the Orionid (look toward Orion) around the nineteenth.
- Cygnus (The Swan or Northern Cross) lies just above the western horizon around 10:00 P.M. This constellation contains Deneb, a first-magnitude star with a luminosity ten thousand times greater than that of our sun.

257

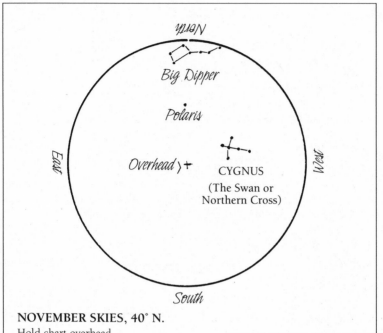

NOVEMBER SKIES, 40° N.
Hold chart overhead

9 PM MST - Early Nov.
8 PM MST - Late Nov.

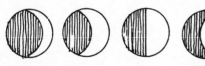

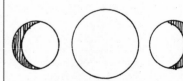

November

"Moon of Storms"
—Cheyenne

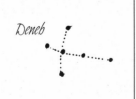

Deneb

CYGNUS (The Swan or Northern Cross)

Cattails at Sawhill Ponds

Bear Canyon

DECEMBER

Chickadees sing. Chickarees chatter. Mounds of snow make marsh-mallow poufs out of rocks in Boulder Creek, where a dipper bobs for bugs. The remnants of prairie grasses flutter like tattered prayer flags. It's finally winter, and we walk or ski into a Christmas card whenever we go outdoors.

All the paintings of winter scenes come to life. Colorado blue spruce trees are flocked with snow, junipers jagged with ice. Canada geese by the thousands fly over frozen lakes, filling the air with wild music.

The weather provides the usual assortment of paradoxes. Although the shortest days of the year come now, December is only the second coldest month. After the winter solstice, around December 21, days become longer. However, to our yearly bemusement, the sun rises at a later time each day until early in January.

The northern hemisphere now tilts away from the sun, which lies low in the southern sky. Shadows are longer, and the quality of the light seems more somber. Some people find the diminishing daylight depressing—an ailment doctors call Seasonal Affective Disorder, or SAD. Emily Dickinson wrote, "There's a certain Slant of light, / on Winter Afternoons— / That oppresses, like the Heft / Of Cathedral Tunes." Others of us savor the cathedral quality of December's light—especially since it often follows days as bright as October's.

By now many animals have turned as white as winter. It's only when a mound of snow winks that it metamorphoses into a ptarmigan, bird of a thousand disguises. Ermine (weasels in winter coats) and snowshoe

---

December

Greens

Since junipers in the yard need
occasional trimming, do it now and
use the cuttings for Christmas
greenery. We frequently create
our Christmas tree from these
trimmings rather than
buy one.

---

hares become visible only when they move. On one December ski outing, white flashed against white, and a long-tailed weasel dashed across the snow. It disappeared into the bloody head of a decapitated elk and began to feed. Aware of our presence but relatively unconcerned, the weasel ducked in and out of the skull. The white coat stained with red reminded us that "Nature, red in tooth and claw" is not only beautiful but also deadly, and that the death of one creature sustains the life of another.

At night, stars in the sky twinkle like frost on the ground. Star scintillation and dancing are especially noticeable near the horizon on cold winter nights, when the star's light travels through a longer column of atmosphere. As the light passes through layers of air with different densities, it is bent in different directions and appears to dance. Sirius, the brightest star in the sky, seems as brilliant as Bethlehem's star could have been. We hold our breath, waiting for miracles.

One perfect Christmas Eve, as snowflakes drifted down and the light deepened to a Maxfield Parrish blue, a doe stepped up to our front door. She stood there several minutes, gazing (but not grazing) at the evergreen wreath. Suddenly seeing us on the other side of the window, she bounded away across the junipers and into the night—another bit of December magic.

DECEMBER WEATHER

DECEMBER 1
Sunrise: 7:02 AM MST
Sunset: 4:36 PM MST

	Boulder	**Allens Park**	**Niwot Ridge**
	5,445'	8,500'	11,565'
Ave. Max.	49°F	37°F Ave. December high	16°F Ave. December high
Ave. Min.	26°F	17°F Ave. December low	5°F Ave. December low

DECEMBER 31
Sunrise: 7:21 AM MST
Sunset: 4:45 PM MST

Ave. Max.	42°F	37°F Ave. December high	16°F Ave. December high
Ave. Min.	18°F	17°F Ave. December low	5°F Ave. December low

DECEMBER CHANGES (December 1–December 31)
Day Length: 9 hours, 34 minutes to 9 hours, 24 minutes=change of −10 minutes

Change: Max.	−7°F	−7°F	−8°F
Change: Min.	−8°F	−4°F	−7°F

DECEMBER EXTREMES

Max. Temp.	76°F	63°F	See note
Min. Temp.	−24°F	−15°F	See note
Max. Wind	120 mph	184 mph	Not available
Ave. Precip.	.71 in.	1.1 in.	7.5 in.
Max. Precip.	4.20 in.	3.6 in.	12.9 in.
Min. Precip.	Trace	.3 in.	1.3 in.
Ave. Snow	10 in.	17 in.	Not available
Max. Snow	31 in.	34 in.	Not available
Min. Snow	00 in.	6 in.	Not available

Note. 77°F is highest for any summer and −31°F is lowest for any winter on Niwot Ridge.

DECEMBER NOTES:
Remarkable Temperature Rise: 31 December 1990, temperature rose 28 degrees in 5 minutes (2°F to 30°F)

FLORA

WINTER SCAVENGING

December can be bitter cold with long periods of below-freezing temperatures. In December 1983, the city of Boulder experienced sixty-nine consecutive hours of temperatures below 0°F. Sub-zero temperatures have been recorded on every date in December, with the record low set on December 22, 1990, at −24°F.

These cold spells are often moderated by periods of remarkably mild weather. Some highs in the seventies can be expected, and sunny days outnumber snowy ones. During warm spells, opportunistic plants may actually begin their annual growth. Winter annuals, which begin their growth cycle in the fall, may also show touches of green. It's always fun to go out hiking on winter solstice searching for these and other signs of the warmer seasons.

On the mesas and in the foothills, look for the tiny silvery blue leaves of prairie sage (*Artemisia ludoviciana*) poking up at the base of last year's desiccated stems; the hairy, cuplike leaves of common mullein (*Verbascum thapsus*); and the lime green leaves of common horehound

(*Marrubium vulgare*) and other mints. Getting an early start may give these plants a competitive advantage over their neighbors, but it also exposes them to risks during long periods of drought or cold. It's interesting to return a few months later to see how these early-greening plants are faring.

The first wildflowers of winter often appear on south-facing shale beds in the foothills. A few days of warm weather combined with adequate soil moisture bring these microhabitats to life. On January 2, 1993, after the snowiest and one of the coldest November-Decembers on record, we found Easter daisies (*Townsendia hookeri* and *T. exscapa*) beginning to bloom in Bear Canyon below the National Center for Atmospheric Research.

During winter, the starch content in roots of some tuberous plants reaches its highest level. Wild licorice (*Glycyrrhiza lepidota*), which grows in moist areas on the plains, is chewy but sweet if dug at the right time. For wild-tuber fanciers with time on their hands, there is the bush morning glory or "man root" (*Ipomoea leptophylla*). This tuber, said to be

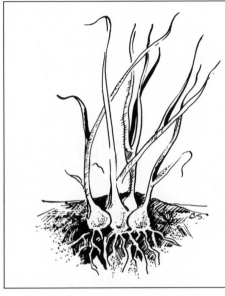

Garlic

In mild winters it's possible to dig up garlic chives and Jerusalem artichokes from the garden for Christmas dinner.

more or less edible, grows up to 1 foot in diameter and extends 10 or more feet into the ground. Historically, botany professors who wanted to get rid of obnoxious graduate students found the phrase, "Why don't you go dig me up a sample of that morning glory bush?" very useful. Red rose hips persist till spring and can be brewed into a rather mild tea. Seeds extracted from the desiccated fruits of prickly pears and then roasted and crushed are reputed to make a zesty addition to winter soups and stews.

CONIFEROUS SEED CROPS

While walking through foothills ponderosa pine forests in December, look for pine cones and listen for bird songs. Every few years, local pine forests produce bumper cone crops. Pine grosbeaks, red-breasted nuthatches, Clark's nutcrackers, and red crossbills flock to the forest to harvest the seeds. These birds, known as irruptive seed-eaters, follow seed crops throughout North American coniferous forests. Seed-crop failures in boreal (cold northern) forests may also

Seeds

Many parts of ponderosa pines are edible, including the seeds that nourish many bird and mammal species. The small seeds are contained in narrow gray sheaves at the base of the cone. They have little taste and are difficult to extract, but eating one or two is a good way to become initiated into the complex food chain of ponderosa pine forests.

stimulate an invasion of our area by irruptive seed-eaters.

Some ecologists suggest that cyclical variation in seed production by conifers serves as a defense against predators. By producing poor seed crops every few years, conifers may control populations of seed-dependent species such as Abert's squirrels and pine grosbeaks.

University of Colorado ecologist Carl Bock, who studied conifer seed crops and songbird irruptions in North America and Asia, concluded that seed-crop fluctuations are synchronized over large geographic areas. Amazingly, conifers in northern Siberia and northern Canada tend to produce poor seed crops during the same years. Bock theorized that trees growing at high latitudes may have evolved "a common sensitivity for a group of regularly fluctuating climatic variables." Seed-crop production of some northern conifers, including Engelmann spruce and subalpine fir, appears to follow predictable cycles. Ponderosa pine seed-crop production is more irregular.

Enchanted Mesa, in the Boulder Mountain Park, is a perfect outdoor laboratory for observing the dynamics and effects of ponderosa pine seed-crop fluctuations. During some winters, Abert's squirrels are hard to miss as they scamper across the forest floor or forage high in the treetops. The "cheep, cheeps" of red crossbills, raucous calls of Clark's nut-crackers, and nasal cries of red-breasted and white-breasted nuthatches fill the air with energy and excitement. In other years the forest is quiet, seeming al-most abandoned. The difference illus-trates the complexity of forest ecology and the remarkable ability of conifers to exert control over their environ-ment.

HINTS ON BIRD FEEDING

Singing trees that bloom in December are an everyday miracle that anyone can have for a few sunflower seeds and a chunk of suet. The "blooms" are actually birds in assorted colors and shapes waiting their turn at the feeder, and even in December some of them sing through the storms. To attract birds you need provide only a few basic necessities: food, water, and cover.

Variety and consistency are the secrets to attracting the greatest number and species of birds. Use different types of feeders placed at different levels and filled with different foods. Black oil sunflower seeds are the most universally popular seeds. However, jays prefer peanuts and corn, juncos also like white proso millet, and goldfinches prefer thistle seeds along with sunflower seeds. Woodpeckers and many other birds go for suet. The mixed wild seed often sold in grocery stores is the least popular with birds.

If sunflower hulls accumulate on the ground, they can kill plants or grass—a disaster that can be prevented by periodically cleaning up the area or by using hulled seeds. Feeders should be cleaned periodically to prevent them from spreading avian diseases.

"If you segregate the seeds, you get a greater variety of birds," says Steve Frye, owner of the Wild Bird Center in Boulder. Frye recommends putting only sunflower or thistle seed in tube feeders, mixed seed in hopper feeders, and millet in platform feeders. Suet can be placed in a wire-mesh cage and fastened to a tree. Some birds, such as juncos, prefer feeding on the ground. Separating types of seed reduces competition and seed loss while increasing variety.

Then come the squirrels. A cartoon caption once asked, "What *did* squirrels eat before bird feeders were invented?" In some cases, a properly placed baffle keeps them off the feeder. However, squirrels can jump at least 8 feet horizontally and 4 feet vertically, so feeders should also be placed out of jumping range. Peaceful coexistence may be the best solution.

Birdbaths should be placed away from "ambush" spots to protect birds from cats. Electrical heaters prevent the water from freezing in winter, and fountain misters or drippers enhance the bath's attraction in summer.

Shrubbery provides cover—a place where birds can shelter from storms and hide from predators. Recycled Christmas trees can be hung with edible "ornaments" made from seed and rendered suet or from peanut butter, thus providing cover, food, and an extension of the Christmas season. Fruiting shrubs and trees, such as crabapples, chokecherries, hawthorns, mountain ash, and junipers, also attract birds. Mountain ash and juniper frequently retain berries until late winter, when more appetizing fruits are gone.

For more information, consult the Wild Bird Center (address in Appendix 5, page 311) or one of the books listed in the bibliography.

FAUNA

WINTER SURVIVORS

For species that do not migrate or hibernate, surviving winter requires effort, resourcefulness, and luck. Raccoons may shiver from the cold as they probe for invertebrates in the icy waters of Boulder Creek. Voles of different species that compete for territories during the summer may share winter nests under the snow to conserve heat. Elk populations may be decimated if the snowpack is unusually deep and long-lasting.

It seems incredible that tiny birds such as chickadees, juncos, and finches can endure night after night of subzero temperatures. Because heat loss in birds and mammals is directly related to the ratio of body mass to body surface area, these lightweight songbirds must burn a lot of calories to maintain steady body temperatures. Studies of goldfinches show that they undergo physiological changes in winter that enable them to convert fat to energy more efficiently. By rapidly burning fuel consumed during the day and by allowing their body temperatures to drop a few degrees, goldfinches are just able to make it through the coldest nights.

Some birds, including poorwills, enter a state of "torpor" on cold nights, with their body temperatures dropping to 50°F or lower. They conserve heat this way but also subject themselves to increased risk from predators. Poorwills are migratory, but a few may remain in Colorado each winter.

Songbirds roost in areas that are sheltered from the wind and where they can absorb heat radiating from trees or boulders. Roosting songbirds fluff out their feathers to trap body heat, and they remain almost motionless through the night. The arteries and veins in the feet of many birds touch, enabling warm blood flowing from the heart to quickly warm the colder blood flowing from the extremities.

The National Institute for Science and Technology property, on South Broadway in Boulder, is a good place to observe roosting songbirds in winter. Black-capped chickadees, dark-eyed juncos, and pine siskins look like tiny puffed-up Christmas ornaments as they cling to the Virginia creeper vine under the eaves of the main building. The birds usually fly into their roosts shortly after sunset.

Many species of songbirds store food during winter. Redpolls and crossbills, which winter in the Arctic and subarctic, have a croplike structure in their throats for storing seeds. Seeds gathered during the day are processed through the digestive tract at night, while the birds are resting. Red-breasted nuthatches store seeds in the bark of ponderosa pines. Clark's nutcrackers cache seeds in the ground, usually on south-facing slopes. During late summer and fall, a single Clark's nutcracker may cache 22,000 to 33,000 seeds. Nutcrackers transport seeds over great distances, making use of a sublingual pouch to carry up to ninety-five seeds per trip.

During December and January, crossbills, nuthatches, Clark's nutcrackers, and pine grosbeaks often forage in foothills ponderosa pine forests. These species are particularly abundant when ponderosa pine seed crops are large. Crossbills wander throughout the year, seeking out areas of the coniferous forest with good seed crops. You can tell whether crossbills are "right- or left-handed" by looking at their bills. The tips of the mandibles cross over, some to the right, others to the left, giving the birds greater leverage for opening pine cones. Crossbills insert their mandibles into cones to force open and hold apart the scales, and then lift the seeds out with their tongues. Since conifer seeds are available throughout the year, crossbills will nest during any month. If you see a reddish songbird sitting on a nest in December, you can almost be sure it's a crossbill.

Winter flocking helps songbirds detect predators and feed more efficiently. In mixed winter flocks of chickadees, nuthatches, and woodpeckers, the woodpeckers help to find food for the smaller birds, and the smaller birds warn the woodpeckers of approaching predators.

Birds traveling in flocks are able to invade winter territories held by other species. Townsend's solitaires, which defend winter territories containing junipers, can do little to resist the onslaught of a flock of several hundred Bohemian waxwings. The waxwings fly from juniper bush to juniper bush, resembling giant aerial schools of fish as they wheel through the air in a pulsating mass. Sometimes the waxwings set up "berry brigades," passing the juniper berries from beak to beak in a bizarre and little-understood example of cooperative feeding.

Like crossbills, Bohemian waxwings move freely from day to day, depending on the availability of wild foods. Winter populations of Bohemian waxwings in Boulder County may vary from zero to tens of thousands.

White-tailed ptarmigan winter high in the mountains, where heat conservation is vital. At night, ptarmigan avoid the elements by burrowing into the snow. When temperatures are well below zero, ptarmigan stay in their snow roosts from sundown to sunrise. Roosting ptarmigan remain alert, and their metabolic rate stays high. However, temperatures in snow roosts are moderate (20°F or higher), and the ptarmigan are able to maintain constant body temperatures with a minimum expenditure of energy.

White-tailed ptarmigan are the only birds that typically winter in the alpine tundra region of Boulder County. Models of heat conservation, they are feathered from head to toe, with only eyes and the bills exposed. Even the nostrils are feathered. The feathers are layered to provide "loft," and barbules within each feather contain air pockets, which provide additional insulation.

Camouflage also helps ptarmigan conserve energy because they don't have to burn precious calories eluding predators. During September and October, their mottled, rock-colored feathers are replaced by a pure white winter plumage that blends with the snowy surroundings. Ptarmigan are so difficult to see in winter that the first hint of a ptarmigan flock may be the sight of a handful of black dots – the birds' eyes and beaks – bobbing across the snow.

Searching for ptarmigan in winter can be frustrating. Clues include a soft, chickenlike clucking; small cylindrical droppings; and feathery three-toed tracks. Look for females in willow thickets around high-country lakes; wintering males are usually found higher up in cirques and willow thickets near tree line. The most popular ptarmigan-watching spot in our area is Guanella Pass, south of Georgetown, where a dirt road winds up into the tundra.

Like ptarmigan, weasels undergo a molt in fall, when their honey brown summer fur is replaced by a snowy winter coat. The white fur helps to conceal them from prey and predators. Because short-tailed weasels (one of two weasel species found in Boulder County) are very active and small, they must consume the equivalent of one-half their body weight in prey each day to maintain a constant body temperature. Fortunately, these fast-moving, sharp-toothed predators, weighing only 1 to 3 ounces, are able to kill mammals much larger than themselves, including rats, pikas, and small rabbits. Short-tailed weasels use the fur of their prey to line winter nests placed in burrows under the snow.

Short-tailed weasels are mostly confined to the county's coniferous forests. The long-tailed weasel, weighing 3 to 7 ounces, is more common and widespread, ranging from the plains to the alpine tundra. Look for the distinctive tracks of weasels along ski trails in the high country. The dumbbell-shaped tracks reveal the weasels' galloping gait.

A variety of other animals shield themselves from winter's harshest elements by maintaining quarters beneath the snow. Northern pocket gophers tunnel and forage on the ground surface, at the base of the snowpack. When the snow melts, their earthen casts look like sections of garden hose scattered across the tundra. Voles and mice also burrow and nest under the snow.

In their book *Winter*, James Halfpenny and Roy Ozanne point out that some species of mammals living under the snow may actually fare best during winters when the snowpack is deepest. A deep snowpack on Niwot Ridge in the spring of 1988 coincided with "a vole population irruption of greater magnitude than had been observed in perhaps thirty years."

Beavers take advantage of ice and water to maintain a comfortable winter environment. Beaver lodges are partially submerged, with underwater entrances. When ponds freeze, beavers swim to and from their lodges under the layer of ice, where the temperature never falls far below 32°F. They feed on tree limbs and herbaceous plants stored on the pond bottom and within the lodge. Yearlings and newborns share the lodge with their parents, so there is plenty of body heat to keep the surroundings warm and cozy. If you stand next to a beaver lodge in winter, you may see steam rising up from below or hear the soft chatter of beavers conversing in the dark.

Beavers are found throughout Boulder County, from the plains to tree line, and they may be as abundant now as they were when the first white fur trappers arrived in Colorado. Beavers are fairly easy to observe if you follow their schedule (mostly nocturnal) and sit absolutely still. Look for beavers at Walden and Sawhill ponds, White Rocks,

Ermine and Marmots

Seasonal adaptive strategies of local wildlife are extremely varied. For example, while marmots hibernate, ermine (winter form of short-tailed weasels) are active through the winter.

The term "ermine" applies only to the winter form of the short-tailed weasel, not to the long-tailed weasel, even though both are white during winter.

along Boulder Creek east of the city of Boulder, and at middle elevations throughout the mountains of Boulder County.

For animals that are able to control their environment, such as beavers, marmots, and bears, winter survival is relatively easy. But for many species, including the superbly adapted ptarmigan and weasel, winter is a time of attrition. High birth rates in spring and summer are necessary to replace those who succumb to the cumulative effects of cold, starvation, and predation.

CHRISTMAS BIRD COUNTS

The first National Audubon Society Christmas Bird Count was held in 1900 as an alternative to Christmas bird shoots. The first Boulder count was held on December 25, 1909. The count summary, reported to *Bird Lore* magazine by Norman Betts, contained the following details:

Boulder, Col. (creek bottom) – 2–5 PM, clear; ground covered with 6 inches of snow, wind west, brisk; temperature about 25 . . . 12 species, 110 individuals.

Now the Boulder Christmas counts run from sunrise to sunset. They attract over one hundred participants, who usually find about one hundred bird species. In addition to the Boulder count, there is a Longmont count, also held in mid- to late December, and an Indian Peaks count, usually held in January. The Indian Peaks count, centered in Eldora, claims the national record for most miles skied by participants and highest elevation reached. The three counts are open to all members of the public, including beginning bird-watchers.

Christmas bird counts have contributed substantially to our understanding of bird populations. Sharp declines in brown pelican and peregrine falcon populations during the 1950s and 1960s were first reported by the Christmas bird-count network. These species were saved from extinction when subsequent studies led to the banning of DDT in the United States. Christmas bird-count statistics help determine the Audubon Society's "Blue List" of North American birds with declining populations.

Christmas bird counts follow a stan-dardized methodology. Each count area is a circle 15 miles in diameter. Participants go out in groups to search every part of the count circle. Those who cannot go out watch feeders at home. Counts are held from Fort Clayton, Panama, where 338 species were seen in 1990, to Prudhoe Bay, Alaska, where 1 species was seen.

To find out more about local counts, call or write the Boulder County Audubon Society, the Foothills Audubon Club, or the Boulder County Nature Association (see Appendix 5, page 311, for addresses).

Boulder Christmas Bird Count Highlights

Most species seen: 108 in 1974

Fewest species seen: 12 in 1909

Most human participants: 154 in 1974

Fewest human participants: 1 in 1909

Most individuals of one species: 55,000 mallards in 1945

Most Bohemian waxwings seen: 11,284 in 1987

Most bald eagles seen: 36 in 1985

First European starling seen: 1945

First house sparrow seen: 1922

Only species seen on every count: Common flicker and black-billed magpie

(black-capped chickadee and mountain chickadee were seen every year but 1945)
Most miserable count day: Possibly 1968, when it was 10–13°F and snowed all day. Twenty-two observers somehow found 12,787 birds (77 species)

WHERE TO GO IN DECEMBER

WILD BASIN

This corner of Rocky Mountain National Park lies in Boulder County and is ideal for early-season ski-touring or snowshoeing because the flat 2-mile road leading to the trailhead needs only a few inches of snow to make a decent track. From the trailhead, continue another 3 miles past Copeland Falls and Calypso Cascade to Ouzel Falls. Beautiful at any time of year, in winter these frozen waterfalls outsparkle a tree strung with fairy lights. For directions to Wild Basin, see the June chapter.

Many excellent snowshoe/ski-touring trails originate in Rocky Mountain National Park. Check at the visitor center or in the park brochure. Herds of elk, deer, and bighorn sheep are commonly seen along park roads in winter.

MIDDLE ST. VRAIN

Also good for early-season ski-touring, snowshoeing, or wildlife-watching, this area offers both a wide road appropriate for beginners and a slightly more difficult trail that avoids snowmobiles. The trail climbs past Timberline Falls (about 2 miles) and heads past the wilderness boundary (about 5.5 miles) to Red Deer Lake at about 8.5 miles. The road continues for about 3 miles beyond Camp Dick. (Also see the July chapter.)

Take either SR 7 or SR 72 to Peaceful Valley and park at the pull-out along the wide curve.

ELDORADO SPRINGS STATE PARK ROAD

An easy winter hike along the road through Eldorado Springs State Park to the picnic area is especially satisfying because of the ice formations – jade and opal studded with diamonds – in South Boulder Creek. Dippers like the rapids in this stretch and, in the spring, canyon wrens can be seen and heard. It's also fun to watch the technical rock climbers who come from all over the world to scale the Bastille and other rocks at the gateway to the park. From the road you can continue up Rattlesnake Gulch, described in the November chapter, or take the Eldorado Canyon Trail to Walker Ranch, described in the May chapter.

Turn west off US 93 onto Eldorado Springs Drive and continue to the west end of town. A state parks pass is required beyond the sign.

BETASSO PRESERVE

The Canyon Trail goes down and up for a 2.75-mile loop through ponderosa pine groves and meadows with views of the plains. This is an agreeable winter hike if the snow is not too deep. Listen for nuthatches and crossbills, and watch for mule deer and soaring bald eagles. Winter plants, such as the green and red rosettes of filaree

and fragrant clumps of sage, may also be found.

From Boulder Canyon, turn north on Sugarloaf Road and go about 1 mile; turn right at the sign for Betasso.

HEATHERWOOD-WALDEN TRAIL

Treated sewage flows into Boulder Creek near 75th Street, creating a warmer microenvironment that attracts ducks in winter and forms frost on nearby weeds and shrubs. Mallards rising suddenly through a cloud of steam make even effluent seem picturesque. Snipe, Virginia rails, great blue herons, kingfishers, and red foxes have also been seen along this stretch.

If snow falls overnight and the temperature remains cold, this trail and the adjoining network of trails at Walden and Sawhill ponds are perfect for a combination birding-skiing-tracking tour. But beware of skiing on the iced-over creek; more than one skier has fallen through. Look overhead for enormous flocks of Canada geese.

Park where 75th Street crosses Boulder Creek just south of Jay Road. It's also possible to follow the creek east of 75th for a short distance (there is no trail) on Boulder Open Space land.

BOULDER VALLEY RANCH

This is still a working ranch, but a network of trails and old farm roads go across mesas and meadows, giving access to both prairie and riparian habitats. A shallow pond near the east end of Eagle Trail attracts waterfowl, and the prairie dogs attract various predators, including coyotes, hawks, and both golden and bald eagles. Great horned owls usually nest in the cottonwoods early in the year.

The first time we hiked this area we searched diligently for Mesa Reservoir and failed to find it, although maps showed a large body of water. Later we learned it has been dry since the 1970s and is being rehabilitated as a wildlife habitat. Boulder Valley Ranch is also a good place to visit in spring, when prairie flowers bloom extravagantly along the shale cliffs.

Three trailheads give access to this area: the Boulder Valley Ranch trailhead on Longhorn Road, 1 mile east of SR 36; the Foothills trailhead, 0.4-mile north of

the intersection of 36 and North Broadway; and the Eagle trailhead, on the west side of 51st Street, half a mile north of the entrance gate to Boulder Reservoir. Eagle, Broken Arrow, Sage, Mesa Reservoir, Cobalt, Degge, and Hidden Valley trails make various loops and permutations throughout the ranch. One of the most interesting routes follows Eagle Trail all the way from 51st to SR 36, passing by the pond, wetlands, and the dry reservoir. One-way distance is 3.4 miles.

WILD BIRD CENTER

Every Saturday morning throughout the year, Steve Frye, owner of the Wild Bird Center at 1641 28th Street in Boulder, leads beginning bird walks along Boulder Creek. The center also provides information on where rare (or just interesting) birds have been spotted.

DECEMBER OUT-OF-COUNTY EXCURSIONS

The Denver Museum of Natural History (2001 Colorado Boulevard) and the

Chautauqua Ranger's Cottage

This is an excellent place to ask questions, pick up maps or nature brochures, and check out the wildflower garden—all plants are native to the mountain backdrop and one section features native butterfly plants.

Denver Botanic Gardens (1005 York Street) are good choices for gloomy winter days and should be prescribed as antidotes to Seasonal Affective Disorder. Actually, they are a delight in any weather and at any time of year. Both have excellent displays and experts to answer natural history or gardening questions. A visit to the conservatory at the Botanic Gardens is like a mini-vacation in the tropics, and in December there's usually a special exhibit, such as Christmas trees through the ages. Plant workshops and classes are offered throughout the year.

Martha Maxwell

If you enjoy museum dioramas, give thanks to one of the first female naturalists and taxidermists: Martha Maxwell. She opened The Rocky Mountain Museum in Boulder in the 1870s, and in 1876 she exhibited her "Rocky Mountain Fauna" at the Philadelphia Centennial Exposition. This may have been the first time that mounted animals and birds were displayed in habitat groupings and naturalistic settings in the United States—a forerunner of today's dioramas. Earlier, she had discovered a subspecies of the screech owl, which was named *Scops asio Maxwelliae* in her honor.

DECEMBER AT A GLANCE

MAMMALS

- Mule deer begin to shed antlers in December and January.
- As deer mating ends, the sexes start to move about in separate groups, with the does, fawns, and yearlings staying together and the bucks traveling in bachelor groups.
- Bighorn sheep dueling and breeding extends from November to January and peaks in December.

BIRDS

- Dippers move down from the high country and are active in creeks at lower elevations.
- Large flocks of Canada geese congregate around open water as migrants from the north join resident geese.

OTHER CRITTERS

- Stone, black, caddis, and crane flies continue their aquatic activities; springtails and snow fleas remain active.

PLANTS

- The forest service opens some areas for Christmas-tree cutting.
- In urban areas, winter pansies continue to bloom, their bright faces peering out from the snow.
- If the ponderosa pines produce bountiful cone crops, invasions of seed-eaters such as crossbills and nuthatches may occur.

SPECIAL EVENTS

- The Audubon Christmas Count takes place across the United States, usually in the week before Christmas.

IN THE SKY

- Winter solstice occurs around December 21, and days begin to lengthen. Traditionally, this was a day to celebrate and hope for the sun's return from the south.
- The Geminid meteor shower, one of the most spectacular of the year, peaks around the twelfth.
- Look for Sirius, The Dog Star and centerpiece of the constellation Canis Major, low in the southeastern sky around 9:00 P.M. Sirius is the brightest star in the heavens. To locate it, extend a line southeastward from the belt of Orion (see the January chapter).

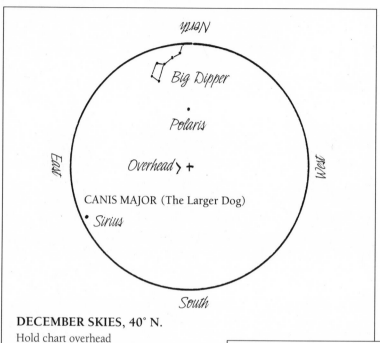

North

Big Dipper

Polaris

Overhead ⟩ +

CANIS MAJOR (The Larger Dog)

• *Sirius*

East

West

South

DECEMBER SKIES, 40° N.

Hold chart overhead

9 PM MST - Early Dec.
8 PM MST - Late Dec.

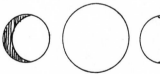

December

"Long Night Moon"
—Sioux

Sirius

CANIS MAJOR (The Larger Dog)

APPENDIXES

SUNSET AND SUNRISE TIMES

BLOOMING TIMES

CHECKLIST OF BIRDS OF BOULDER COUNTY

MAMMALS OF BOULDER COUNTY

LOCAL AND REGIONAL NATURE ORGANIZATIONS

APPENDIX 1
SUNSET & SUNRISE TIMES
(Boulder County)

DAY	JAN Rise A.M.	JAN Set P.M.	FEB Rise A.M.	FEB Set P.M.	MAR Rise A.M.	MAR Set P.M.	APR Rise A.M.	APR Set P.M.	MAY Rise A.M.	MAY Set P.M.	JUNE Rise A.M.	JUNE Set P.M.
1	7 21	4 46	7 08	5 19	6 34	5 52	5 45	6 24	5 01	6 54	4 34	7 22
2	7 21	4 47	7 07	5 21	6 32	5 53	5 43	6 25	5 00	6 55	4 34	7 22
3	7 21	4 48	7 07	5 22	6 31	5 54	5 42	6 26	4 59	6 56	4 33	7 23
4	7 21	4 49	7 06	5 23	6 29	5 55	5 40	6 27	4.57	6 57	4 33	7 24
5	7 21	4 50	7 05	5 24	6 28	5 56	5 38	6 28	4 56	6 58	4 33	7 24
6	7 21	4 50	7 03	5 25	6 26	5 57	5 37	6 29	4 55	6 59	4 32	7 25
7	7 21	4 51	7 02	5 27	6 25	5 58	5 35	6 30	4 54	7 00	4 32	7 26
8	7 21	4 52	7 01	5 28	6 23	5 59	5 34	6 31	4 53	7 01	4 32	7 26
9	7 21	4 53	7 00	5 29	6 22	6 00	5 32	6 32	4 52	7 02	4 32	7 27
10	7 21	4 54	6 59	5 30	6 20	6 01	5 31	6 33	4 51	7 03	4 32	7 27
11	7 21	4 55	6 58	5 31	6 18	6 02	5 29	6 34	4 50	7 04	4 31	7 28
12	7 21	4 56	6 57	5 32	6 17	6 03	5 28	6 35	4 49	7 05	4 31	7 28
13	7 20	4 57	6 56	5 34	6 15	6 04	5 26	6 36	4 48	7 06	4 31	7 29
14	7 20	4 59	6 54	5 35	6 14	6 06	5 25	6 37	4 47	7 06	4 31	7 29
15	7 20	5 00	6 53	5 36	6 12	6 07	5 23	6 38	4 46	7 07	4 31	7 30
16	7 19	5 01	6 52	5 37	6 11	6 08	5 22	6 39	4 45	7 08	4 31	7 30
17	7 19	5 02	6 50	5 38	6 09	6 09	5 20	6 40	4 44	7 09	4 31	7 30
18	7 18	5 03	6 49	5 39	6 07	6 10	5 19	6 41	4 43	7 10	4 31	7 31
19	7 18	5 04	6 48	5 41	6 06	6 11	5 17	6 42	4 42	7 11	4 32	7 31
20	7 17	5 05	6 47	5 42	6 04	6 12	5 16	6 43	4 41	7 12	4 32	7 31
21	7 17	5 06	6 45	5 43	6 01	6 13	5 14	6 44	4 41	7 13	4 32	7 31
22	7 16	5 08	6 44	5 44	6 01	6 14	5 13	6 45	4 40	7 14	4 32	7 32
23	7 15	5 09	6 42	5 45	5 59	6 15	5 12	6 46	4 39	7 15	4 32	7 32
24	7 15	5 10	6 41	5 46	5 58	6 16	5 10	6 47	4 38	7 15	4 33	7 32
25	7 14	5 11	6 40	5 47	5 56	6 17	5 09	6 48	4 38	7 16	4 33	7 32
26	7 13	5 12	6 38	5 48	5 54	6 18	5 07	6 49	4 37	7 17	4 33	7 32
27	7 13	5 13	6 37	5 50	5 53	6 19	5 06	6 50	4 37	7 18	4 34	7 32
28	7 12	5 15	6 35	5 51	5 51	6 20	5 05	6 51	4 36	7 19	4 34	7 32
29	7 11	5 16	6 35	5 52	5 50	6 21	5 04	6 52	4 35	7 19	4 34	7 32
30	7 10	5 17			5 48	6 22	5 02	6 53	4 35	7 20	4 35	7 32
31	7 09	5 18			5 46	6 23			4 34	7 21		

Source: The Nautical Almanac Office of the U.S. Naval Observatory.

Sunrise and sunset times are in Mountain Standard Time at approximately 105°W, 40°N, and are considered valid for any year in the twentieth century. Add one hour for Daylight Saving Time if and when in use.

DAY	JULY Rise A.M.	JULY Set P.M.	AUG Rise A.M.	AUG Set P.M.	SEPT Rise A.M.	SEPT Set P.M.	OCT Rise A.M.	OCT Set P.M.	NOV Rise A.M.	NOV Set P.M.	DEC Rise A.M.	DEC Set P.M.
1	4 35	7 32	4 58	7 13	5 28	6 32	5 56	5 43	6 28	4 58	7 02	4 36
2	4 36	7 32	4 59	7 12	5 28	6 30	5 57	5 41	6 29	4 57	7 03	4 36
3	4 36	7 32	5 00	7 11	5 29	6 29	5 58	5 40	6 31	4 56	7 04	4 36
4	4 37	7 31	5 01	7 10	5 30	6 27	5 59	5 38	6 32	4 55	7 05	4 36
5	4 37	7 31	5 02	7 09	5 31	6 25	6 00	5 37	6 33	4 54	7 06	4 35
6	4 38	7 31	5 03	7 08	5 32	6 24	6 01	5 35	6 34	4 53	7 06	4 35
7	4 39	7 31	5 04	7 07	5 33	6 22	6 02	5 33	6 35	4 52	7 07	4 35
8	4 39	7 30	5 05	7 06	5 34	6 21	6 03	5 32	6 36	4 51	7 08	4 35
9	4 40	7 30	5 06	7 04	5 35	6 19	6 04	5 30	6 37	4 50	7 09	4 35
10	4 41	7 30	5 07	7 03	5 36	6 17	6 05	5 29	6 39	4 49	7 10	4 35
11	4 41	7 29	5 08	7 02	5 37	6 16	6 06	5 27	6 40	4 48	7 11	4 36
12	4 42	7 29	5 09	7 01	5 38	6 14	6 07	5 26	6 41	4 47	7 12	4 36
13	4 43	7 28	5 10	6 59	5 39	6 12	6 08	5 24	6 42	4 46	7 12	4 36
14	4 43	7 28	5 11	6 58	5 40	6 11	6 09	5 23	6 43	4 45	7 13	4 36
15	4 44	7 27	5 12	6 57	5 41	6 09	6 10	5 21	6 44	4 45	7 14	4 36
16	4 45	7 27	5 13	6 55	5 42	6 08	6 11	5 20	6 45	4 44	7 14	4 37
17	4 46	7 26	5 13	6 54	5 42	6 06	6 12	5 18	6 47	4 43	7 15	4 37
18	4 46	7 25	5 14	6 53	5 43	6 04	6 13	5 17	6 48	4 42	7 16	4 37
19	4 47	7 25	5 15	6 51	5 44	6 03	6 14	5 15	6 49	4 42	7 16	4 38
20	4 48	7 24	5 16	6 50	5 45	6 01	6 15	5 14	6 50	4 41	7 17	4 38
21	4 49	7 23	5 17	6 48	5 46	5 59	6 16	5 13	6 51	4 40	7 17	4 39
22	4 50	7 23	5 18	6 47	5 47	5 58	6 17	5 11	6 52	4 40	7 18	4 39
23	4 51	7 22	5 19	6 45	5 48	5 56	6 18	5 10	6 53	4 39	7 18	4 40
24	4 51	7 21	5 20	6 44	5 49	5 54	6 19	5 09	6 54	4 39	7 19	4 40
25	4 52	7 20	5 21	6 42	5 50	5 53	6 20	5 07	6 55	4 38	7 19	4 41
26	4 53	7 19	5 22	6 41	5 51	5 51	6 22	5 06	6 56	4 38	7 20	4 41
27	4 54	7 18	5 23	6 39	5 52	5 50	6 23	5 05	6 58	4 37	7 20	4 42
28	4 55	7 17	5 24	6 38	5 53	5 48	6 24	5 03	6 59	4 37	7 20	4 43
29	4 56	7 16	5 25	6 36	5 54	5 46	6 25	5 02	7 00	4 37	7 21	4 44
30	4 57	7 15	5 26	6 35	5 55	5 45	6 26	5 01	7 01	4 36	7 21	4 44
31	4 58	7 14	5 27	6 33			6 27	5 00			7 21	4 45

The sunrise and sunset times are defined as the time at which the upper edge of the sun's disk appears to be exactly on the horizon. Normal atmospheric conditions, a constant sun diameter, and an unobstructed and unelevated horizon are assumed. Thus, the effects of the mountains are eliminated.

APPENDIX 2
BLOOMING TIMES:
SKUNK CREEK VALLEY 1992

The blooming times shown here indicate that at least a few individual plants were in flower some place along Skunk Creek between Broadway (5,400 feet ±) and the Mesa Trail (6,400 feet ±).

Introduced garden plants are included along with native plants, because they are often excellent indicators of the effects of prolonged periods of "unusual" weather.

PLANT	JAN	FEB	MAR	APR	MAY	JUN
Crocus spp.						
Anemone blanda						
Phlox subulata						
Narcissus spp.						
Eranthis spp.						
Hyacinthus spp.						
Iris danfordiae & I. reticulata						
Mahonia repens (N)						
Galanthus spp.						
Townsendia hookeri & T. exscapa (N)						
Tulipa turkestanica						
Anemone patens (N)						
Prunus armeniaca						
Forsythia sp.						
Prunus tomentosa						
Viola sp. (common blue)						
Cercis canadensis						
Aurinia saxatilis						
Clematis columbiana (N)						
Viola pedatifida (N)						
Ribes aureum (N)						
Claytonia rosea (N)						

1992, as always, had its share of unusual weather. Spring was very warm, with some plants blooming as much as a month earlier than average. Summer was a record-setting cold period, and by September most plants showed about average timing for flowers, seeds, and fall color. The first frost was on October 7.

X indicates fruits, berries, or seeds present
(N) indicates Skunk Creek Valley native plant

PLANT	JUL	AUG	SEPT	OCT	NOV	DEC
Crocus spp.						
Anemone blanda						
Phlox subulata						
Narcissus spp.						
Eranthis spp.						
Hyacinthus spp.						
Iris danfordiae & I. reticulata						
Mahonia repens (N)						
Galanthus spp.						
Townsendia hookeri & T. exscapa (N)						
Tulipa turkestanica						
Anemone patens (N)						
Prunus armeniaca						
Forsythia sp.						
Prunus tomentosa						
Viola sp. (common blue)						
Cercis canadensis						
Aurinia saxatilis						
Clematis columbiana (N)						
Viola pedatifida (N)						
Ribes aureum (N)						
Claytonia rosea (N)						

Appendix 2

PLANT	JAN	FEB	MAR	APR	MAY	JUN
Viola nuttallii (N)						
Malus (crab)						
Amelanchier alnifolia (N)						
Linum perenne (N)						
Rubus deliciosus (N)						
Malus spp. (naturalized)						
Thermopsis divaricarpa (N)						
Mertensia lanceolata (N)						
Delosperma nubigenum						
Verbena bipinnatifida						
Iris missouriensis (N)						
Nepeta X faassenii						
Lonicera tatarica						
Cerastium tomentosum						
Eschscholzia californica						
Crataegus sp. (N)						
Syringa vulgaris						
Spirea X Vanhouttei						
Prunus virginiana (N)						
Scutellaria brittonii (N)						
Oxytropis lambertii (N)						
Leucocrinum montanum (N)						
Arnica fulgens (N)						
Penstemon virens (N)						
Geranium caespitosum (N)						
Lithospermum incisum (N)						
Achillea millefolium ssp. lanulosa (N)						
Prunus americana (N)						
Delphinium nuttallianum (N)						
Lupinus sp. (N)						
Most trees leafed out						
Philadelphus sp.						
Chrysopsis spp. (N)						
Amorpha nana (N)						

Appendix 2

PLANT	JUL	AUG	SEPT	OCT	NOV	DEC
Viola nuttallii (N)						
Malus (crab)						
Amelanchier alnifolia (N)						
Linum perenne (N)	▨					
Rubus deliciosus (N)						
Malus spp. (naturalized)		▨	▨			
Thermopsis divaricarpa (N)						
Mertensia lanceolata (N)						
Delosperma nubigenum						
Verbena bipinnatifida	▨	▨	▨			
Iris missouriensis (N)						
Nepeta X faassenii		▨	▨	▨		
Lonicera tatarica						
Cerastium tomentosum						
Eschscholzia californica	▨	▨	▨	▨		
Crataegus sp. (N)			▨			
Syringa vulgaris						
Spirea X Vanhouttei						
Prunus virginiana (N)						
Scutellaria brittonii (N)						
Oxytropis lambertii (N)						
Leucocrinum montanum (N)						
Arnica fulgens (N)						
Penstemon virens (N)						
Geranium caespitosum (N)	▨	▨	▨			
Lithospermum incisum (N)	▨					
Achillea millefolium ssp. lanulosa (N)	▨	▨	▨			
Prunus americana (N)			▨	▨		
Delphinium nuttallianum (N)						
Lupinus sp. (N)						
Most trees leafed out						
Philadelphus sp.						
Chrysopsis spp. (N)		▨	▨			
Amorpha nana (N)						

Appendix 2

PLANT	JAN	FEB	MAR	APR	MAY	JUN
Aesculus hippocastanum					▓	
Yucca glauca (N)					▓	
Holodiscus dumosus					▓	▓
Penstemon jamesii (N)					▓	▓
Penstemon pinifolius					▓	▓
Oryzopsis hymenoides					▓	▓
Chrysanthemum leucanthemum					▓	▓
Penstemon barbatus					▓	▓
Psilostrophe tagetina					▓	▓
Penstemon grandiflorus					▓	▓
P. palmeri					▓	▓
P. hirsutus					▓	▓
Epilobium angustifolium					▓	▓
Lychnis coronaria					▓	▓
Paeonia sp.					▓	▓
Coreopsis lanceolata					▓	▓
Penstemon cobaea					▓	▓
Anacyclus depressus					▓	▓
Philadelphus lewisii					▓	
Argemone sp. (N)						▓
Mirabilis multiflora						▓
Psoralea sp.					▓	▓
Rosa woodsii (N)					▓	▓
Castilleja sp. (N)					▓	▓
Sphaeralcea coccinea (N)						▓
Fallugia paradoxa						▓
Fendlera rupicola						▓
Iris X germanica						▓
Jamesia americana (N)						▓
Townsendia grandiflora (N)					▓	▓
Cowania mexicana						▓
Penstemon strictus						▓
Achillea taygetea 'Moonshine'						▓
Berlandiera lyrata						▓

Appendix 2

PLANT	JUL	AUG	SEPT	OCT	NOV	DEC
Aesculus hippocastanum						
Yucca glauca (N)						
Holodiscus dumosus	▨					
Penstemon jamesii (N)	▨	▨	▨			
Penstemon pinifolius						
Oryzopsis hymenoides	▨		▨			
Chrysanthemum leucanthemum	▨	▨	▨	▨		
Penstemon barbatus						
Psilostrophe tagetina						
Penstemon grandiflorus	▨	▨	▨	▨		
P. palmeri	▨	▨				
P. hirsutus		▨				
Epilobium angustifolium						
Lychnis coronaria	▨					
Paeonia sp.						
Coreopsis lanceolata	▨	▨	▨	▨	▨	
Penstemon cobaea			▨			
Anacyclus depressus						
Philadelphus lewisii						
Argemone sp. (N)						
Mirabilis multiflora	▨	▨	▨	▨		
Psoralea sp.						
Rosa woodsii (N)	▨	▨	▨			
Castilleja sp. (N)		▨	▨	▨	▨	
Sphaeralcea coccinea (N)						
Fallugia paradoxa						
Fendlera rupicola	▨					
Iris X germanica						
Jamesia americana (N)						
Townsendia grandiflora (N)						
Cowania mexicana						
Penstemon strictus	▨					
Achillea taygetea 'Moonshine'	▨	▨	▨			
Berlandiera lyrata						

PLANT	JAN	FEB	MAR	APR	MAY	JUN
Saponaria ocymoides						■
Salvia officinalis						■
Delosperma cooperi						■
Viguiera multiflora						■
Aquilegia chrysantha						■
Penstemon linarioides						■
P. clutei						■
Oenothera caespitosa						■
Campanula rotundifolia (N)						■
Vitis riparia (N)						■
Elaeagnus angustifolia						■
Koeleria cristata (N)						■
Penstemon secundiflorus (N)						■
Gaillardia aristata (N)						■
Eriogonum umbellatum (N)						■
Callirhoë involucrata						■
Physocarpus monogynus (N)						■
Sisyrinchium montanum (N)						■
Lavandula angustifolium						■
Rosa glauca						■
Philadelphus microphyllus						■
Ratibida columnifera (N)						■
Calochortus sp. (N)						■
Gaura coccinea (N)						■
Monarda fistulosa (N)						■
Gypsophila paniculata						■
Penstemon digitalis 'Husker Red'						■
Anthemis tinctoria						■
Penstemon murrayanus						■
Gaura lindheimeri						■
Penstemon pseudospectabilis						■
P. angustifolius						■
Coreopsis verticillata 'Moonbeam'						■
Sambucus canadensis						■

Appendix 2

PLANT	JUL	AUG	SEPT	OCT	NOV	DEC
Saponaria ocymoides						
Salvia officinalis						
Delosperma cooperi						
Viguiera multiflora						
Aquilegia chrysantha						
Penstemon linarioides						
P. clutei						
Oenothera caespitosa						
Campanula rotundifolia (N)						
Vitis riparia (N)						
Elaeagnus angustifolia						
Koeleria cristata (N)						
Penstemon secundiflorus (N)						
Gaillardia aristata (N)						
Eriogonum umbellatum (N)						
Callirhoë involucrata						
Physocarpus monogynus (N)						
Sisyrinchium montanum (N)						
Lavandula angustifolium						
Rosa glauca						
Philadelphus microphyllus						
Ratibida columnifera (N)						
Calochortus sp. (N)						
Gaura coccinea (N)						
Monarda fistulosa (N)						
Gypsophila paniculata						
Penstemon digitalis 'Husker Red'						
Anthemis tinctoria						
Penstemon murrayanus						
Gaura lindheimeri						
Penstemon pseudospectabilis						
P. angustifolius						
Coreopsis verticillata 'Moonbeam'						
Sambucus canadensis						

Appendix 2

PLANT	JAN	FEB	MAR	APR	MAY	JUN
Penstemon alpinus						▓
Cirsium undulatum (N)						▓
Echinacea purpurea						▓
Asclepias speciosa (N)						▓
Sphaeralcea incana						▓
Clematis tangutica						▓
Silene laciniata						▓
Penstemon cardinalis						▓
Achillea X 'Coronation Gold'						▓
Dalea purpurea (N)						▓
Lotus corniculatus						▓
Amorpha canescens						
Stanleya pinnata						
Thelesperma megapotamicum						
Asclepias tuberosa						
Perovskia atriplicifolia						
Aster porteri (N)						
Caryopteris X clandonensis						
Ruellia humilis						
Machaeranthera bigelovii						
Cichorium intybus						
Cosmos bipinnatus						
Gilia aggregata						
Chamaebatiaria millefolium						
Solidago sp. (N)						
Liatris punctata (N)						
Grindelia squarrosa (N)						
Achillea millefolium 'Summer Pastels'						
Gutierrezia sarothrae (N)						
Datura meteloides						
Agastache cana						
Aster laevis (N)						
Gentiana affinis (N)						
Zinnia grandiflora						

PLANT	JUL	AUG	SEPT	OCT	NOV	DEC
Penstemon alpinus						
Cirsium undulatum (N)						
Echinacea purpurea	▨	▨				
Asclepias speciosa (N)	▨	▨				
Sphaeralcea incana		▨	▨			
Clematis tangutica		▨	▨	▨	▨	
Silene laciniata		▨				
Penstemon cardinalis		▨	▨	▨		
Achillea X 'Coronation Gold'		▨	▨	▨		
Dalea purpurea (N)	▨	▨				
Lotus corniculatus	▨	▨				
Amorpha canescens	▨					
Stanleya pinnata	▨	▨				
Thelesperma megapotamicum		▨	▨	▨		
Asclepias tuberosa	▨					
Perovskia atriplicifolia		▨	▨	▨		
Aster porteri (N)	▨	▨				
Caryopteris X clandonensis	▨	▨				
Ruellia humilis	▨	▨				
Machaeranthera bigelovii		▨	▨	▨		
Cichorium intybus		▨	▨	▨		
Cosmos bipinnatus		▨	▨	▨	▨	
Gilia aggregata		▨	▨	▨		
Chamaebatiaria millefolium		▨				
Solidago sp. (N)	▨	▨				
Liatris punctata (N)		▨	▨	▨		
Grindelia squarrosa (N)		▨	▨	▨		
Achillea millefolium 'Summer Pastels'		▨	▨	▨		
Gutierrezia sarothrae (N)		▨	▨	▨		
Datura meteloides	▨					
Agastache cana		▨	▨	▨	▨	
Aster laevis (N)		▨	▨	▨	▨	
Gentiana affinis (N)		▨	▨	▨		
Zinnia grandiflora		▨	▨	▨		

Appendix 2

PLANT	JAN	FEB	MAR	APR	MAY	JUN
Sorghastrum nutans						
Andropogon gerardii (N)						
Lobelia siphilitica						
Bouteloua curtipendula (N)						
Agastache barberi						
Anaphalis margaritacea						
Rudbeckia trilobata						
Mirabilis longiflora						
Talinum calycinum						
Senecio spartioides (N)						
Chrysothamnus sp. (green)						
Lobelia cardinalis						
Thelesperma filifolium						
Eustoma grandiflorum						
Eriogonum niveum						
Cyclamen hederifolium						
Senecio longilobus						
Penstemon kunthii						
Sedum X 'Autumn Joy'						
Zauschneria arizonica						
Helianthus maximiliana						
Clematis paniculata						
Eriogonum corymbosum						
Haplopappus spinulosus						
Chrysothamnus sp. (silver)						
Fall color peak						

Appendix 2

PLANT	JUL	AUG	SEPT	OCT	NOV	DEC
Sorghastrum nutans						
Andropogon gerardii (N)						
Lobelia siphilitica						
Bouteloua curtipendula (N)						
Agastache barberi						
Anaphalis margaritacea						
Rudbeckia trilobata						
Mirabilis longiflora						
Talinum calycinum						
Senecio spartioides (N)						
Chrysothamnus sp. (green)						
Lobelia cardinalis						
Thelesperma filifolium						
Eustoma grandiflorum						
Eriogonum niveum						
Cyclamen hederifolium						
Senecio longilobus						
Penstemon kunthii						
Sedum X 'Autumn Joy'						
Zauschneria arizonica						
Helianthus maximiliana						
Clematis paniculata						
Eriogonum corymbosum						
Haplopappus spinulosus						
Chrysothamnus sp. (silver)						
Fall color peak						

APPENDIX 3
CHECKLIST OF BIRDS
OF BOULDER COUNTY

This list is adapted from the Boulder County Audubon Society's *Birds of Boulder County Field Checklist*, compiled by Jim Holitza, Joe Krieg, Alex Brown, and Gillian Brown. We have included only those birds likely to be seen every year. Abundance may vary from year to year, so abundance codes represent most probable occurrences: **C**–Common, **FC**–Fairly Common, **U**–Uncommon, **R**–Rare. Most likely locations are given as follows: **Pl**–Plains (below 5,500 feet), **Fh**–Foothills (5,500–8,000 feet), **Mt**–Mountains (above 8,000 feet).

Species	Winter	Spring	Summer	Fall	Location
LOONS, GREBES, AND PELICAN					
☐ Common Loon		R		U	Pl
☐ Pied-billed Grebe	U	FC	FC	FC	Pl
☐ Horned Grebe	U	FC		FC	Pl
☐ Eared Grebe		U		U	Pl
☐ Western Grebe	U	FC	FC	C	Pl
☐ Clark's Grebe	U	U	U	FC	Pl
☐ American White Pelican		U	FC	U	Pl
CORMORANTS, HERONS, AND IBIS					
☐ Double-crested Cormorant		U	FC	U	Pl
☐ American Bittern		U	U	U	Pl
☐ Least Bittern		R	R		Pl
☐ Great Blue Heron	U	C	C	FC	Pl,Fh
☐ Great Egret		U	U	U	Pl
☐ Snowy Egret		R	R	R	Pl
☐ Green-backed Heron			R	R	Pl
☐ Black-crowned Night Heron		FC	FC	U	Pl
☐ White-faced Ibis		U	R	R	Pl

Appendix 3

Species	Winter	Spring	Summer	Fall	Location
SWANS AND GEESE					
☐ Tundra Swan	R			R	Pl
☐ Snow Goose	R	R		R	Pl
☐ Canada Goose	C	C	C	C	Pl,Fh
DUCKS					
☐ Wood Duck		R	U	R	Pl
☐ Green-winged Teal	FC	C	U	C	Pl,Fh,Mt
☐ Mallard	C	C	C	C	Pl,Fh,Mt
☐ Northern Pintail	FC	C	U	FC	Pl
☐ Blue-winged Teal		FC	FC	U	Pl
☐ Cinnamon Teal		FC	FC	R	Pl
☐ Northern Shoveler	FC	C	U	FC	Pl
☐ Gadwall	FC	C	U	C	Pl
☐ American Wigeon	FC	C	U	C	Pl
☐ Canvasback	U	FC		U	Pl
☐ Redhead	FC	C	U	C	Pl
☐ Ring-necked Duck	C	C	U	C	Pl,Mt
☐ Lesser Scaup	FC	C	R	U	Pl
☐ Common Goldeneye	FC	FC		U	Pl
☐ Bufflehead	U	FC		FC	Pl
☐ Hooded Merganser	FC	U		U	Pl
☐ Common Merganser	C	FC	R	U	Pl
☐ Red-breasted Merganser	U	U		R	Pl
☐ Ruddy Duck	R	U	U	U	Pl
GULLS AND TERNS					
☐ Franklin's Gull		FC	FC	FC	Pl,Fh
☐ Bonaparte's Gull		R		R	Pl
☐ Ring-billed Gull	C	C	U	C	Pl
☐ California Gull		FC	U	U	Pl,Fh
☐ Herring Gull	FC	U		U	Pl
☐ Forster's Tern		FC	U	U	Pl
☐ Black Tern		U	U	R	Pl

A p p e n d i x 3

Species	Winter	Spring	Summer	Fall	Location
HAWKS, EAGLES, AND FALCONS					
☐ Turkey Vulture		FC	FC	U	Pl,Fh,Mt
☐ Osprey		U	R	U	Pl,Fh,Mt
☐ Bald Eagle	FC			U	Pl,Fh
☐ Northern Harrier	FC	FC	R	FC	Pl
☐ Sharp-shinned Hawk	U	FC	U	FC	Pl,Fh,Mt
☐ Cooper's Hawk	U	FC	U	FC	Fh
☐ Northern Goshawk	U	U	U	U	Fh,Mt
☐ Broad-winged Hawk	·	R		R	Fh
☐ Swainson's Hawk		FC	FC	U	Pl
☐ Red-tailed Hawk	FC	C	FC	C	Pl,Fh,Mt
☐ Ferruginous Hawk	FC	U	R	FC	Pl
☐ Rough-legged Hawk	FC	U		FC	Pl
☐ Golden Eagle	FC	FC	U	FC	Pl,Fh,Mt
☐ American Kestrel	C	C	C	C	Pl,Fh
☐ Merlin	R	R		R	Pl
☐ Prairie Falcon	U	FC	U	FC	Pl,Fh
☐ Peregrine Falcon	R	R	R	R	Pl,Fh
PHEASANT AND GROUSE					
☐ Ring-necked Pheasant	U	U	U	U	Pl
☐ Blue Grouse	U	FC	FC	U	Fh,Mt
☐ White-tailed Ptarmigan	U	U	U	U	Mt
☐ Wild Turkey	U	U	U	U	Fh
RAILS, COOT, AND CRANE					
☐ Virginia Rail	R	U	U	U	Pl
☐ Sora		U	U	R	Pl,Fh,Mt
☐ American Coot	FC	C	C	C	Pl,Fh
☐ Sandhill Crane		R		U	Pl
SHOREBIRDS					
☐ Semipalmated Plover		U		R	Pl
☐ Killdeer	U	C	C	FC	Pl,Fh
☐ American Avocet		FC	FC	U	Pl
☐ Greater Yellowlegs		FC	R	FC	Pl

A p p e n d i x 3

Species	Winter	Spring	Summer	Fall	Location
☐ Lesser Yellowlegs		FC	U	FC	Pl
☐ Solitary Sandpiper		U	R	R	Pl
☐ Willet		U			Pl
☐ Spotted Sandpiper		FC	FC	R	Pl,Fh,Mt
☐ Marbled Godwit		U			Pl
☐ Semipalmated Sandpiper		U	R	R	Pl
☐ Western Sandpiper		U	R	R	Pl
☐ Least Sandpiper		FC	U	R	Pl
☐ Baird's Sandpiper		FC	U	U	Pl
☐ Long-billed Dowitcher		FC	R	FC	Pl
☐ Common Snipe	U	FC	FC	FC	Pl,Fh,Mt
☐ Wilson's Phalarope		FC	U	U	Pl

DOVES AND CUCKOOS

Species	Winter	Spring	Summer	Fall	Location
☐ Rock Dove	C	C	C	C	Pl,Fh
☐ Band-tailed Pigeon		U	U	U	Fh,Mt
☐ Mourning Dove		FC	C	FC	Pl,Fh
☐ Yellow-billed Cuckoo		R	R		Pl

OWLS

Species	Winter	Spring	Summer	Fall	Location
☐ Common Barn Owl	R	R	R	R	Pl
☐ Eastern Screech Owl	U	U	U	U	Pl
☐ Great Horned Owl	FC	FC	FC	FC	Pl,Fh,Mt
☐ Flammulated Owl		FC	U		Fh
☐ Northern Pygmy Owl	U	U	U	U	Fh,Mt
☐ Burrowing Owl		U	R	R	Pl
☐ Long-eared Owl	R	R	R	R	Pl,Fh
☐ Short-eared Owl	R	R			Pl
☐ Northern Saw-whet Owl	U	U	U	U	Fh,Mt
☐ Boreal Owl	R	U	U	U	Mt

GOATSUCKERS AND SWIFTS

Species	Winter	Spring	Summer	Fall	Location
☐ Common Nighthawk		U	FC	U	Pl,Fh
☐ Common Poorwill		U	FC	U	Fh
☐ Black Swift			R		Mt
☐ Chimney Swift		U	U	R	Pl
☐ White-throated Swift		FC	FC	U	Fh

Appendix 3

Species	Winter	Spring	Summer	Fall	Location
HUMMINGBIRDS AND KINGFISHER					
☐ Broad-tailed Hummingbird		FC	C	U	Fh,Mt
☐ Rufous Hummingbird			U	R	Fh,Mt
☐ Belted Kingfisher	FC	FC	FC	FC	Pl,Fh
WOODPECKERS					
☐ Lewis's Woodpecker	R	U	U	U	Pl
☐ Red-headed Woodpecker		R	U	R	Pl
☐ Yellow-bellied Sapsucker	U	R		U	Pl
☐ Red-naped Sapsucker		U	FC	U	Mt
☐ Williamson's Sapsucker		FC	FC	U	Fh,Mt
☐ Downy Woodpecker	FC	FC	FC	FC	Pl,Fh,Mt
☐ Hairy Woodpecker	FC	FC	FC	FC	Fh,Mt
☐ Three-toed Woodpecker	U	U	U	U	Mt
☐ Northern Flicker	C	C	C	C	Pl,Fh,Mt
FLYCATCHERS					
☐ Olive-sided Flycatcher		U	U	R	Fh,Mt
☐ Western Wood-pewee		U	C	U	Fh,Mt
☐ Willow Flycatcher		R	U	R	Pl,Fh,Mt
☐ Hammond's Flycatcher		U	FC	U	Fh,Mt
☐ Dusky Flycatcher		U	FC	U	Fh,Mt
☐ Cordilleran Flycatcher		U	FC	U	Fh,Mt
☐ Say's Phoebe		U	U	U	Pl,Fh
☐ Western Kingbird		U	FC	U	Pl
☐ Eastern Kingbird		U	FC		Pl
LARKS AND SWALLOWS					
☐ Horned Lark	FC	FC	FC	FC	Pl,Mt
☐ Tree Swallow		C	FC	U	Pl,Fh,Mt
☐ Violet-green Swallow		FC	FC	U	Pl,Fh,Mt
☐ Northern Rough-winged Swallow		FC	FC	U	Pl
☐ Bank Swallow		U	U	R	Pl
☐ Cliff Swallow		FC	C	U	Pl
☐ Barn Swallow		C	C	FC	Pl,Fh

Species	Winter	Spring	Summer	Fall	Location
CROWS AND JAYS					
☐ Gray Jay	FC	FC	FC	FC	Mt
☐ Steller's Jay	C	C	C	C	Fh,Mt
☐ Blue Jay	FC	FC	FC	FC	Pl
☐ Scrub Jay	U	U	U	U	Fh
☐ Pinyon Jay		U		U	Fh
☐ Clark's Nutcracker	FC	FC	FC	FC	Fh,Mt
☐ Black-billed Magpie	C	C	C	C	Pl,Fh
☐ American Crow	C	C	C	C	Pl,Fh
☐ Common Raven	C	C	C	C	Pl,Fh,Mt
TITMICE AND RELATIVES					
☐ Black-capped Chickadee	C	C	C	C	Pl,Fh
☐ Mountain Chickadee	C	C	C	C	Fh,Mt
☐ Bushtit	R	R	R	R	Fh
☐ Red-breasted Nuthatch	FC	FC	FC	FC	Fh,Mt
☐ White-breasted Nuthatch	FC	FC	FC	FC	Pl,Fh,Mt
☐ Pygmy Nuthatch	C	C	C	C	Fh
☐ Brown Creeper	FC	FC	FC	FC	Fh,Mt
WRENS					
☐ Rock Wren		U	U		Fh,Mt
☐ Canyon Wren	FC	FC	FC	FC	Fh
☐ Northern House Wren		FC	C	U	Pl,Fh,Mt
☐ Winter Wren	R	R		R	Pl,Fh
☐ Marsh Wren	R	R		R	Pl
DIPPER, KINGLETS, AND GNATCATCHER					
☐ American Dipper	FC	FC	FC	FC	Fh,Mt
☐ Golden-crowned Kinglet	U	U	U	U	Pl,Mt
☐ Ruby-crowned Kinglet	U	FC	C	FC	Pl,Mt
☐ Blue-gray Gnatcatcher		R	R		Fh
THRUSHES AND THRASHERS					
☐ Western Bluebird		U	R	U	Fh
☐ Mountain Bluebird	U	C	FC	U	Pl,Fh,Mt

Appendix 3

Species	Winter	Spring	Summer	Fall	Location
☐ Townsend's Solitaire	FC	FC	FC	FC	Fh,Mt
☐ Veery		R	R		Mt
☐ Swainson's Thrush		U	U		Pl,Fh,Mt
☐ Hermit Thrush		U	FC	U	Fh,Mt
☐ American Robin	FC	C	C	C	Pl,Fh,Mt
☐ Gray Catbird		U	U	U	Fh
☐ Northern Mockingbird	R	R	R	R	Pl,Fh
☐ Sage Thrasher		R	R	U	Pl,Fh
☐ Brown Thrasher	R	U		R	Pl

PIPIT, WAXWINGS, AND SHRIKES

☐ American Pipit		U	FC	U	Pl,Mt
☐ Bohemian Waxwing	FC/U	FC/U		U	Pl
☐ Cedar Waxwing	FC	FC	U	FC	Pl
☐ Northern Shrike	U	R		U	Pl
☐ Loggerhead Shrike	R	U	U	U	Pl

STARLING

☐ European Starling	C	C	C	C	Pl,Fh

VIREOS

☐ Solitary Vireo		U	FC	U	Fh
☐ Warbling Vireo		FC	C	U	Fh,Mt
☐ Red-eyed Vireo		R	U	R	Pl

WARBLERS

☐ Tennessee Warbler		U		U	Pl
☐ Orange-crowned Warbler		FC		FC	Pl,Fh,Mt
☐ Nashville Warbler		U		U	Pl
☐ Virginia's Warbler		C	FC	U	Fh
☐ Northern Parula		R			Pl
☐ Yellow Warbler		FC	FC	U	Pl,Fh
☐ Chestnut-sided Warbler		R	R		Pl,Fh
☐ Black-throated Blue Warbler		R		R	Pl,Fh
☐ Yellow-rumped Warbler	R	C	C	FC	Pl,Fh,Mt
☐ Townsend's Warbler		U	R	U	Fh,Mt

Species	Winter	Spring	Summer	Fall	Location
☐ Bay-breasted Warbler		R		R	Pl
☐ Blackpoll Warbler		R			Pl
☐ Black and White Warbler		U		R	Pl
☐ American Redstart		U	R	R	Pl,Fh
☐ Northern Waterthrush		U		R	Pl
☐ Macgillivray's Warbler		FC	FC	U	Fh,Mt
☐ Ovenbird		R	R	R	Fh
☐ Common Yellowthroat		FC	FC	U	Pl
☐ Wilson's Warbler		FC	FC	U	Pl,Mt
☐ Yellow-breasted Chat		U	FC	U	Pl,Fh

TANAGERS, GROSBEAKS, AND BUNTINGS

Species	Winter	Spring	Summer	Fall	Location
☐ Western Tanager		FC	FC	U	Fh
☐ Rose-breasted Grosbeak		R	R	R	Pl
☐ Black-headed Grosbeak		FC	FC	U	Fh
☐ Blue Grosbeak		R	U	R	Pl
☐ Lazuli Bunting		FC	FC	R	Fh
☐ Indigo Bunting		U	U		Fh

TOWHEES

Species	Winter	Spring	Summer	Fall	Location
☐ Green-tailed Towhee		U	FC	U	Pl,Fh,Mt
☐ Rufous-sided Towhee	U	FC	C	FC	Fh

SPARROWS

Species	Winter	Spring	Summer	Fall	Location
☐ American Tree Sparrow	C	FC		FC	Pl
☐ Chipping Sparrow		C	C	FC	Pl,Fh,Mt
☐ Clay-colored Sparrow		U		U	Pl
☐ Brewer's Sparrow		FC	U	U	Pl,Fh
☐ Vesper Sparrow		C	FC	FC	Pl,Fh
☐ Lark Sparrow		FC	FC	FC	Pl,Fh
☐ Lark Bunting		U	U	U	Pl
☐ Savannah Sparrow		U	U	U	Pl,Fh
☐ Grasshopper Sparrow		U	U	U	Pl
☐ Fox Sparrow	R	U	U	R	Pl,Mt
☐ Song Sparrow	FC	FC	FC	FC	Pl,Fh,Mt
☐ Lincoln's Sparrow		U	FC	U	Pl,Mt

Appendix 3

Species	Winter	Spring	Summer	Fall	Location
☐ White-throated Sparrow	R	R		R	Pl,Fh
☐ White-crowned Sparrow	FC	FC	FC	FC	Pl,Mt
☐ Harris's Sparrow	U	U		U	Pl
☐ Dark-eyed Junco	C	C	C	C	Pl,Fh,Mt

ICTERIDS

☐ Bobolink		R	U		Pl
☐ Red-winged Blackbird	C	C	C	C	Pl,Fh
☐ Western Meadowlark	C	C	C	C	Pl,Fh
☐ Yellow-headed Blackbird		FC	FC	U	Pl
☐ Rusty Blackbird	R			R	Pl
☐ Brewer's Blackbird	U	FC	FC	FC	Pl,Fh
☐ Common Grackle		FC	FC	FC	Pl,Fh
☐ Brown-headed Cowbird		FC	FC	U	Pl,Fh,Mt
☐ Northern Oriole		U	FC	R	Pl,Fh

FINCHES

☐ Rosy Finch	FC	FC	FC	FC	Mt
☐ Pine Grosbeak	U	U	U	U	Mt
☐ Cassin's Finch	FC	FC	FC	FC	Fh,Mt
☐ House Finch	C	C	C	C	Pl,Fh
☐ Red Crossbill	FC/U	FC/U	FC/U	FC/U	Fh,Mt
☐ Common Redpoll	R			R	Pl
☐ Pine Siskin	C	C	C	C	Fh,Mt
☐ Lesser Goldfinch		U	FC	FC	Pl,Fh
☐ American Goldfinch	FC	FC	FC	FC	Pl,Fh
☐ Evening Grosbeak	FC	FC	FC	FC	Pl,Fh,Mt

WEAVER FINCHES

☐ House Sparrow	C	C	C	C	Pl,Fh

APPENDIX 4
MAMMALS OF BOULDER COUNTY

Information for this list was provided by Dr. David Armstrong of the University of Colorado Museum, and Dave Hallock of the Boulder County Parks and Open Space Department. For a slightly more detailed list, see David Armstrong, "Mammalian Fauna of Boulder County," *Boulder County Comprehensive Plan: Environmental Resources Element*, 1984, pp. 3-94 to 3-100.

Italicized species have been extirpated from Boulder County. Asterisked species are believed to be present based on their range and habitat requirements but have not been documented within Boulder County. Likely habitats are indicated by the following codes: **A**–Aspen, **C**–Coniferous Forest, **D**–Deciduous Woodland (riparian), **G**–Grasslands and Meadows, **R**–Rock and Talus, **S**–Shrublands, **T**–Tundra, **U**–Urban, **W**–Wetlands (marshes and ponds). Location codes are as follows: **Pl**–Plains (below 5,000 feet), **Fh**–Foothills (5,500–8,000 feet), **Mt**–Mountains (above 8,000 feet).

Species	Habitat	Location
MARSUPIALS		
☐ Virginia Opossum	D	Pl
INSECTIVORES		
☐ Masked Shrew	A,C,D,G,R,T,W	Pl,Fh,Mt
☐ Pygmy Shrew*	C,T,W	Mt
☐ Montane (Dusky) Shrew	A,C,D,G,R,T,W	Fh,Mt
☐ Dwarf Shrew*	A,C,D,G,R,S,T,W	Fh,Mt
☐ Water Shrew	A,C,D,T,W	Mt
☐ Merriam's Shrew	C,G,S	Fh
☐ Least Shrew	D,G,W	Pl
BATS		
☐ Little Brown Bat	A,C,D,G,S,U,W	Pl,Fh,Mt
☐ Long-eared Myotis	C,G,W	Fh
☐ Fringed Myotis*	C,G	Fh
☐ Long-legged Myotis	A,C,D,G,U,W	Pl,Fh,Mt
☐ Western Small-footed Myotis	D,G,S,W	Pl,Fh

A p p e n d i x 4

Species	Habitat	Location
☐ Silver-haired Bat	A,C,D,G,W	Pl,Fh,Mt
☐ Big Brown Bat	A,C,D,G,S,U,W	Pl,Fh,Mt
☐ Red Bat	D,G	Pl
☐ Hoary Bat	A,C,D,G	Pl,Fh,Mt
☐ Townsend's Big-eared Bat	C,G,S	Fh

RABBITS AND ALLIES

☐ Eastern Cottontail*	D	Pl
☐ Nuttall's Cottontail	A,C,D,G,S	Fh,Mt
☐ Desert Cottontail	G	Pl
☐ Showshoe Hare	A,C,D	Mt
☐ White-tailed Jackrabbit	A,C,G,R,T	Pl,Fh,Mt
☐ Black-tailed Jackrabbit*	C,G,S	Pl,Fh
☐ Pika	R,T	Mt

RODENTS

☐ Least Chipmunk	A,C,D,R,S,T	Fh,Mt
☐ Colorado Chipmunk	C,R,S	Fh,Mt
☐ Uinta Chipmunk	A,C,R	Mt
☐ Yellow-bellied Marmot	A,C,G,R,S,T	Fh,Mt
☐ Wyoming (formerly Richardson's) Ground Squirrel	C,G	Fh,Mt
☐ Thirteen-lined Ground Squirrel	G	Pl
☐ Spotted Ground Squirrel	G	Pl
☐ Rock Squirrel	C,D,G,S	Pl,Fh
☐ Golden-mantled Ground Squirrel	A,C,G,R,S,T	Fh,Mt
☐ Black-tailed Prairie Dog	G	Pl,Fh
☐ Fox Squirrel	D,U	Pl,Fh
☐ Abert's Squirrel	C	Fh
☐ Chickaree (Pine Squirrel)	C	Fh,Mt
☐ Northern Pocket Gopher	A,C,G,R,S,T	Pl,Fh,Mt
☐ Plains Pocket Gopher	C,G	Pl,Fh
☐ Olive-backed Pocket Mouse	G,C	Pl,Fh
☐ Plains Pocket Mouse	G	Pl
☐ Silky Pocket Mouse*	G	Pl
☐ Hispid Pocket Mouse	G	Pl

A p p e n d i x 4

Species	Habitat	Location
☐ Ord's Kangaroo Rat*	G	Pl
☐ Beaver	A,D,W	Pl,Fh,Mt
☐ Plains Harvest Mouse*	G	Pl
☐ Western Harvest Mouse	G	Pl
☐ Deer Mouse	A,C,D,G,R,S,T,U,W	Pl,Fh,Mt
☐ Rock Mouse	C,G,S	Fh
☐ Northern Grasshopper Mouse	G	Pl
☐ Mexican Wood Rat	C,G,R,S	Fh
☐ Bushy-tailed Wood Rat	C,G,R,S,T	Fh,Mt
☐ Southern Red-backed Vole	A,C,D,W	Mt
☐ Heather Vole	A,C,D,G,T	Mt
☐ Meadow Vole	A,D,G,W	Pl,Fh,Mt
☐ Montane Vole	A,C,D,G,T,W	Fh,Mt
☐ Long-tailed Vole	A,C,D,G,T	Fh,Mt
☐ Prairie Vole	C,D,G	Pl,Fh
☐ Muskrat	D,W	Pl,Fh,Mt
☐ Norway Rat (introduced)	U	Pl,Fh
☐ House Mouse (introduced)	U	Pl,Fh
☐ Meadow Jumping Mouse	D,W	Pl
☐ Western Jumping Mouse	A,D,G,W	Mt
☐ Porcupine	A,C,D,S	Pl,Fh,Mt

CARNIVORES

Species	Habitat	Location
☐ Coyote	A,C,D,G,R,S,T	Pl,Fh,Mt
☐ *Gray Wolf*	A,C,D,G,R,S,T	Pl,Fh,Mt
☐ Red Fox	A,C,D,G,R,S,T,W	Pl,Fh,Mt
☐ Swift Fox*	G	Pl
☐ Gray Fox	C,S,R	Fh
☐ Black Bear	A,C,D,S	Fh,Mt
☐ *Grizzly Bear*	A,C,D,G,R,S,T	Pl,Fh,Mt
☐ Raccoon	C,D,U,W	Pl,Fh
☐ Ringtail*	S	Fh
☐ Pine Marten	A,C,T	Mt
☐ Short-tailed Weasel (Ermine)	A,C,D,G,R,T	Fh,Mt
☐ Long-tailed Weasel	A,C,D,G,R,S,T	Pl,Fh,Mt
☐ *Black-footed Ferret*	G	Pl

Species	Habitat	Location
☐ Mink	D,W	Pl,Fh,Mt
☐ *Wolverine*	C	Mt
☐ Badger	C,G,R,S,T	Pl,Fh,Mt
☐ Western Spotted Skunk	C,R,S	Fh
☐ Striped Skunk	A,C,D,G,R,S,U,W	Pl,Fh,Mt
☐ River Otter	D,W	Pl,Fh,Mt
☐ Mountain Lion	C,G,R,S	Fh,Mt
☐ Lynx	C	Mt
☐ Bobcat	C,D,S,T	Pl,Fh,Mt

EVEN-TOED UNGULATES

Species	Habitat	Location
☐ Wapiti (Elk)	A,C,G,T	Pl,Fh,Mt
☐ Mule Deer	A,C,D,G,R,S,T	Pl,Fh,Mt
☐ White-tailed Deer	D,W	Pl,Fh
☐ *Pronghorn*	G	Pl
☐ *Bison*	G	Pl,Fh
☐ Mountain Goat	R,T	Mt
☐ Bighorn Sheep	C,G,R,T	Fh,Mt

APPENDIX 5
LOCAL AND REGIONAL
NATURE ORGANIZATIONS

Addresses and phone numbers are subject to change. Phone numbers are given here only when they do not change with a change in officers of a specific organization.

Boulder Bird Club
(Contact Wild Bird Center, later in this listing, for current information.)

Boulder City Open Space Operations
 Center
66 South Cherryvale Road
Boulder 80303
441-4142

Boulder City Parks & Recreation
 Department
3198 North Broadway
Boulder 80302
441-3400

Boulder County Audubon Society
P.O. Box 2081
Boulder 80306

Boulder County Nature Association
P.O. Box 493
Boulder 80306

Boulder County Parks & Open Space
 Department
2045 13th Street
P.O. Box 471
Boulder 80302
441-3950

Cloud Ridge Naturalists
8297 Overland Road
Ward 80481
459-3248

Colorado Bat Society
1085 14th Street
Suite 1337
Denver 80302

Colorado Environmental Coalition
777 Grant, Suite 606
Denver 80203
837-8701

Colorado Field Ornithologists
13401 Piccadilly Road
Brighton 80601

Appendix 5

Colorado Mountain Club of Boulder
900 Baseline
Boulder 80302
449-1135

Colorado Mycological Society
P.O. Box 9621
Denver 80209
320-6569

Colorado Native Plant Society
P.O. Box 200
Fort Collins 80522

Denver Botanic Gardens
1005 York Street
Denver 80206
331-4000

Denver Museum of Natural History
2001 Colorado Boulevard
Denver 80205
370-6357

Foothills Audubon Club
P.O. Box 946
Boulder 80306
722-1854

National Audubon Society, Rocky
  Mountain Regional Office
4150 Darley Avenue, Suite 5
Boulder 80303
499-0219

Nature Conservancy, Colorado Field
  Office
1244 Pine
Boulder 80302
444-2950

Rocky Mountain Nature Association
Rocky Mountain National Park
Estes Park 80517

Sierra Club, Southwest Office
1240 Pine
Boulder 80303
449-5595

University of Colorado Museum
Henderson Building
CU Campus
Boulder 80309
492-6892

Wild Bird Center
1641 28th Street
Boulder 80301
442-1322
(Check here for current "rare bird
alert" phone numbers and for
information on birding activities
and organizations.)

Xerces Society
P.O. Box 3092
University Station
Laramie, Wyoming 82071

SUGGESTED READING

MAPS

Boulder County Road Map. 1991. Available from Boulder Chamber of Commerce: 2440 Pearl Street, Boulder, Co. 80302.

Open Space/Parks and Trails Map. 2d ed. 1991. Available from sporting goods and map stores or Open Space offices.

Roosevelt National Forest map. 1975. U.S. Department of Agriculture, Forest Service. Available from U.S. Forest Service Office: 2995 Baseline Road, Boulder, Co. 80303.

Boulder County Colorado 1:50,000 scale topographic map. 1980. U.S. Department of the Interior, Geological Survey. Available from sporting goods and map stores. Individual USGS topographic maps for smaller areas are also available.

GENERAL

Benedict, Audrey. *The Southern Rockies.* San Francisco: Sierra Club Books, 1991.

Cassells, E. Steve. *The Archaeology of Colorado.* Boulder, Colo.: Johnson Books, 1983.

Chronic, Halka. *Roadside Geology of Colorado.* Missoula, Mont.: Mountain Press, 1986.

Cushman, Ruth Carol, and Stephen R. Jones. *The Shortgrass Prairie.* Boulder, Colo.: Pruett Publishing Co., 1988.

Dillard, Annie. *Pilgrim at Tinker Creek.* Toronto: Bantam Books, 1981.

Leopold, Aldo. *A Sand County Almanac.* New York: Oxford University Press, 1966.

McLaughlin, Marie L. *Myths and Legends of the Sioux.* Lincoln: University of Nebraska Press, 1990.

Mutel, Cornelia Fleisher, and John C. Emerick. *From Grassland to Glacier: The Natural History of Colorado.* 2d ed. Boulder, Colo.: Johnson Books, 1992.

Teale, Edwin Way. *Autumn Across America.* New York: Dodd, Mead, 1956.

———. *Journey Into Summer.* New York: Dodd, Mead, 1960.

———. *North With the Spring.* New York: Dodd, Mead, 1951.

———. *Wandering Through Winter.* New York: Dodd, Mead, 1957.

Suggested Reading

Tinbergen, Niko. *Curious Naturalists.* Garden City, N.Y.: Anchor Books, 1968.
Veblen, Thomas T., and Diane C. Lorenz. *The Colorado Front Range: A Century of Ecological Change.* Salt Lake City: University of Utah Press, 1991.
Zwinger, Ann. *Beyond the Aspen Grove.* New York: Random House, 1970.

WEATHER

Callahan, William G. *The Boulder Weather Log.* Boulder: Upslope Press, 1986.
————. *The Weather Enthusiasts of Boulder Newsletter.* Boulder: Upslope Press, monthly.
Gallant, Roy A. *Rainbows, Mirages and Sundogs.* New York: Macmillan, 1987.
Kirk, Ruth. *Snow.* New York: William Morrow & Co., Inc., 1978.
LaChapelle, Edward R. *Field Guide to Snow Crystals.* Seattle: University of Washington Press, 1969.
Halfpenny, James C., and Roy Douglas Ozanne. *Winter: An Ecological Handbook.* Boulder: Johnson Publishing Company, 1989.
Keen, Richard A. *Skywatch: The Western Weather Guide.* Golden, Colo.: Fulcrum Publishing, 1987.
Schaefer, Victor J., and John A. Day. *A Field Guide to the Atmosphere.* Peterson Field Guide Series, no. 26. Boston: Houghton Mifflin Co., 1981.
Weather Guide Calendars. Denver: Accord Pub. Co. Published annually.
Williams, Terry Tempest. *The Secret Language of Snow.* San Francisco: Sierra Club/ Pantheon Books, 1984.

FLORA

Arora, David. *Mushrooms Demystified.* 2d ed. Berkeley, Calif.: Ten Speed Press, 1986.
Colorado Native Plant Society in cooperation with the Rocky Mountain Nature Association. *Rare Plants of Colorado.* Estes Park: Colorado Native Plant Society, 1989.
Craighead, John J., and Frank C. Craighead. *A Field Guide to Rocky Mountain Wildflowers.* Peterson Field Guide Series, no. 14. Boston: Houghton Mifflin Co., 1963
Freeman, Craig C., and Eileen K. Schofield. *Roadside Wildflowers of the Southern Great Plains.* Lawrence: University Press of Kansas, 1991.

Suggested Reading

Kindscher, Kelly. *Edible Wild Plants of the Prairie: An Ethnobotanical Guide*. Lawrence: University Press of Kansas, 1987.

Knobel, Edward. *Field Guide to the Grasses, Sedges and Rushes of the United States*. 2d rev. ed. New York: Dover, 1980

Knopf, Jim. *The Xeriscape Flower Gardener*. Boulder, Colo.: Johnson Books, 1991.

Lincoff, Gary. *Audubon Society Field Guide to North American Mushrooms*. New York: Alfred A. Knopf, 1981.

Marr, John W. *Ecosystems of the East Slope of the Colorado Front Range*. Boulder: Colorado Associated University Press, 1967.

McGregor, Ronald L., and T. M. Barkley. *Flora of the Great Plains*. Lawrence: University Press of Kansas, 1986.

Nelson, Ruth Ashton. *Handbook of Rocky Mountain Plants*. 4th rev. ed., Roger L. Williams. Boulder, Colo.: Roberts Rinehart Publishers, 1992.

Van Bruggen, Theodore. *Wildflowers, Grasses, and Other Plants of the Northern Plains and Black Hills*. Interior, S. Dak.: Badlands Natural History Association, 1983.

Weber, William A. *Colorado Flora: Eastern Slope*. Niwot, Colo.: Colorado Associated University Press, 1990.

Weber, William A., and Ronald C. Wittman. *Catalog of the Colorado Flora: A Biodiversity Baseline*. Niwot, Colo.: Colorado Associated University Press, 1992.

Whitson, Tom D., ed. *Weeds of the West*. rev. ed. Newark, Calif.: Western Society of Weed Science in cooperation with the Western United States Land Grant Universities Cooperative Extension Services, 1992.

Willard, Beatrice E., and Michael T. Smithson. *Alpine Wildflowers of Rocky Mountain National Park*. Estes Park, Colo.: Rocky Mountain Nature Association, 1988.

Zwinger, Ann H. *Aspen: Blazon of the High Country*. Salt Lake City: Peregrine Smith Books, 1991.

Zwinger, Ann H., and Beatrice E. Willard. *Land Above the Trees: A Guide to American Alpine Tundra*. Tucson: University of Arizona Press, 1989.

FAUNA

Armstrong, David. *Rocky Mountain Mammals*. Boulder: Colorado Associated University Press, 1987.

Bailey, Alfred Marshall, and Robert J. Niedrach. *Birds of Colorado*. Denver: Denver Museum of Natural History, 1965.

Suggested Reading

Barbour, Roger William, and Wayne H. Davis. *Bats of America*. Lexington: University Press of Kentucky, 1969.

Craighead, John J., and Frank C. Craighead, Jr. *Hawks, Owls, and Wildlife*. New York: Dover, 1969.

Erlich, Paul R., David R. Dobkin, and Darryl Wheye. *The Birder's Handbook: A Field Guide to the Natural History of North American Birds*. New York: Simon & Schuster Inc., 1988.

Ferris, Clifford D., and F. Martin Brown, eds. *Butterflies of the Rocky Mountain States*. Norman: University of Oklahoma Press, 1981.

Halfpenny, James A. *A Field Guide to Mammal Tracking in Western North America*. Boulder, Colo.: Johnson Books, 1986.

Hammerson, Geoffrey A. *Amphibians and Reptiles in Colorado*. Denver: Colorado Division of Wildlife, 1982.

Holt, Harold R., and James A. Lane. *A Birder's Guide to Colorado*. rev. ed. of *A Birder's Guide to Eastern Colorado*. Denver: ABC Sales, 1988.

National Geographic Society. *Field Guide to the Birds of North America*. 2d ed. Washington, D.C.: National Geographic Society, 1983.

Peterson, Roger Tory. *Field Guide to Western Birds*. 3d ed. Peterson Field Guide Series, no. 2. Boston: Houghton Mifflin Co., 1990.

Pyle, Robert Michael. *The Audubon Society Field Guide to North American Butterflies*. New York: Alfred A. Knopf, 1981.

————. *The Handbook for Butterfly Watchers*. Boston: Houghton Mifflin Co., 1992.

Ryden, Hope. *Lily Pond*. New York: William Morrow, 1989.

True, Dan. *A Family of Eagles*. New York: Everest House, 1980.

Turbak, Gary. *America's Great Cats*. Flagstaff, Ariz.: Northland Press, 1986.

————. *Twilight Hunters: Wolves, Coyotes and Foxes*. Flagstaff, Ariz.: Northland Press, 1987.

Whitaker, John O., and Robert Elman. *Audubon Field Guide to North American Mammals*. New York: Alfred A. Knopf, 1980.

HIKING GUIDES

De Haan, Vici. *Hiking Trails of the Boulder Mountain Parks and Plains*. 3d ed. Boulder: Pruett Publishing Co., 1991.

Folzenlogen, Darcy, and Robert Folzenlogen. *Walking the Denver-Boulder Region*. Littleton, Colo.: Willow Press, 1992.

Ormes, Robert M. *Guide to the Colorado Mountains*. 9th ed. Randy Jacobs, ed. Denver: Colorado Mountain Club, 1992.

BOTANICAL INDEX

Plant names in the *Boulder County Nature Almanac* have been taken mostly from *Flora of the Great Plains* and *Hortus Third* because these two sources are widely available and list many botanic synonyms. However, in recent years considerable taxonomic studies have led to many suggested changes in botanic names. The following index may help in keeping up with these changes. It is based on *Colorado Flora: Eastern Slope,* by William A. Weber, and *Catalog of the Colorado Flora: A Biodiversity Baseline,* by William A. Weber and Ronald C. Wittmann.

In this index, each plant is listed under both its English-language name and its older botanic name. When a plant has a newer botanic name, this appears in parentheses after the English-language and older botanic names.

The following abbreviations are used in this index: ssp.=subspecies; var.=variety; spp.=several species unknown or unidentified; sp.=one species unknown or unidentified.

Fungi

(Fungi, although plantlike, are placed in their own taxonomic kingdom. For this reason, they are grouped separately from plants in this index.)

Agaricus campestris; Meadow Mushrooms, 129, 185

Amanita verna; Destroying Angel, 185
Armillaria bulbosa, 184
Armillaria ostoyae, 184

Boletus edulis; Steinpilz, 146, 185

Calvatia spp., *Lycoperdon* spp.; Puffballs, 129, 145, 185

Destroying Angel; A. verna, 185
Hydnum imbricatum; Scaly Urchin, 185

Lycoperdon spp., *Calvatia* spp.; Puffballs, 129, 145, 185

Meadow Mushrooms; *Agaricus campestris,* 129, 185
Morchella spp.; Morels, 186
Morels; *Morchella* spp., 186

Puffballs; *Calvatia* spp., *Lycoperdon* spp., 129, 145, 185

Scaly Urchin; *Hydnum imbricatum,* 185
Steinpilz; *Boletus edulis,* 146

Botanical Index

Other Nonvascular Plantlike Organisms

Map Lichen; *Rhizocarpon geographicum,* 134

Old-man's-beard; Usnea spp., 20

Rhizocarpon geographicum; Map Lichen, 134

Usnea spp; Old-man's-beard, 20

Vascular Plants

Abies lasiocarpa; Subalpine Fir, 27, 109, 136, 138

Acer glabrum; Rocky Mountain Maple, 38

Acer grandidentatum; Bigtooth Maple, 204

Acer negundo; Box Elder, (*Negundo aceroides*), 83

Acer platanoides; Norway Maple, 204

Acer platanoides 'Schwedleri'; Schwedler Maple, 230

Acer rubrum; Red Maple, 230

Acer saccharinum; Silver Maple, 229–30

Acer saccharum; Sugar Maple, 219

Achillea filipendulina 'Coronation Gold'; Coronation Gold Yarrow, 294

Achillea millefolium ssp. *lanulosa;* Wild White Yarrow, 288, 294

Achillea taygetea 'Moonshine'; Moonshine Yarrow, 290

Aconitum columbianum; Monkshood, 172

Actaea rubra; Baneberry, 200–201

Adder's-mouth, White; *Malaxis monophyllos* ssp. *brachypoda,* 16

Aesculus hipposcastanum; Horse Chestnut, 290

Agastache Barberi; *Agastache barberi,* 296

Agastache cana; Double Bubble Mint, 294

Agropyron smithii; Western Wheatgrass, (*Pascopyrum smithii*), 9, 158

Amelanchier alnifolia; Juneberry, 288

Amelanchier spp.; Juneberries, 107

Amorpha canescens; Lead Plant, 294

Amorpha nana; Dwarf Lead Plant, 288

Anacyclus depressus; Atlas Daisy, 290

Anaphalis margaritacea; Pearly Everlasting, 296

Andropogon gerardii; Big Bluestem, 9, 158, 254, 296

Andropogon scoparius; Little Bluestem, (*Schizachyrium scoparium*), 158

Androsace spp.; Rock Jasmines, 130

Anemone blanda; Wind Flower, 286

Anemone patens; Pasque Flower, (*Pulsatilla patens*), 44, 66–68, 86, 119, 286

Antelope Bitterbrush; *Purshia tridentata,* 83, 86

Anthemis; *Anthemis tinctoria,* 292

Apache Plume; *Fallugia paradoxa,* 290

Apocynum spp.; Dogbane, 200

Apples, Crabapples; *Malus* spp., 65, 100, 223–24, 288

Apricot; *Prunus armeniaca,* 65, 286

Aquilegia caerulea; Colorado Columbine, 129

Aquilegia chrysantha; Yellow Columbine, 292

Arctostaphylos uva-ursi; Kinnikinnick, 22, 200

Argemone spp.; Prickly Poppies, 129, 159, 290

Arizona Zauschneria; *Zauschneria arizonica,* 296

Arnica; *Arnica fulgens,* 288

Botanical Index

Botanical Index

Botanical Index

Botanical Index

Botanical Index

Kobresia, 134

Koeleria cristata; June Grass, 292

Koenigia islandica; Koenigia, 133, 176

Lady's Slipper, Brownie; *Cypripedium fasciculatum*, 147

Lady's-tresses, Hooded; *Spiranthes romanzoffiana*, 172

Lady's-tresses, Ute; *Spiranthes diluvialis*, 172

Larkspur; *Delphinium nuttallianum*, 117, 288

Lavender; *Lavandula angustifolium*, 292

Lead Plant; *Amorpha canescens*, 294

Lead Plant, Dwarf; *Amorpha nana*, 288

Leucocrinum montanum; Sand Lily, 44–45, 288

Liatris punctata; Dotted Gay-feather, 294

Licorice, Wild; *Glycyrrhiza lepidota*, 264

Lilacs; *Syringa* spp., 125, 288

Lilium philadelphicum; Wood Lily, 119

Linum perenne; Blue Flax, (*Adenolinum lewisii*), 98, 288

Lithospermum incisum; Puccoon, 288

Lobelia cardinalis; Cardinal Flower, 296

Lobelia, Great blue; *Lobelia siphilitica*, 296

Locoweed, Lambert's; *Oxytropis lambertii*, 75, 288

Lomatium spp.; Biscuit-roots, 166

Lonicera tatarica; Tatarian Honeysuckle, 288

Lotus corniculatus; Bird's-foot Trefoil, (*L. tenuis*), 294

Lupines; *Lupinus* spp., 288

Lychnis coronaria; Rose Campion, 290

Machaeranthera bigelovii; Bigelow's Aster, 294

Magnolia spp.; Magnolia species, 100

Magnolia X soulangiana; Saucer Magnolia, 107

Mahonia repens; Creeping Mahonia, 8, 42, 86, 200, 240, 243–44, 286

Malaxis monophyllos ssp. *brachypoda*; White Adder's-mouth, 16

Malus spp.; Apples, Crabapples, 65, 100, 223–24, 288

Man Root, or Bush Morning-glory; *Ipomoea leptophylla*, 264

Maple, Bigtooth; *Acer grandidentatum*, 204

Maple, Norway; *Acer platanoides*, 204

Maple, Red; *Acer rubrum*, 230

Maple, Rocky Mountain; *Acer glabrum*, 38

Maples; *Acer* spp., 42

Maple, Schwedler; *Acer platanoides* 'Schwedleri', 230

Maple, Silver; *Acer saccharinum*, 229

Maple, Sugar; *Acer saccharum*, 219

Mariposa Lily; *Chalocortus* sp., 292

Marrubium vulgare; Common Horehound, 264

Marsh Marigold; *Caltha palustris*, (*Psychrophila leptosepala*), 130

Mentzelia decapetala; Ten-petal Blazing-star, (*Nuttallia decapetala*), 75

Mentzelia spp.; Blazing-stars, (*Acrolasia* spp., *Nuttallia* spp.), 195

Mertensia spp.; Mertensia, or Chiming Bells, 11, 83, 86, 288

Mexican Campion; *Silene laciniata*, 294

Milk-vetch, Drummond; *Astragalus drummondii*, 75

Milkweed, Butterfly; *Asclepias tuberosa*, 294

Milkweeds; *Asclepias* spp., 160–61

Milkweed, Showy; *Asclepias speciosa*, 159, 294

Botanical Index

Mimulus spp.; Monkey Flowers, 172
Mirabilis multiflora; Wild Four O'Clock, 290
Mirabilis longiflora; Long-flowered Four O'Clock, 294
Mockorange, Lewis's; *Philadelphus lewisii,* 290
Mockoranges; *Philadelphus* spp., 288, 290, 292
Monarda fistulosa; Monarda, (*M. fistulosa* var. *menthifolia*), 164, 292
Moneses uniflora; Wood Nymph, 181
Monkey Flowers; *Mimulus* spp., 172
Monkshood; *Aconitum columbianum,* 172
Monument Plant; *Frasera speciosa,* 129
Morning-glory, Bush, or Man Root; *Ipomoea leptophylla,* 264
Moss Campion; *Silene acaulis,* 132, 134
Mountain Ash, European; *Sorbus aucuparia,* 204
Mountain Ash, Greene's, or Western; *Sorbus scopulina,* 204
Mountain Mahogany, deciduous; *Cercocarpus montanus,* 241
Mountain Mahoganies; *Cercocarpus* spp., 243
Mountain Ninebark; *Physocarpus monogynus,* 292
Mountain Parsley; *Cymopterus lemmonii,* (*Pseudocymopterus montanus*), 166
Mountain Spray; *Holodiscus dumosus,* 290
Mullein, Common; *Verbascum* spp., 264
Mustard, Blue; *Chorispora tenella,* 98, 107

Nanking Cherry; *Prunus tomentosa,* 286
Narcissus spp.; Daffodils, 86, 286
Navajo Tea, or Cota; *Thelesperma megapotamicum,* 294

Nepeta X faassenii; Faassen's Nepeta, 288

Oak, Pin; *Quercus palustris,* 205
Oenothera caespitosa; White Stemless Evening Primrose, 98, 292
Oenothera spp.; Evening Primroses, 129
Old-man-of-the-mountains; *Hymenoxys grandiflora,* (*Rydbergia grandiflora*), 132
Orchids, Bog; *Plantanthera* spp., (*Limnorchis* spp.), 172
Oryzopsis hymenoides; Indian Ricegrass, (*Stipa hymenoides*), 290
Ox-eye Daisy; *Chrysanthemum leucanthemum,* (*Leucanthemum vulgare*), 290
Oxytropis lambertii; Lambert's Locoweed, 75, 288

Paeonia spp.; Peonies, 290
Paintbrushes; *Castilleja* spp., 145, 153, 290
Panicum virgatum; Switchgrass, 9, 158
Paperflower; *Psilostrophe tagetina,* 290
Parnassia spp.; Grass-of-Parnassus, 172
Parthenocissus quinquefolia; Virginia Creeper, 231
Pasque Flower; *Anemone patens,* (*Pulsatilla patens*), 44, 66–68, 86, 119, 286
Pearly Everlasting; *Anaphalis margaritacea,* 296
Pedicularis groenlandica; Elephanthead, 172

Pediocactus simpsonii; Ball Cactus, 118
Penstemon alpinus; Penstemon Alpinus, 294
Penstemon angustifolius; Narrowleaf Penstemon, 292

Botanical Index

Botanical Index

Botanical Index

Spruce, Engelmann; *Picea engelmannii*, 10–12, 27, 109, 136, 138

Stanleya pinnata; Prince's Plume, 294

Stonecrop; *Sedum lanceolatum*, (*Amerosedum lanceolatum*), 132

Storksbill, or Filaree; *Erodium cicutarium*, 42, 45

Streptopus fassettii; Twisted-stalk, 201

Sugar Bowls; *Clematis hirsutissima*, (*Coriflora hirsutissima*), 120

Sulphur Flower; *Eriogonum umbellatum*, 240

Sumac, Smooth; *Rhus glabra* var. *cismontana*, 200, 232

Sumac, Three-leaf; *Rhus trilobata*, (*R. aromatica* ssp. *trilobata*), 10

Sunflower, Common; *Helianthus annuus*, 159

Sunflower, Maximilian's; *Helianthus maximiliana*, 296

Switchgrass; *Panicum virgatum*, 9, 158

Syringa spp.; Lilacs, 125, 288

Talinum calycinum; Fameflower, 296

Teasel, Common; *Dipsacus fullonum*, (*D. sylvestris*), 241

Thelesperma filifolium; Greenthread, 296

Thelesperma megapotamicum; Navajo Tea, or Cota, 294

Thermopsis divaricarpa; Golden Banner, 117, 288

Thistle, Wavy-leaf; *Cirsium undulatum*, 294

Tickseed; *Coreopsis lanceolata*, 290

Townsendia exscapa, *T. hookeri*; Early Easter Daisy, 38, 44, 75, 264, 286

Townsendia grandiflora; Easter Daisy, 290

Toxicodendron rydbergii; Poison Ivy, 200

Tradescantia sp.; Spiderwort, 98

Tragopogon dubius; Western Salsify, 159

Trefoil, Bird's-foot; *Lotus corniculatus*, (*L. tenuis*), 294

Trollius laxus var. *albiflorus*; Globeflower, (*T. albiflorus*), 130

Tulipa spp.; Hybrid Tulips, Wild Tulips, 86

Tulipa turkestanica; Turkestan Tulip, 286

Tulips, Hybrid and Wild; *Tulipa* spp., 86

Tulip, Turkestan; *Tulipa turkestanica*, 286

Twisted-stalk; *Streptopus fassettii*, 201

Ulmus americana; American Elm, 231

Vaccinium spp.; Blueberries, 11

Verbascum thapsus; Common Mullein, 264

Verbena bipinnatifida; Dakota Verbena, Dakota Vervain (*Glandularia bipinnatifida*), 287

Viguiera multiflora; Showy Golden Eye, (*Heliomeris multiflora*), 292

Viola nuttallii; Nuttall's Violet, Yellow Violet, 44–45, 75, 288

Viola pedatifida; Bird's-foot Violet, 286

Violet, Nuttall's, or Yellow; *Viola nuttallii*, 44–45, 75, 288

Virginia Creeper; *Parthenocissus quinquefolia*, 231

Vitis riparia; Wild Grape, 292

Vitis spp.; Grapes, 65

Wallflowers; *Erysimum* spp., 117

Waxflower, or Jamesia; *Jamesia americana*, 200, 290

Wheatgrass, Western; *Agropyron smithii*, (*Pascopyrum smithii*), 9, 158

329

Botanical Index

INDEX

Only those words deemed most useful to the reader are indexed here. Place names in bold type refer to destinations described in the Where To Go sections, and the page number on which directions are given is listed first. When there is substantial information in the text about a specific plant, it is included here; otherwise, see the Botanical Index on page 317.

Index

Index

Index

Index

Index

Index

Index

Index